PONDERINGS
OF A CITIZEN OF
THE MILKY WAY

PONDERINGS OF A CITIZEN OF THE MILKY WAY

*The Fantastic Arising
of Padraic Clancy Muldoon*

The Legend of Sharon Shashanovah

Journey to Jerusalem

The Argument

ALEXANDER FRANCIS HORN

A Nadder Book

ELEMENT BOOKS LTD

The Fantastic Arising of Padraic Clancy Muldoon, Journey to Jerusalem and *The Argument* © Alexander Francis Horn 1978

The Legend of Sharon Shashanovah © Alexander Francis Horn 1987

The Fantastic Arising of Padraic Clancy Muldoon, Journey to Jerusalem and *The Argument* first published in the USA in 1978 by Everyman Publications, San Francisco
This edition first published in Great Britain 1987
by Element Books Ltd, Longmead, Shaftesbury, Dorset

Printed in Great Britain by
Billings, Hylton Road, Worcester
Cover design by Howard Coale
Supervised by David Robey and Janice Crosby

(British Library Cataloguing in Publication Data)

British Library Cataloguing in Publication Data
Horn, Alexander Francis
Ponderings of a citizen of the milky way.
— (A Nadder book).
I. Title II. Horn, Alexander Francis.
Fantastic arising of Padraic Clancy
Muldoon III. Horn, Alexander Francis.
Legend of Sharon Shashanovah IV. Horn,
Alexander Francis. Journey to Jerusalem
V. Horn, Alexander Francis. The Argument
812'.54   PS3558.068/

ISBN 1-85230-000-0

Contents

Author's Preface

The theatre — a reflector of reality, a celebration of life, the conscience of the nation, the conscience of the world . . . The murders of John Kennedy, Robert Kennedy, Martin Luther King . . . The sixties, Vietnam, the peace marches, the Kent State shootings . . . These plays begin here.

But their real history began the day I met the woman who was to become my wife. It may be a pardonable offense against the spirit of our times for a man to love his wife: to also sing her praises as teacher, actress, director, producer is surely unforgivable.

Yet the truth must be stated. If ever a playwright had a teacher, she has been mine: if ever a work has been a collaboration, these plays have. For me, writing has been the most difficult of tasks, and I am grateful to have such a comrade by my side.

Socrates had his Diotima, Dante his Beatrice, Shakespeare his Dark Lady of the Sonnets, and I, my Sharon. I cannot compare myself to these giants in greatness, they outdistance me as the stars the earth; yet I hold myself their equal in grace and fortune, for I have been blessed with a love that completes my life and my work.

It's time to send these children of ours out into the world. May they be robust and strong and have long life. May they help you attain that happiness I wish for you with all my heart.

Alexander Francis Horn

ALEXANDER FRANCIS HORN

Theatre and the Esoteric Tradition

In *The Idea of the Theatre,* Francis Ferguson states that there have been three great theatres in the Western tradition: the Greek, Aeschylus and Sophocles; the Elizabethan, Shakespeare; and the medieval, Dante (taken as theatre). All three were cosmic theatres. All theatres since Shakespeare have been partial perspectives. In Racine there is a split between reason and passion, in which reason triumphs over passion. In Wagner passion is triumphant over reason.

The modern theatre founded by Ibsen, great as he is, is also a partial perspective, which culminates in Chekhov, the pathetic modality, and which is inferior to heroic man seen in the round, as part of the universe, and part of divinity. Modern theatre lacks cosmic dimension. Hebbel, Ibsen, Chekhov, Brecht, Miller, Williams, Strindberg, Shaw, Cocteau, Anouilh, O'Neill, Ionesco all remarkable, each a partial perspective.

For theatre to become truly great again, it must be restored to its cosmic dimension, lost to it since the theatre of Shakespeare.

The mirror has cracked, that great mirror of Man which in Hamlet is held up to the world to reveal all the multiple facets on various levels of Man, the microcosmos that reflects his entire society and the great world, the macrocosmos. This mirror of man is now in fragments, in as many fragments as there are different varieties of theatre. Therefore, for the restoration of cosmic theatre there must be a restoration of man. Man, fallen into multiplicity, must be restored to his original unity. The great work of the cosmic theatres in the past: the *Orestia,* the Oedipus trilogy of Sophocles, *Hamlet, King Lear, The Tempest, The Divine Comedy* contain the psychology of man's development, from multiplicity to unity, and are in fact the restoration of the divinity of man. This is his evolution. The Eleusinian mystery, the transformation of man symbolized as an ear of corn that can die to be reborn, the sacred drama of cosmic dimensions performed in the Egyptian temples to select initiates, is made public in the Christ drama, the passion play, the death and resurrection of man's spirit. This single universal theme is implicit in all the great works.

These plays are an effort to create a cosmic theatre for our time.

They embody many esoteric traditions: Western theosophy (the Pythagorean Platonic tradition and the great sage philosophers, Thales, Heraclitus, Parmenides, Empedocles), the Cabala, Egyptian Hermetic teaching, Zen Buddhism, Sufism, and of course the teaching of G.I. Gurdjieff, Peter Ouspensky, Dr. Maurice Nicoll, and Rodney Collin, known to us in the twentieth century as representatives of a system called The Work. This work was in earlier periods called The Work of Law, the Work of Love, and in our time, as Rodney Collin has said, should be called the Work of Harmony, because never before in our recorded history, in our war-torn, fragmented, computer-driven society, never has HARMONY been such an IMPERATIVE.

With the culmination of the nineteenth century, Nietzsche proclaimed God dead; by the middle of the twentieth century Sartre had proclaimed man dead, a useless passion. Surely the old God is dead, as surely as man as we have known him is dead, and has been since the 1600's when divinity was banished from the world, from man's consciousness. God, once the greatest pride of man, gave way to a mechanistic universe — Kepler, Galileo, Newton — where a magical living universe, God-informed, was replaced by a mechanistic and functional universe, informed by the Void. Man fell into dualism, the universe was ruptured, man's psyche became divorced from Reality, his consciousness diminished to the idols of the cave. From this time the science of faith was replaced by the science of doubt. The Cartesian world view triumphed. Man became the servant of the scientific method which cut off the heads of Kings, replaced the Pope with the Mob, and gave birth to the Frankenstein of the French Revolution. The new tyrant, reason, seceded from the heart, and all the children of that revolution arose: Darwin, Marx, Freud, Einstein, and the humanistic tradition, in which man danced gaily away from his creator to the edge of the precipice, following the siren song of the carpetbaggers of the twentieth century — the logical positivists, the deconstructionists, and all the other professors of meaninglessness. The adulteration of all sacred traditions, the confusion of tongues, the cafeteria of the spiritual supermarket where the great teachings are consumed like a Bloomingdale's potpourri, have so unsettled what little is left of man's sanity that only a thorough housecleaning of all the sophistries that beset us can now redeem us. We are all the lost children of Israel, suffering the Egyptian plagues.

There are two lines in all sacred traditions — not only the Old

Testament and the New Testament, but the Mahabarata, the Homeric, the Chaldean, and Babylonian, as well as the Chinese, Indian and Persian traditions — that is the line of kings and the line of priests, the Brahmins and Shatiras. Whether it be the Arthurian cycle of the wizard Merlin and King Arthur, or the Old Testament of Samuel and Saul which unites in the great priest-king David (giving birth to the splendor and wisdom of Solomon when Israel reaches its apex of glory), always the contemplative priest is seen side by side with the king, the leader of sacred action, Bhakti, Raja and Jana yoga — that is the yogas of devotion, consciousness and knowledge side by side with Karma yoga — the yoga of action.

In the ancient theocracies, such as the Hebraic and Egyptian the two functions are united: the sacred priest king, Moses, Hermes Trismegistus, the sage kings of ancient China, the divine priest kings of Babylonia and Chaldea, and South America.

Sometimes we see these two functions running side by side in two separate beings, or together in one being; sometimes the lines diverge, or clash — as in the long conflict between the popes and kings of Western Europe. These dual functions are exemplified in the sacred books of the *Tarot* (the Magician and the Emperor), the *I Ching*, the *Po Vuvul* of South America.

Ponderings of a Citizen of the Milky Way is the line of contemplatives; its companion volume, *In Search of a Solar Hero* the line of kings. Yet this sharp division can only exist in discursive thinking; in reality they are never apart. In *I*, the last play of *The King Trilogy*, which comprises *In Search of a Solar Hero*, the two lines unite in the Magician and Daniel.

Referring to these distinct lines, Plato makes clear that when a man leaves the cave and achieves true contemplation, i.e. the vision of God, he must return to the cave and aid his fellow men. When these two lines are sundered, false esotericism arises; when they are united they produce true esotericism. This is the main point upon which all esotericism inevitably founders and degenerates in the course of time, giving rise to the need for the esoteric impulse to be constantly revivified and redefined.

When the line of priests, or contemplatives, loses its true vision of God, or retaining it loses its connection with the line of kings, or conversely when the line of kings loses its true validity, which can only stem from the vision of God imparted to it by the true priests, then esotericism becomes false and the civilization which is based upon it inevitably degenerates. For example, the transcendental Indian civilization became sterile and life-denying when the yogis became so divorced from the line of kings that they ended up on mountaintops and lost their union with action.

This problem, which can be called the central problem of esotericism, and therefore of all civilizations, is apparent in our time. When contemplatives and men of action find each other mutually despicable, this rupture produces the barbarism of today. The line of kings has so degenerated that the men who rule the world are simply shopkeepers in a universal assembly line turning out objects of consumption for a debased humanity. With the rarest of exceptions, the contemplatives have degenerated into sterile pseudo-intellectuals teaching courses in universities that have no relation to active life. Consequently we have no civilization, no contemplatives pondering the meaning of existence (philosophy having ended with Nietzsche), and no true men of action. Thus the vision of God actualized in a living community has been lost. And Yeats could only cry "The centre cannot hold;/ Mere anarchy is loosed upon the world,/ The blood-dimmed tide is loosed, and everywhere/ The ceremony of innocence is drowned;/ The best lack all conviction, while the worst/ Are full of passionate intensity." Rilke lamented in the *Duino Elegies,* "Earth! invisible! What is your urgent command, if not transformation?" While Elliot despaired throughout *The Wasteland* of modern life. The last time in our tradition there was a struggle for a unified world view was the Renaissance — all efforts since being quickly aborted.

Plato has stated that until philosophers are kings or kings are philosophers there will never be an end to the miseries of the world. Nothing ever said could be truer. All civilizations of the past prove this axiom. Wisdom and love must be united with courage and strength for there to be real doing. When these are separated the end is idle states of mind: pseudo-mystical states, or power-mad dictators. Consequently, to understand the central dilemma of Western civilization, which is usually stated as the split between idealism and realism, spirit and matter, as stemming from the sundering of the lines of philosophers and kings, is to understand not only the main problem of human life, but the solution to it.

The King Trilogy is an example of the two lines united: Adam King, Luke King and Matthew King in the line of kings, and the line of priests exemplified by Joseph Man. In *The Magician* Luke exemplifies the line of kings and the Magician the line of priests. In *I* these two lines unite in the Magician and Daniel to overcome the problem of

Evil, i.e. Tyrant, and transform evil to restore the Golden Age. *In Search of a Solar Hero* is *the* search for Man who unites these two separate functions, the line of contemplatives and the line of action, long sundered, into one, and thereby restores Man to his primordial unity and the world to its primeval simplicity, the Garden of Eden, when Man was one with Nature and God. Psychologically, in the work of Gurdjieff, these lines are called the line of knowledge and the line of Being. Their union produces divine understanding which leads to great Doing.

The King Trilogy traces this evolution psychologically and cosmologically.

Journey to Jerusalem, empowered by many traditions, such as the Sufi, is a cabalistic, hermetic, alchemical work. Adam and Eve (Eros) and the Serpent of Wisdom (the Logos) journey through all space and time to the kingdom of consciousness, Jerusalem, where the two halves of Man, the female and the male, divided since the fall, are reunited in the mystic marriage of Christ (Eros united with Wisdom). In an ever recurring spiral, exemplifying paradise lost and paradise regained, man and women together struggle to unite themselves and all worlds to their source, that first principle of their existence, God. The history of the world in time and eternity.

The Legend of Sharon Shashanovah expresses the idea found in the sacred tradition that, as he is, man is a puppet waxing and waning under the power of the moon, but who can, under the right conditions and with proper help, transform himself into a human being. The theatre, a sacred discipline, is the transforming force that shocks and awakens man from his sleep of death in the puppet theatre, and which can enable man to enter the cosmic theatre whereby he becomes a spectator of all time and all existence.

The Fantastic Arising of Padraic Clancy Muldoon is a demonstration that the gods, willfully banished from the modern drawing room, have in fact always been with us, and that only man asleep has failed to see them. When he awakens to his blindness, his illusions, his self-deceit, his paralyzed state of impotence, and takes the decisive step of dying to himself, he can be reborn as a conscious being in their company — to the heavenly kingdom that lies within him, and which has always awaited him, and inherit the Earth at last.

The Argument has been going on since the beginning of time. Man, under the authority of his own self will, versus Man, under the authority of the one true God. Two religions: the religion of power and money versus the religion of true power, derived from God.

All of these plays are mystery plays deriving from the great tradition: Aeschylus, Sophocles, Dante, Shakespeare, and, to a lesser degree, Goethe. They are a complete break with the psychology and the aesthetic of modern drama, and are a return to the ancient psychology, metaphysics, ethics, and natural philosophy. They are an attempt to move toward a cosmic theatre and away from our present theatre, which, with the rarest of exceptions, is disgraced with an exclusive attention to the trivial, the mundane, the incomprehensible, the absurd, the nihilistic.

The objective science of Aeschylus, Sophocles, Shakespeare, and Dante depicts the true relationship of the part to the whole: of the individual to humanity, humanity to Nature, and Nature to God, in one unified world vision. These philosopher-kings unite science with art, philosophy and religion. This fusion accounts for the primordial force of their works and is a demonstration of the unity of priest and king, of contemplative and active, of visionary and empiricist.

The barbarism of our time once again is exemplified in the fragmentation of art, religion, science and philosophy. Once united in one body of wisdom-knowledge, it has become fragmented in separate domains, again a sign of the barbarism of our times. When these sacred disciplines lose their primordial unity with one another, we have knowledge instead of wisdom and all the accumulation of data without meaning of modern science, so that science now degenerates into pseudo-science, pseudo-art, pseudo-religion, pseudo-philosophy, technicians running around like squirrels gathering nuts. The return to true science, art, religion, and philosophy can only come about through the union of man's heart and mind, which have been at war with one another since Descartes.

The prophetic insight of Tolstoy, who cried out against a pseudo-science and a pseudo-art that could only lead to man's destruction (first speaker in *The Argument*), passionately pleaded for the wisdom of a true science and a true art that would contribute to true greatness — man's transformation under God.

Tyrant, the fallen angel, who is both a cosmic principle without man and within man, is that Luciferian rebellion against God which leads to the fall of man. This rebellion is occurring in the cosmic levels outside man and the psychological levels within man, since man as a citizen of the galaxy embraces higher worlds as well as the lower. The rebellion of fallen man, Tyrant, against God and His universe, which we retrace throughout all the ancient scriptures culminates in the nihilism of today. Man, led by the spirit of Tyrant within him, seeks to destroy his Creator and His universe, and authorize himself as the god of the Void.

It is clear to all men and women of good will that man is at the end of the line; that the medieval natural order of man in nature installed under the spiritual order of God, which was broken by a Renaissance maimed irreparably by a tyrannical inquisition, and which refused to recognize the perfect equality of men and women, and therefore turned Eros into a Cinderella living in terror of her life, of her two step-sisters, obscenity and heartless rationality, was a wrong turning in the life of mankind. For four hundred years we have been descending into deeper and deeper hells. Since the reformation (Luther), and the counter-reformation, which produced the religious wars that destroyed the civilization of Europe and plunged man into the Thirty Years War of the seventeenth century, the enlightenment of the eighteenth century, which could better be called the endarkenment, the gross materialism of the nineteenth century which produced the atheism of industrialism and the collectivism of communism, socialism, Americanism, Utopianism and every other ism, and the twentieth century technology of two world wars, the horrors of Buchenwald and Hiroshima, three quarters of the population of the earth going to sleep hungry, the murder of man's spirit, the mass starvation of the body and the soul, a growing universal illiteracy, the beginning of the Third World War the day the Second World War ended, that Third World War we have been in forty years during which time we have witnessed the mass deaths of Korea, Vietnam, Cambodia, Indonesia, Nicaragua, Guatemala, Brazil, the enslavement of an entire continent of Africa, and the wholesale murder of an entire people, the rape of our youth, deaths, maiming and tortures of five million in the First World War, fifty million in the Second World War, and untold millions in the Third World War in our terrible and terrifying century of madness; the incalculable psychic damage of all the diverse cultures of the world being uprooted and thrown into the blender of America which has churned them up and produced a new species of man: unthinking, unfeeling — clones — the perfect victims of the Anti-Christ, we have reached the lowest hell of Dante's *Inferno* yet. Man, who has followed the spirit of that fallen angel, Tyrant, spirit of darkness and denial, of daemonic defiance of our creator and His created order, in our rebellion against Heaven whereby we have made a tyranny of life on this earth, both for our neighbors and ourselves, has cast this earth, which is designed to be a heaven, into a cauldron of Hell. It is clear that unless we make the turning now, and recognize, with Dante's pilgrim, that midway in our life we are lost in a dark forest and that we seek to find the true way back, that we will have irretrievably damned ourselves and that *our* humanity, at least, will perish from off the face of this earth. The return to our original selves is imperative, because beings, no longer men, but masquerading as such, have so fallen under the tyrannical impulse of their own false nature, that not content with having raped and exploited God's earth and humanity, seek now to put hotels on Mars and divide the planets of our Solar System into profitable parcels of real estate toward the greater glory of their own comfort and freakhood. It is now either lights-out, or a return to Love united with Wisdom. These plays are written out of the desperate need of our time: ponderings of a citizen of the Milky Way in search of a solar hero.

AFH

January 1, 1987

THE FANTASTIC ARISING OF PADRAIC CLANCY MULDOON

A Play in Two Acts

1972

To my father who taught me never to be
ashamed of what I love

To my mother who taught me to fight

And to my Rose of Sharon

If one says he has searched
but not found, do not believe him.

The Talmud

CHARACTERS

Padraic Clancy Muldoon, a college professor

Mary Bordelaise Muldoon, his wife

Michael, a college student ⎫

Katie, a college student ⎬ their children

Sean, age ten ⎪

Molly, age eight ⎭

Great Grandfather, Padraic's grandfather

Grandmother, Padraic's mother

Charles Bordelaise, an industrialist and financier,
   Mary's brother

Father Killian Murphy, a priest,
   Padraic's childhood friend

Nat Williams, a friend of Michael and Katie

The Planetary Gods

PROLOGUE

SEAN: If self-knowledge is the aim of man,
There is no meaning in the life we live.
For man, lawful master of the earth,
Has given up his birthright.
Learned men of high repute,
Philosophers, kings and sages,
All agree we live a life of hollow pretense.
Having touched the length,
The width, the height,
Man at last is out of breath,
Flailing in the depth.
Ten thousand years of seeking
The answer to the same dilemma
Brings no greater wisdom
Than we had before.
We know the bee, the rat, the snail,
But man's the riddle we can't unravel.
We are assailed by treasonous voices,
Mystified, polluted and bewildered,
The issue's still unsolved.
No presidential commission
No papal oath promising absolution,
Can illuminate this strange enigma, man.
Is he monkey, God or devil?
Is he dust or spirit, flesh or vapor?
Lover, hater, God forsaker?
Or compound vegetable, animal, mineral?
A starry hoax, an absurd joke
Or God's impossible ultimate hope?
The greatest mystery on the earth,
The king of apes, the status seeker.

Something must be done, we know,
With this menace who's refused
To be his brother's keeper.
The age of royalty is dead.
Science and priesthood have failed us.
Now dawns the day of ordinary man.
On him we place our final hope.
Ladies and gentlemen, help us if you can.
Usher in the long awaited era
Of the brotherhood of man!

ACT I

(*The entire action of the play takes place in the Muldoon household during the Easter season. The planetary gods stand and recline in various postures on the upper level.*[1] *Sometimes they listen; sometimes they come down and unbeknownst to the characters participate directly as moving forces that direct the actors in the play.*)

MARY: Wake up, man! Paddy, wake up. Come on, get out of bed.

PADRAIC: Wake up, is it? The whole world's going directly to hell and I won't get out of bed 'til it changes its direction!
(*He pulls the sheets up over his head.*)

MARY: Padraic Clancy, do you hear me? It's time to wake up, my darling man. Now don't pretend you're still sleeping.

PADRAIC: Do you love me as I love you?

MARY: You know I do.

PADRAIC: Really? Truly and forever?

MARY: And then some.

PADRAIC: Prove it.

MARY: I'll fill your mouth with kisses.

PADRAIC: More!

MARY: Sweet kisses, and if that's not enough, I brought you this to coax you out of bed.

PADRAIC: What's this? A fig?

MARY: From our own garden bursting with delights — peaches and plums and apricots and everything sweet for my lord and master.

PADRAIC: A feast . . .

MARY: Of love.

PADRAIC: Marvelous. Now I can sleep forever.

MARY: Not on your life! Rise and shine, my honey boy. The world's expecting great things of you today, and so am I. I don't know why, but I feel as if it were the first day of Creation. When I tiptoed into the garden this morning, there was such a heavenly silence I had to stand quite still. There was such a benediction in the air . . . I felt like an intruder in a strange world. So I stood apart, my bare feet grasping the earth, and watched. A little worm crawled on my foot. I picked him up and held him in my hand and wondered at the Power that had made both him and me to live side by side in the same garden. Everything breathed in an immense solitude. Each tree, heavy with fruit, begging to be picked, its branches rustling in the wind . . . and the butterflies dancing in the sky . . . the bees and ants and all the little creatures . . .

PADRAIC: Ah Mary, if you found a unicorn in the garden you'd tame it, for you're made of love.

MARY: (*Laughing.*) I feel so gay; I don't know why. It was as if each bush, each plant, each blade of grass was kissed by heaven, to see them gleaming in the early morning dew.

PADRAIC: That dew must be the tears of God.

MARY: Tears of joy . . .

PADRAIC: Or sadness. Come to the window, love, and look.
"Ah, love, let us be true
To one another!"

MARY: " . . . For the world, which seems
To lie before us like a land of dreams,"

MARY AND PADRAIC: "So various, so beautiful, so new,"

PADRAIC: "Hath really neither joy, nor love, nor light,
Nor certitude, nor peace, nor help for pain;"

MARY: "And we are here as on a darkling plain
Swept with confused alarms of struggle and flight,"

PADRAIC: "Where ignorant armies clash by night."

MARY: "Dover Beach."[2]

PADRAIC: Remember?

MARY: I shall never forget. "Ah, love, let us be true to one another." Those were the first words you ever said to me. And then you kissed me. I nearly fainted. I ran away from you. But in all the streets of Dublin, wherever I turned, you were there, your head thrown back, laughing. I started to tremble. I hid myself in the crowd, but always you were there. I tried to lose you in all the shops, down all the lanes and byways, but always your footsteps sounded behind me. At the post office, the bookstore, even the dressmaker, you sauntered in. You kept looking at me. I began to blush; then I began to cry, and kept crying all that night. In the morning I ran to the city to find you, but you were gone. I went to every gate of Trinity College. I asked the watchman if he had seen you. I didn't even know your name. I looked for you everywhere, but you had vanished. I thought I would die. And then I saw you from a distance. I ran to meet you, and then I was in your arms, your strong arms that have held and protected me from the treachery of the world through all the years. Ah Paddy, I didn't know the meaning of life 'til I met you.

PADRAIC: Ah, you've got it all backwards and upside down. It was you who educated me. You were my lady.

MARY: And you were my knight.

PADRAIC: Hmmm . . . those were the days . . . when I was young and strong . . . Now I'm a tarnished knight.

MARY: You're the finest man I know.

PADRAIC: No . . . it's . . .

MARY: (*Clasps her hand over his mouth.*) Hush! I won't hear you saying bad things about yourself. It's time to be up. The university is calling you.

PADRAIC: I won't be going to the university today, Mary, or any other day. My occupation's gone.

MARY: What are you talking about? You've got a speech to make before the march. They're all expecting you.

PADRAIC: Another speech! That's all I've done my whole life long — talk, talk, talk. I'm sick and tired of the sound of my own voice, and you'd think everyone else would be, too. Oh, if only I could do something.

MARY: Do something! Look what you've done already.

PADRAIC: What? Written a few books to add to the general uproar. The world's a mess. What good are books or talk at a time like this?

MARY: But that's not all you've done. You've taken action.

PADRAIC: The action of a self-conceited braggart braying in the wind.

MARY: You're too hard on people and yourself . . .

PADRAIC: I've just been chasing fame and fortune like all the others.

MARY: That's not true. That's not all there is to it, and you know it. Your books have been written in blood — your blood, and everything else you've done, I know what it's cost you. Tell that to the world, but not to me. I know what your struggle has been, for it's been my struggle too.

PADRAIC: What have I done? Nothing.

MARY: You care for men, Paddy; don't deny it.

PADRAIC: Men . . . don't talk to me of men. I'm disappointed in them. And the worst of it is I'm disappointed in myself.

MARY: I can't bear to see you this way. What is it, Paddy? What's the matter?

PADRAIC: It's as if something broke here inside me. I . . . I . . . can't seem to get a hold of myself.

MARY: You must. Everyone's counting on you. You can't let all those people down . . . your students . . . Michael . . . Katie . . . not after all these years of struggle, just when we're in sight of victory.

PADRAIC: All the little compromises I've made — they've chipped away at me. I didn't think they were anything at the time, but they've taken a part of me and now I've lost my way.

MARY: Oh Paddy, we'll find it again together.

PADRAIC: I feel so bad, Mary, I could cry.

MARY: Oh my darling, let me hold you in my arms.

PADRAIC: I just can't seem to get started. I want to, but I don't know how. Oh, why did you marry a poor sinner like me?

MARY: Because I loved you.

PADRAIC: And why do you stay married to me?

MARY: So I can stand you on your two good feet and point you in the right direction.

PADRAIC: And what way is that?

MARY: The usual way — the way to life.

PADRAIC: Life's the hell a poor devil like me is trying to get out of.

MARY: An end to your dark philosophizing. Come on, my melancholy baby, rise and shine! You've got a speech to make.

PADRAIC: I can't.

MARY: Why not?

PADRAIC: I've resigned.

MARY: Resigned! Why didn't you tell me!

PADRAIC: I've been trying to.

MARY: But why?

PADRAIC: Lies! Lies! Lies! I can't live with all these lies. A university is a place of truth or it's nothing.

MARY: Then tell the truth.

PADRAIC: I can't. No one wants to hear it. Everyone's given up. If I stayed, I'd have to be a hypocrite.

MARY: Everyone hasn't given up, but it's what you want to do.

PADRAIC: Why not? It seems to be the thing to do.

MARY: Padraic Clancy, get out of bed this instant!

PADRAIC: I will not.

MARY: This instant!

PADRAIC: Woman, can't you take no for an answer? You're pecking and clawing me to death.

MARY: No more than you could when you were wooing me.

PADRAIC: That was different. I was madly in love with you.

MARY: Is that why you chased me through half the countries of Europe?

PADRAIC: I couldn't get you out of my blood.

MARY: And still can't. You know you can't resist me. (*Starts tickling him.*)

PADRAIC: Stop it, Mary. (*Laughing.*) You know I can't stand being tickled.

MARY: Exactly. Padraic, you've been lying in bed for three days now.

PADRAIC: Mary, please (*laughing*) . . . Don't take advantage of me.

MARY: And I've let you do it because I knew you needed the rest. But now it's time for all good men to get up.

PADRAIC: For the love of Jesus, cut it out! (*Laughing.*)

MARY: You can stay in bed 'til high noon. That's D-Day. For you're due at the university at one o'clock. Understand?

PADRAIC: No. (*Laughing.*) Yes. Yes!

MARY: And I want you to promise me you'll be up at twelve o'clock and no later.

PADRAIC: (*Laughing*) Anything . . . anything.

MARY: Twelve o'clock. Promise?

PADRAIC: I promise . . . I promise . . . God, but you're a strong-willed woman.

MARY: Well, what would you do if I lay in bed all day?

PADRAIC: What would I do? I'll tell you what I'd do. (*Grabs her and throws her onto bed.*)

MARY: (*Screaming.*) Paddy!

PADRAIC: I'd straddle you with love.

MARY: Oh no you don't!

PADRAIC: Oh yes I do, my sweet, my love. Since when have you lost the desire to take the full weight of the man you love?

MARY: Let me go. I've got to finish decorating the Easter eggs.

PADRAIC: What for?

MARY: Charles will be here any moment.

PADRAIC: Why must he always be hanging around? Damnation on the man!

MARY: Paddy, jealous of my own brother, are you?

PADRAIC: Why doesn't he move in and be done with it? He comes here often enough.

MARY: Now, sweet man, let me up.

PADRAIC: I will not!

(*Enter Sean and Molly.*)

MOLLY: Daddy's making love to Mom again.

SEAN: Doesn't he ever get tired?

MARY: Paddy! The children!

PADRAIC: Bring them to bed with us. We'll educate them early. We'll lie naked as a pair of pagans and let them romp between, recipients of the honey of our love. They'll suck up knowledge like pomegranates from the rind.

MARY: But, angel . . . (*Laughing.*)

PADRAIC: Oh, the stiff formality of the law. It's enough to make you puke, in or out of season. We're all prisoners of the law, and yet this world's unlawful. Let's break the world apart and fly to regions that now we only dream of.

MARY: Oh, oh! Watch out children!

MOLLY: Isn't Daddy ever gonna get out of bed?

PADRAIC: Get away now, you kids.

(*Children begin tickling him. Enter Grandmother.*)

Get away, you rascals. I'm busy sleeping.

SEAN: You're not doing anything but laying on your behind.

PADRAIC: That takes a lot of work. Look at the world: like a bunch of busy bees gathering honey for the gods to eat.

SEAN: Where are they?

PADRAIC: Who?

SEAN: The gods.

PADRAIC: All around us.

MOLLY: I can't see them.

SEAN: I can.

PADRAIC: Oh no! We'll have to go on our magic trip and soon you'll see them for yourselves. But first, promise me you'll never be a success.

SEAN: Grandmother says we have to.

GRANDMOTHER: And that you do!

PADRAIC: Don't you want to imitate your father and be a failure like me?

SEAN: (*To Grandmother.*) Then why does Daddy say we don't?

MARY: Never mind. Just heed what your father says.

GRANDMOTHER: Your father's just telling tales, children. You shouldn't lie to them that way, Paddy. You should let them know what a grand success you are.

PADRAIC: But I'm telling the truth. Will no man here believe me?

MARY: (*Arms around his neck, whispering.*) I do.

GRANDMOTHER: Your father's a very famous man.

PADRAIC: At the end of his tether.

GRANDMOTHER: Now off to school with you.

SEAN: I don't want to go to school.

MOLLY: I do.

GRANDMOTHER: Why not?

SEAN: I'll only have to unlearn everything.

GRANDMOTHER: Who told you that?

SEAN: Daddy.

GRANDMOTHER: Sweet Jesus, why do you let the man talk that way to the children, Mary?

MARY: Because he's right.

GRANDMOTHER: (*Muttering.*) Two of a kind.

(*Enter Father Murphy.*)

PADRAIC: Good morning, Father. Come to give me catechism so early? Better were you to castigate the nation.

FATHER MURPHY: We do our best to keep the flesh on the bones of the world.

PADRAIC: What brings you here so early?

FATHER MURPHY: Katie asked me to have a word with you.

PADRAIC: A word with me? About what?

GRANDMOTHER: Listen to him. You know damn well about what.

PADRAIC: Can't the girl speak for herself? I'm a reasonable man.

MARY: You're the most outrageous man I ever met. That's all she's been trying to do.

FATHER MURPHY: Come on Padraic, give her your blessing and get it over with.

PADRAIC: My daughter's fallen in love with the boy next door. Understandable; that's what he's there for, I suppose. But will someone please tell me why he has to be black?

GRANDMOTHER: A dark horse if I've ever seen one.

MARY: This is liberal America, Paddy.

PADRAIC: Liberal America's turned out to be a libertine whore.

MARY: Is this the famous Professor Muldoon, fighter for the rights of man?

PADRAIC: Just because you fight for the freedom of the blacks doesn't mean you have to marry one.

MARY: You're not marrying him; Katie is.

PADRAIC: It's her happiness I'm thinking of.

MARY: I was happy enough when I ran off with you.

GRANDMOTHER: You're a black Irishman yourself. What are you complaining about?

PADRAIC: Thanks for backing me up, Mum.

GRANDMOTHER: Isn't it enough I gave birth to you? What else do you want?

PADRAIC: These hot and eager maidens burning to gain knowledge of the world.

MARY: What did you say?

PADRAIC: Not a thing. Not a thing.

MARY: Well, that's settled then. She'll marry Nat.

PADRAIC: But he hasn't even proposed.

MARY: Don't worry; he will.

PADRAIC: I won't have it. She won't marry him.

MARY: I say she will.

PADRAIC: And I say she won't.

MARY: I say she will.

PADRAIC: And I say she won't.

MARY: Oh yes, she will.

PADRAIC: Oh no, she won't.

MARY: She will.

PADRAIC: No!

MARY: Yes!

PADRAIC: No! No! No! You're driving me mad. What am I doing in this strange land? How'd I ever get transposed from my native hearth? An Irishman lost in America! It's impossible. Is it a joke the Lord has played upon me?

FATHER MURPHY: The Lord doesn't joke. You know that, Padraic.

PADRAIC: The devil then — whisked off in me dreams. Who's to blame?

MARY: Don't look at me.

PADRAIC: It was you who brought me to this savage land. You promised me the streets were lined with gold and the inhabitants made of milk and honey. That's what I get for falling in love with an American.

MARY: Padraic, you're the greatest liar that ever ran away from Ireland. You insisted on coming to America.

PADRAIC: I loved the energy of her cities, the steam whistles throbbing in the night. How did I ever get sent to this asshole of the universe? God must have been daft. I'll curse Him for wasting such a good man as me on these savages. What crime have I committed that He put me here?

FATHER MURPHY: Well, get out of bed, man. This bed's no good for living.

PADRAIC: Why, this bed is good for everything: eating, sleeping, loving, dreaming. Why, I can sit on it, lie on it, bounce on it, stand on it. It could be the observatory of heaven or the forecastle of a ship. I could be a ploughman at the fields. Here am I at the wheel plowing through the heavy seas. All aboard that's coming aboard.

MOLLY: What is it, Daddy?

PADRAIC: The ship of state for lovers, lunatics and clowns.

SEAN: Where are we going?

PADRAIC: Through the midnight sky. It was a bed; it's now a rocket ship. We're off to find a hole in the sky. Blast off, Lieutenant!

SEAN: Aye, aye, Captain!

PADRAIC: Now to Venus, Saturn and Mars.

GRANDMOTHER: Will you never stop filling their heads with imagination?

PADRAIC: Imagination's divine. The immortal sovereign of the world! The inmost faculty of God! Who will learn the secret of world creation?

MOLLY: Me, me!

SEAN: Me!

PADRAIC: I know a magician named Imagination. The great magician who casts his spell and we the dreamers caught in his web. Watch him take wing. Come on, we'll follow, no matter how far the journey.

(*Both children jump on Padraic's back as he stands on the bed. All the planetary gods become involved in a cosmic dance for the first time during Padraic's romp with the children through the universe.*)

We'll climb on his back and spiral up, up, up throughout the seven worlds. Who follows his sweet reign contains heaven and earth and all the worlds between. I'll follow him to the end of time, for he's immense. But first, are you strong, and are you brave? Who rides Imagination must have a clean, brave mind.

SEAN: Yes, yes!

MOLLY: Yes!

PADRAIC: All right now — up, up, up we go, flying through the rooftop of the world. Here's the first world. That's you, you, you, and you. For each of us is a world entire.

MARY: That's a world. And now for number two.

PADRAIC: Humanity on the earth. If you tire, hold on tight, for here comes number three, this ball of earth. Oh world, within worlds, spinning! Are you dizzy? We've just spun into world four, the solar system within the galaxy. This is a ride you'll never forget. Can you count to five? Things are getting hot. We're swimming in the fire of a billion suns, lost amidst the stars of our galaxy. Here comes six! Our minds are bursting. We've reached the infinite universe itself! And now comes seven! We'll really have to stretch.

MOLLY: Will we find God?

PADRAIC: Let's call out and see. Oh, Lord!

MOLLY: God! God! God!

PADRAIC: Drat, He's on vacation.

MOLLY: What's that?

PADRAIC: He's vacated the universe and left us to our own devices. Look out! We're gonna crash! This world's a prison, that's for sure. If only I could find the exit!

FATHER MURPHY: What's ailing you then, man? Why aren't you romping in the noonday sun?

PADRAIC: I'm in mourning for the nation.

FATHER MURPHY: Poor Ireland.

PADRAIC: Not Ireland. My country. I'm an American now. The president is dead!

FATHER MURPHY: It's full seven years, Paddy.

PADRAIC: It seems like only yesterday. And now the senator, his brother, dead.

GRANDMOTHER: Two years now, Paddy.

PADRAIC: And with him, the priest, the conscience of his race, is dead. Oh God, will murder never end? The Great Beast has freed himself from his dark hole and wends his way toward Calvary again. And the world cries, "Glory to the Beast!" The world cries, "Death, death!" And I'm to march for peace.

MARY: The students expect it, and so do Michael and Katie. You're their spiritual leader.

PADRAIC: Their spiritual enema, you mean.

MARY: They pin all their hopes on you. Your mind has roused them from their slumber.

GRANDMOTHER: And you lying in ease the length of the bed.

PADRAIC: I'm growing stupider by the moment. Oh, to unlearn all the uses of this dull world and slip backward to the womb of time, and exit. What's the way out from this world of grief? Does anyone know?

(*Enter Michael with Great-Grandfather.*)

GREAT-GRANDFATHER: Something's terribly wrong with this country, Michael. Where are the fighting men, men who'll take a stand and not back down to any man?

MICHAEL: They've all been shot down, Great-Grandfather, all our brave leaders shot down.

GREAT-GRANDFATHER: Aye! And there's nothing can be done, no one who'll fight for what's right?

PADRAIC: The evil's too strong.

GREAT-GRANDFATHER: Come on, get out of bed. We'll go out and fight the world ourselves. We'll face up to them.

GRANDMOTHER: You're too old, Father; your fighting days are done.

GREAT-GRANDFATHER: Who says I'm too old, Daughter? Never too old for a good fight. A man who can't fight any more might just as well be dead.

PADRAIC: And I, a peace-loving man, surrounded by fighting men — violence on every side.

GRANDMOTHER: You, peace-loving . . . Huh!

GREAT-GRANDFATHER: Ah, and your father, Paddy, what a proud man was he! Why, he would stand up to the whole world and not budge an inch! He was a man!

GRANDMOTHER: Aye, he was that — every inch a man. He wooed me and, with the same breath, off to the war he went, with barely enough time to conceive you. "Where you going," I says, with my panties half off. "I'm for the revolution," he answered, "to make men free." "What about me," I cried. "Ireland shall be free," he answered. That was your father. He died a hero — betrayed.

GREAT-GRANDFATHER: As Ireland was betrayed.

MICHAEL: As the whole world's betrayed.

PADRAIC: So goes the world: betrayed, betrayed, betrayed . . . Children, promise me you'll be failures. Catch butterfly wings, but not success. Rub your toes in sand; ride lizards' backs, but not success.

GRANDMOTHER: Paddy! That's no way to teach the children.

PADRAIC: This age, Mother, the triumph of mediocrity, would you have me teach them to take part in that?

SEAN: Why not, Daddy?

PADRAIC: It'll make a monkey out of you.

GREAT-GRANDFATHER: Never mind, Sean. He's going to grow up and be a strong fighting man like all the Muldoons, aren't you, lad?

SEAN: Yes sir, a'soldiering I will go.

GREAT-GRANDFATHER: He's going to fight for the honor of his country.

SEAN: Yes sir, like Great-Grandfather.

PADRAIC: You don't understand, Grandfather. There's many ways to fight for the honor of your country.

GREAT-GRANDFATHER: Oh, I understand. I understand better than you think. Don't I, Michael?

MICHAEL: It's one world or bust, Great-Grandfather. We've got to fight for that.

GREAT-GRANDFATHER: Do you hear that? Do you hear that?

PADRAIC: Today's the day you change the world, my son?

MICHAEL: Today's the day we march for peace.

PADRAIC: Peace . . . the very sound of it is music to the ears. But I'm afraid it will never be in our time.

MICHAEL: Peace *now*, and in our time.

PADRAIC: One world. The governments of the world will never allow it.

MICHAEL: Hang the governments of the world!

PADRAIC: A glorious idea! What's the charge?

MICHAEL: Treason — that the governments of the world are leading humanity to war and certain destruction; the charge is disturbing the peace.

GRANDMOTHER: I'm sure you're not right in the head, Michael.

MARY: My son came forth in a passion. His father was cursing night and day when he was born. He tumbled out of my womb looking for a fight.

PADRAIC: Me boy wants to save the world. A world savior he would be. I keep telling him the world refuses to be saved on absolutely all occasions.

GRANDMOTHER: Your father's right. The world can't be saved.

MICHAEL: I don't believe that, Grandmother.

PADRAIC: You can't fight the whole world.

MICHAEL: Why not? You have.

PADRAIC: That was then, son. I'm all through fighting.

MICHAEL: You're just tired, Dad. You don't mean that. You need a rest. I'll go on for both of us.

PADRAIC: Michael, I'm not what you think I am. No man is.

MICHAEL: What do you mean, Dad?

GRANDMOTHER: Oh, Michael, why fight other people's battles for them when they're so cowardly they daren't do it for themselves? People are such damn fools. They'll follow any newfangled thing before they take one step for peace. Who allows the war to go on, the rape of God's green earth to continue? The damn people who remain silent, of course — the ones who are afraid to take a stand — the people who see every atrocity take place before their silly eyes, only to pretend they have no eyes to see. The people with their shenanigans who can create nothin' but who know very well how to destroy the forward march of the world, that's who. The dear sweet people who know only one authority: fear. (*Muttering.*) Damn fools!

MICHAEL: (*Mars descends and raises Michael's arm.*) I can't bear the hypocrisy. I want people to see there's a whole new way to live. I want to raise man up.

PADRAIC: Like Lazarus from the dead.[3]

MARY: My sweet firebrand — my fierce demon. What star shone when I gave birth to you!

PADRAIC: He wants to set fire to the world.

MICHAEL: The world needs fire.

MARY: The world needs love.

MICHAEL: Love's in poverty, running naked in the streets, and no man will have her. The people are crying for freedom. What can love do?

MARY: Here's a tune love can play. You've forgotten Lysistrata of old.[4] I'll tell you what, my love, your sister and I will assemble all the women in the world and withhold love 'til the men, racked with pain, resign themselves to peace. We won't say 'yes' to men until they say 'no' to war.

MICHAEL: It won't work. I'll not live a castrate in a spiritless world. That's no life. I'd rather die.

GRANDMOTHER: You talk as if your head is full of books. You keep wanting to tell the world how ugly it is, and the world keeps hiding in embarrassment. Forget people, Michael. Live for yourself.

MICHAEL: I can't live when everyone around me is suffering.

MARY: Saint Michael and his legion of angels slaying the dragon. Oh,

Mother, are all men such idiots?

GRANDMOTHER: He takes after his father. He was dropped on his head as a tyke. He's not been the same since.

PADRAIC: Old woman, you're a thorn in my side.

GRANDMOTHER: Am I then? Well, let me tell you this. It would have been a tragedy if I hadn't laughed when you turned out to be my son.

(*Enter Katie with Charles.*)

PADRAIC: But quiet now. Here comes the wine of life — sweet grace — my darling daughter, Katie.

KATIE: Good morning Dad, Mum, everyone. Look who I've brought home for Easter.

MARY: Charles! Where did you find him?

KATIE: On campus, as he was getting into his limousine.

CHARLES: Mary! It's been a long time.

MARY: A whole year.

MOLLY: It's Uncle Charles! It's Uncle Charles!

CHARLES: Molly! My darling girl. Did you miss your Uncle Charles?

MOLLY: Oh yes! Did you bring me a present?

CHARLES: Have I ever forgotten?

MOLLY: A dolly . . . a gorgeous Easter dolly.

SEAN: Kid stuff.

KATIE: Isn't he beautiful? So distinguished, and greying at the temples.

CHARLES: I'm getting older.

KATIE: You're handsomer than ever.

CHARLES: Do you think so?

KATIE: Stop it, Uncle Charles. You know you're my favorite.

CHARLES: A good Easter, everyone.

ALL: Happy Easter!

CHARLES: Padraic! . . .

PADRAIC: Charles . . .

CHARLES: Are you ill? What are you doing in bed?

PADRAIC: Ill as this world goes. Father Murphy was about to give me the last rites.

FATHER MURPHY: You must be mad, Padraic. And me a proper pillar of the community! Are you asking the church to bury you alive?

GREAT-GRANDFATHER: It wouldn't be the first time.

GRANDMOTHER: Father!

GREAT-GRANDFATHER: Or the last.

CHARLES: I looked for you at the university.

PADRAIC: I've retired. My kingdom is my bed.

MARY: What took you so long in coming?

CHARLES: The university's in a turmoil. They've called out the National Guard.

PADRAIC: Is it serious then?

CHARLES: You know it is.

MARY: What's to be done?

CHARLES: Where's Michael? (*Calling.*) Michael!

MARY: That's strange, he was here just a moment ago.

CHARLES: I have something for him.

PADRAIC: What is it?

CHARLES: We really must call off this march, Padraic.

MICHAEL: That's impossible, Uncle Charles.

CHARLES: Michael, how good to see you. My, how you've grown. You're a man now.

MICHAEL: Yes.

CHARLES: That reminds me. I haven't given your mother her present.

MARY: What is it?

CHARLES: Find out for yourself.

MARY: Why it's . . . a . . . diamond brooch. You're too extravagant for words.

CHARLES: Nothing's too extravagant for you, Mary. Your other present will be waiting for you Sunday morning. Come to the window, Michael. I've something to show you.

MICHAEL: What is it?

CHARLES: Look for yourself.

SEAN: A brand new convertible. Wow!

MOLLY: It's beautiful.

KATIE: And it drives like a dream.

CHARLES: For your nineteenth Easter. You see, I haven't forgotten.

MICHAEL: Uncle Charles, I . . . I don't know what to say.

CHARLES: There's nothing to say, my boy. Enjoy it.

KATIE: You lucky devil.

MICHAEL: No! I can't take it.

CHARLES: Why not?

MICHAEL: I just can't . . .

MARY: Michael, what are you saying? It's what you've always wanted. Your uncle promised he would get it for you, and he has. What's the matter?

MICHAEL: I . . .

MOLLY: You're wrong, Michael . . .

MICHAEL: I can't go on the peace march and take this gift.

CHARLES: Peace march . . . what are you talking about? You're not going.

MICHAEL: I am. I'm leading it.

CHARLES: But you're a scholar. This is a far cry from the dreamy-eyed young philosopher, mad for Plato, who used to take long walks with me in the woods. Then, you were dedicated to the pursuit of truth, beauty and goodness.

MICHAEL: Thought that doesn't lead to action is sterile. Plato taught me that too.

CHARLES: Michael, you amaze me. When I saw you last, you couldn't have cared less.

MICHAEL: A lot can happen in a year, Uncle Charles.

CHARLES: So I see. Your father's been filling your head with his ideas, hmm?

MICHAEL: Dad's got nothing to do with this; leave him out of it. I make my own decisions.

PADRAIC: I keep telling Michael to agree with you and the dean and adjust, Charles; but he and his friends have their own ideas.

CHARLES: I don't think you know how critical the situation is, Michael. The governor has threatened to call in the militia.

MARY: But certainly your influence can prevent that.

CHARLES: There's nothing I can do.

MARY: As Chairman of the Board . . .

CHARLES: My hands are tied. The campus is in riot. The students have gone too far.

MICHAEL: I don't think they've gone far enough.

CHARLES: You know I'm in sympathy with the students. Our family has endowed the university richly. They're free to do what they want. But why this violence?

MICHAEL: Violence! When the whole country is one gigantic arsenal for war.

CHARLES: Gentle persuasion carries a lot more weight than force. Surely we can discuss our differences.

MICHAEL: It's too late for that. You speak of sympathy; but have you ever listened to us?

CHARLES: I'm listening now.

MICHAEL: You know what we want — an end to nuclear testing, and an end to the training of students for military purposes.

CHARLES: That's out of the question, Michael.

MICHAEL: For you, and the men you do business with. You're turning all the universities of the country into war machines.

MARY: Michael, that's no way to talk to your uncle.

MICHAEL: Behind his back then?

MARY: What's the matter with you? What's got into you?

CHARLES: It's all right, Mary. We're all under a strain. We'll talk more of this later. I think I'll just tidy up a bit before breakfast.

MARY: Yes, there'll be no arguing in this household. It's Easter. What's the matter with me? I haven't even showed you to your room.

CHARLES: The same old room, Mary?

MARY: The same old room. Come on everybody, breakfast. You'll be dining with us, won't you, Father?

FATHER MURPHY: Thank you, I will.

PADRAIC: We'll be along.

(*Exit Mary, Charles, Great-Grandfather, Grandmother, Father Murphy, Sean and Molly.*)

KATIE: Where's Nat? He should have been here by now.

MICHAEL: He'll be here any moment.

KATIE: Why has Uncle Charles never married?

PADRAIC: He's half in love with your mother.

KATIE: Oh Dad!

PADRAIC: It's true. He can't stay away from her very long.

KATIE: That's why he comes so often . . . an important man like him.

(*Padraic nods his head yes.*)

MICHAEL: Why? Did you think he was stuck on you?

KATIE: When I want your opinion, Michael Muldoon, I'll ask for it. It must be sad for Uncle Charles.

PADRAIC: What?

KATIE: Not having a family of his own.

(*Exit Katie.*)

MICHAEL: Dad . . .

PADRAIC: Yes, son.

MICHAEL: Doesn't . . . Mother . . . know about Uncle Charles?

PADRAIC: No, son, I don't think she does.

MICHAEL: But why?

PADRAIC: When you love somebody, it's sometimes hard to see them as they are.

MICHAEL: Has Mother always been close to Uncle Charles?

PADRAIC: Always.

MICHAEL: Dad . . .

PADRAIC: Yes, Michael . . .

MICHAEL: Why is everything so sad?

PADRAIC: The world's a hard place, my boy. It's got a terrible sting. It's brought many a good man down, and many a good woman low.

MICHAEL: Is that what happened to Uncle Charles?

PADRAIC: I think so. You used to love him, didn't you?

MICHAEL: Yes. When I was a kid I used to think he was the greatest man in the world next to you. That was before I found out what he was doing.

PADRAIC: Ah, we're all poor sinners I guess.

MICHAEL: Not you, Dad. You're the foremost authority on what's wrong with the world. You say so yourself.

PADRAIC: Poking fun at your old man, are you, rascal? Well, it's true your old man's full of hot air.

MICHAEL: No one else thinks so. I sometimes think the students have chosen me to lead the march because of you.

PADRAIC: That's nonsense and you know it.

MICHAEL: I guess so. Just the same I wish you were marching with us. I wish you were feeling better.

PADRAIC: I do too, my boy. I do too.

MICHAEL: What is it, Dad?

PADRAIC: I can't explain it, my boy. It's nothing. It will pass. It will pass.

MICHAEL: Can I help?

PADRAIC: Just being what you are is all the help I need. You're a son that would be a credit to any man.

MICHAEL: Ah, Dad! (*Hugs his father.*) I'll make you proud of me today. (*Pause.*) What do you do about doubts, Dad? How can I lead others when there's so many things I'm not sure of?

PADRAIC: Follow your highest thought, and you can't go wrong.

MICHAEL: Always?

PADRAIC: Always.

(*Enter Grandmother.*)

GRANDMOTHER: You think you're going to get breakfast in bed, don't you? But you're not. Michael, will you please show your father to the dining room so he can eat with his family like a civilized man.

MICHAEL: Yes, Grandmother. Come on, Dad.

PADRAIC: I'm not hungry.

MICHAEL: For me, Dad.

PADRAIC: All right, my boy.

(*Exit Padraic, Michael, and Grandmother. Katie enters the room. Everyone is gone. She begins combing her hair, her hand guided by Venus, goddess of love. Nat, unseen by her, enters, pushed in by Mercury, god of devotion, and stands behind her for a moment or two. He carries a small suitcase.*)

NAT: Golden locks have golden tresses, golden in the sun.

KATIE: Tresses gleaming golden sunlight, as bright as dreams on summer mornings, when golden hearts are one.

NAT: Hello, Katie.

KATIE: Nat!

NAT: I came to say goodbye.

KATIE: Goodbye?

NAT: I'm going. Where's Michael?

KATIE: Going? Why? But all our plans . . . ?

NAT: Feet just feel like moving. And when feet say let's go mister, it's time to go.

KATIE: Just like that? Pick up and go?

NAT: Do you need a reason for living or dying? When it's time, it's time.

KATIE: But I don't want you to go! I want you to stay here with me . . . and Michael.

NAT: Katie, Katie, Katie!

KATIE: Oh, sometimes I hate you, Nat Williams, you devil.

NAT: Now you know you don't mean that, angel.

KATIE: I do. Michael needs you.

NAT: He'll get along just fine without me.

KATIE: No he won't.

NAT: I got tracks to make.

KATIE: Today's the day. All our hopes are riding on today.

NAT: Not mine. The sun didn't rise for Nat Williams today. And those people out there aren't my people.

(*Michael enters and listens quietly in background.*)

Their hopes aren't my hopes. Today's not my day.

KATIE: I'm part of today.

NAT: You can have today. I'll take tomorrow.

KATIE: Will tomorrow be any different?

NAT: Where I'm going it will. I'm leaving this country.

KATIE: All alone?

NAT: Just me, myself and I.

MICHAEL: Where will you go?

NAT: I'll follow the wind. The world is wide.

MICHAEL: I thought you were with me.

NAT: You thought wrong; I'm with myself. And you better get with it too. When are you gonna wake up?

MICHAEL: I was counting on you to march with me.

NAT: When are you gonna stop dreaming? This land's so sick, man. The angel of death is calling. You're gonna lead a peace march in a land boiling in blood. They cry peace and they march to the sound of war. "We love you black man," but "Hello, nigger!" I've had it! I'm getting out!

KATIE: Running away won't help, Nat.

NAT: Who's running?

MICHAEL: We've got to fight!

NAT: It's your fight, not mine. Don't lay your trip on me.

KATIE: But it's your dream! All our dreams!

NAT: My dream, yes; but it ain't here, and it ain't now.

KATIE: Freedom! And you won't fight for it?

NAT: I'll fight for it in my own way, and on my own terms.

MICHAEL: That's what we're marching for — to change this world.

NAT: I've seen a million marches. They all go in a circle and end up where they started from — the same place: nowhere. Mission accomplished — nothing accomplished! A lot of hooting and hollering, and clapping each other on the back, yelling and screaming: "We did it this time!" Then everybody goes home. And nothing happens. Nothing changes. Nothing ever changes. Same old world — 'til the next time around. What a comedy! Are you kidding me, man? Go out in front of that mob again?

MICHAEL: I want you with me.

NAT: Shooting my mouth off! What for! They can't hear you; they won't listen. Just end up with a head full of busted dreams. (*Breaks down crying.*) (*Stunned silence.*)

KATIE: Nat . . .

NAT: They fired my mother.

MICHAEL: Fired your mother . . . what are you talking about? For what?

NAT: For having a son who's a radical, and a black radical at that.

KATIE: But that's crazy, why would they want to do that? What's your mother got to do with you?

NAT: They call it "harassment."

MICHAEL: Why didn't you tell me, Nat? I'll talk to my father. He won't let them get away with this.

NAT: Won't he?

KATIE: How could they? I never heard of anything so horrible in my life. Oh, it doesn't matter, there are other jobs.

NAT: Yeah, second-class jobs for second-class citizens.

MICHAEL: What a world.

KATIE: What will you do?

NAT: I told you I'm leaving. I'm going to find me a place, and one for my mother where she can live as she should.

KATIE: We've got to fight this. That's what we're marching for.

NAT: I'm to be your dark supporter.

MICHAEL: You're my friend.

NAT: Yes, I'm your friend, but it's a white man's world.

KATIE: We're gonna march on this old world and make it listen.

NAT: Not me, sister. I've been on all the marches I'm ever gonna go on: peace marches, protest marches, anger marches — sit down, stand up, lie down, walk around, run away, turn around, turn about — glory marches. Tear gas, club in the head — sit-in-jail marches. I marched with the King. I saw some of my own people turn against him. I was sixteen. I saw it happen. I never saw a man take so much pain. I used to wonder what kept him going. I said to myself, then: "Nat Williams, you don't wanna travel with crowds." Since that day I travel alone. It's faster and I'm sure to get where I'm going quicker.

MICHAEL: I need you, Nat.

NAT: I can't hear you. Let the dead bury the dead. I'm going to the land of the living.

MICHAEL: Where's that?

NAT: I don't know. But wherever it is, I'm going . . . where they don't kill your family for what a man is. I'm leaving misery behind.

MICHAEL: Somebody's got to face misery or misery will never end.

NAT: Ever been a nigger on the open road?

MICHAEL: America's dying, Nat.

NAT: I know it. I hear its death rattle; ugly sounds crying in the night.

MICHAEL: It's sad.

NAT: It's so sad; it's enough to tear your heart out.

MICHAEL: How could it go so fast?

NAT: Everybody's running scared. The people in this country got their heads up their asses. Nothin' but turkeys in office. All the good guys get shot down! And now no one's got the courage to stand up and tell it like it is.

MICHAEL: I know.

NAT: So what can we do?

MICHAEL: We've got to reach the people.

NAT: What people? They've given up. The promise of America . . . Shoot! An insurance man's dream: life guaranteed, a ride to the moon! I've rode this country from Canada to the Mexican border, from Maine to New Orleans and what did I find: gas stations, supermarkets, drive-in restaurants and traffic jams. There's the bank where they spend your money for you, the insurance company where they kill you, and the graveyard where they bury you.

(*Michael puts his hand on Nat's shoulder.*)

MICHAEL: I understand how you feel, Nat, and I'm with you . . . Don't leave until I get back, huh? So we can say goodbye right. (*They embrace; Michael starts to go, turns and gives high sign to Nat.*) I love you.

(*Michael turns to go again, but before he reaches the door . . .*)

KATIE: (*To Nat.*) You're not going to let him go like that!

NAT: Michael, wait! Is it that important that I walk with you?

MICHAEL: Yes.

NAT: All right. But just this last time — after that I'm on my way. And don't try to stop me!

MICHAEL: I won't. I'll get the others.

(*Exit Michael.*)

KATIE: Marry me, Nat.

NAT: What?

KATIE: Marry me.

NAT: Are you crazy, Katie?

KATIE: I love you, Nat.

NAT: Katie, what are you talking about?

KATIE: You know what I'm talking about. You want me, Nat, but you're too scared to admit it.

NAT: We gotta go, they're waiting for us. We'll talk about this later.

KATIE: If you walk out of here, don't you ever look at me again.

NAT: Katie!

(*Katie starts stalking him around the room. Nat tries to get away from her.*)

KATIE: There's only now, Nat.

NAT: That's what I'm afraid of. I'm getting out of here.

KATIE: You're not going anywhere.

NAT: Yes, I am.

KATIE: Oh no, you're not!

NAT: Katie, be reasonable.

KATIE: You're not getting past me, Mr. Williams. I see you . . .

NAT: Now, Katie . . .

KATIE: Admit that you love me.

NAT: I can't hear you.

KATIE: You love me and you want to marry me.

NAT: (*His back against the wall, cornered.*) Katie, I swear . . .

KATIE: Yes, swear it, you're crazy about me. You can't keep your hands off me . . . my skin, my flesh . . . all you dream about is Katie, Katie, Katie!

NAT: Katie, you're milk and honey. But, oh baby, I can't have you.

KATIE: You love me Nat, and if you leave me, you'll be sorry.

NAT: Katie, Katie, Katie, you're driving me crazy!

KATIE: Do I dazzle you, Nat?

NAT: Razzle, dazzle! . . .

KATIE: Afraid to bring a little white girl home to your mamma?

NAT: Hell, no! On my sacred honor!

KATIE: You're hiding. Nat Williams, the invisible man. When are you going to show your true color? You're not yellow, are you, Nat? What if I came in black?

NAT: If you came in all the colors of the rainbow, the answer is *no*. Black and white don't mix. Black is black is black . . .

KATIE: Black is the beauty of the brightest day.

NAT: We can't make it.

KATIE: Is there a law against it?

NAT: It's against the law for black and white to love in the U.S.A.

KATIE: Whoever made that law, I'm breaking it.

NAT: You can't break it; the nice decent folks won't let you.

KATIE: Let them try and stop me!

(*Katie reaches out for him and they both fall over armchair and topple onto floor.*)

NAT: What is this? White supremacy?

KATIE: No, it's women's liberation. I'm going to liberate you. Be brave, Nat; it'll just hurt a little.

(*They kiss and hug. As they do so, Charles enters and watches in the background. His mouth falls open as they roll on the floor, hugging and kissing and laughing.*)

CHARLES: Excuse me, I didn't mean to intrude.

(*Nat and Katie look up as he walks out.*)

NAT: This old world is standing between us.

KATIE: Then this old world will just have to move over.

NAT: This old world casts a tall shadow.

KATIE: Then we'll jump over it and reach for the sun, and this old world will just have to catch up.

NAT: The sun is hot — it burns.

KATIE: Does the sun burn hot? My love burns hotter than a thousand suns.

NAT: Oh Lord, help me!

KATIE: The Lord has answered your prayers. All the help you need is me. Oh Nat, let me love you! I won't betray you. Trust me, oh trust me! Oh God, how I love you! Oh Nat, love me; please love me!

NAT: Oh Katie! I'd lie for you; I'd steal for you! I'd kill for you! But I can't marry you!

KATIE: Afraid they'd kill you for daring to take the sacred white skin? Don't you want to walk with me — talk with me — know me as I am — know you as you are? This wondrous thing called me?

NAT: I'd die for you.

KATIE: And I for you. We'll streak right through the eye of the sun, and die and be reborn — cool and collected before the Milky Way — a thousand Milky Ways . . .

NAT: Ah, to be human in the light!

KATIE: Star-studded night, dazzling light, bring my lover home to me.

NAT: Ah, Katie, you're beautiful; but it's only a dream.

KATIE: Then dare to live a dream. You'd die for me, but you won't live for me. It's easier to die for someone than to live for them. Say yes, Nat, say yes! We'll live like a bird on the wing — the singing lark. Come on Nat! We can do it! We can make it! Dare to be a butterfly and not a caterpillar! We'll fly the sky, heaven for our pillow — the green grass for our meat and drink. The daffodil our home — the peony, the tulip and the bright-eyed azalea our playmates. I love your mind! I love your heart! I want to dance and sing when I'm near you! I want you for my very own! I'll not be cheated! I won't let anyone steal you from me! I'm not afraid, Nat. I'll stand against the world!

NAT: All right, then it's true, Katie. You're innocent and clean and pure and everything in this world I love.

KATIE: Say yes, Nat! I love you! I love you! Oh yes, say yes, you belong to me! I belong to you! And yes, yes, yes . . . you're mine, you're mine, please . . .

NAT: And from the moment I saw you all the bitterness poured out of me. The filth of life, like a canker in my heart, was torn away. I was a black cat streaking through the alleyways of the world and suddenly you appeared. You've turned my world upside down.

KATIE: Right side up.

NAT: Where I'm going, you can't follow.

KATIE: I'm a Kate can follow you through every alley. I'll follow you wherever you go.

NAT: You're a babe, seventeen . . . a virgin.

KATIE: My mother knows a thing or two. She taught me to fight for the one I love. She teaches heavenly things — that I'm a child of heaven, and heaven's mine by nature. I'll not be a traitress to myself. You're my haven, and I'm your home.

NAT: Can you live a secret love, hidden from this world of filth?

KATIE: No. I'll sing my love throughout the world. I call on you — fairies, elves and trolls – all creatures of the woods and earth — all rhythms and seasons . . . nights and days . . . to be witness to my love. The whole world's singing "Kate for Nat, and Nat for Kate."

NAT: I'll not drag my love through the gutter.

KATIE: I'll haunt you in your dreams. I'll wreck you in your sleep. You'll not sleep or eat 'til you're mine.

NAT: I can't sleep; I can't eat — prowling through the dark alleys of the world, and suddenly you're there, and all at once the world's renewed. Crack! Dazzling white light and, oh Lord, I'm all undone. I swore I'd cut your image out of my heart; but heaven's in your eye, and all the bitter anger in my heart has melted.

KATIE: You'll never get rid of me, Nat Williams!

NAT: I'll cut you out of my heart.

KATIE: A good story for our grandchildren. Meanwhile, I'll have what's fine — the earth, the stars and you.

NAT: Pain, pain, pain. The pain of this world. And then the sweetness in your eyes melting all the pain away.

KATIE: Give me your pain; I'll take it all.

NAT: What do you know of pain? You're from the world of light.

KATIE: The light comes out of darkness and must to darkness return. This dark pain is not light. It's a burden only you can ease.

NAT: Can you go the distance?

KATIE: I'm my father's daughter. I'm Katie Muldoon, and I can do anything I set my heart to.

NAT: But can you go the distance?

KATIE: I can if you want me to.

NAT: Trapped, trapped . . .

KATIE: Do you want me to, Nat?

NAT: Oh God! I'm a dead man!

KATIE: If you couldn't say no to my brother, how can you say no to me? That settles that.
(*Enter Mary and Padraic.*)
Mommy, Nat proposed to me, and I accepted. Are you happy for me?

MARY: Oh yes, my darling.

KATIE: Oh Daddy, Daddy, Daddy! Nat Williams the Third loves me! He loves me! Do we have your blessing?

PADRAIC: I . . .

KATIE: Oh thank you, Daddy. I knew you would. Come on, Nat! (*Pulling him by the hand.*) We've got to tell your mother. Tell Michael we'll be right back.
(*They exit.*)

PADRAIC: (*As he climbs into bed.*) The world is growing madder every day.
(*Enter Charles and Grandmother.*)

CHARLES: No one can cook like you, Mother. I haven't had a meal like that since the last time I was here.

GRANDMOTHER: I bet you say that to all the girls, you scoundrel.

CHARLES: Only to you.

GRANDMOTHER: You are a flatterer, Charles. Even though you're the most charming man in America, it's all wasted on me. Let's talk about something important.

CHARLES: Such as . . .

GRANDMOTHER: Such as what you brought me for Easter.

CHARLES: You'll find out Sunday.

GRANDMOTHER: Is it the new pots and pans you promised me, you villain?

CHARLES: Wait and see.

(*Exit Grandmother.*)

Who was that fellow?

PADRAIC: What?

CHARLES: That black fellow.

PADRAIC: Oh, you mean that nigger rolling on the floor with Katie.

MARY: Paddy!

CHARLES: What's he doing here with . . .

PADRAIC: He's about to become our son-in-law.

CHARLES: A Negro in our family! That's outrageous!

PADRAIC: Yes, I suppose it is.

CHARLES: You can't be serious!

MARY: It's true, Charles.

CHARLES: But you surely can't approve of this.

PADRAIC: To tell you the truth, Charles, I'm against it. But now that I see you agree with me, I'll have to re-examine my position.

CHARLES: Mary?

MARY: She loves him.

CHARLES: What has love got to do with it? You must put an end to it.

MARY: (*She shakes her head no.*) It would break her heart.

CHARLES: You can't be for it.

MARY: I am, Charles.

CHARLES: *Marie, tu es trop irresponsable. Elle est trop jeune pour se connaître.*

MARY: *Je ne crois pas.*

CHARLES: *Elle n'est qu'une enfant.*

MARY: *Elle est assez âgée.*

CHARLES: *Mais les conséquences!*

MARY: *Peu importe les conséquences!*

CHARLES: But this is insane! They'll have black babies. Black babies — do you understand what that means?

PADRAIC: I should think everyone will understand what that means. The babies will be black.

CHARLES: This is absurd.

PADRAIC: I don't see why. You're known as a humanitarian, a man who has an overwhelming desire to raise the oppressed races of the earth. You even make speeches on the subject. Out of an uncontrollable sympathy for the plight of the downtrodden, you've taken a black man into your family line. It will be very good for your image. You'll be more popular than ever. They'll raise a statue to your benevolence. Who knows . . . the grateful masses

might even make you president — a prize you've long wished for.
It will be the making of you, Charles!

CHARLES: Oh God, how could this happen to me?

PADRAIC: It's life, Charles. It happens to the best of us.

CHARLES: I won't allow it.

PADRAIC: There doesn't seem much you can do. Of course you can
shoot the boy. That might dispense with the problem. But, then
again, she might find another one.

CHARLES: That's in bad taste, Padraic.

PADRAIC: Sorry, I was just trying to be helpful.

MARY: He's a fine boy. You'll get to like him.

CHARLES: A fine boy? Why he's nothing but a common . . .

PADRAIC: I'm a common man, Charles.

MARY: Now let's not have a fracas between you two. You're wrong,
Charles. This marriage will work. Just as you were wrong about
Paddy and me. I've had a wonderful marriage.

CHARLES: That's different.

PADRAIC: You mean I'm not a nigger? But I am a common man.

CHARLES: You said it, Padraic. I didn't. Now, mind you, I have
nothing personal against him. I don't even know the boy.

PADRAIC: But there's a principle at stake?

CHARLES: Well, after all . . . Katie is so far beyond him, he can only
resent her and try to drag her down to his level.

MARY: The life we were born to is not the only one that produces
good men, Charles.

CHARLES: My dear sister . . . the same old illusion. How can you
compare men and women of breeding and education and every
worldly advantage with the common run of men?

MARY: Sometimes there is gold in the common run of men.
Sometimes, when you least expect to find it, there are pearls of
great price.

(*Enter Michael. Stunned by what he hears, he remains unseen in
background.*)

CHARLES: The common man! Hah! I'll tell you about the common
man. We feed him. We clothe him. We educate him. Without us he
is nothing — a spineless, shiftless creature — his horizon no
broader than the sporting page. A dull tool who'd starve to death if
it weren't for men of our class. One can't exactly say this on the
front page of our newspapers, but it's true nevertheless.

MARY: Oh, Charles, why must you exaggerate so, just because you're in a temper? You're speaking of human beings.

CHARLES: Human? Don't make me laugh. Why our greyhounds have more intelligence — the thoroughbreds in our stables are more spirited — our hawks better trained. The mass of men are simply spiritless clay to be molded by us. Insensible to any real culture, they live only for the moment and must be used as such. For hundreds of years they've stood in our way with their sniveling little dreams — their petty bourgeois ideas of democracy. Why must we, we who would make the earth great — our vision of splendor — have to cater to the moods and inane folly of the democratic crowd? Why must we pander to their whims? I'm sick to death of it. But the day will be coming — and shortly — when all that will be over. For now we have what we have always lacked — the resources, the science, the mass communications, to bend the masses to our will and better yet — to replace them.

PADRAIC: You seem to have uh . . . plans for the little people of the earth, Charles. You know, it's always been a puzzle to me why I find you so personally attractive, when I find your principles so utterly despicable!

MARY: You're a great fool, darling, if you believe him. (*Laughing.*) He doesn't mean a word he says. Why Charles has always been one of the kindest and gentlest persons I know.

MICHAEL: I think Uncle Charles means what he's saying, Mother.

CHARLES: Michael, I didn't know you were listening.

MICHAEL: Yes, Uncle Charles, I was listening.

MARY: Michael, were you eavesdropping?

MICHAEL: Yes Mother, in a way; I learn a lot that way. Have you ever thought that all those little people you talk about suffer, Uncle Charles? I have. I think about it a lot, and it hurts me. Your vision of life, Uncle Charles, is based on trampling their faces in the mud.

MARY: Michael, your uncle has always helped people. You mustn't pay attention to what a man says, but to what he does. I've always taught you that.

MICHAEL: Yes Mother, I know all about it. It's called the welfare state. In ancient Rome it was called bread and circuses; but whatever you call it, Uncle Charles is the head of it. He's everywhere with his grants and endowments, his stipends and his subsidies, sapping the lifeblood of the country — of the world. I don't think there's a more subtle way to corrupt men's souls than to steal their initiative and give them the illusion of freedom.

That's what all your benevolence comes to, Uncle Charles. That's why I couldn't accept your offer to get me out of the draft while others had to go. I won't be a cheat. I'd rather die.

MARY: Oh, Michael!

MICHAEL: I love you, Uncle Charles, but I'm going to fight you. And I'm not alone. Millions of students are on the march, all over the world: Tokyo, Paris, Mexico City, New York, and everywhere in our country. And we're going to end this war, this senseless slaughter you carry on just to make your billions.

CHARLES: The war can't be stopped, Michael. We have a wartime economy. The nation would be ruined.

MICHAEL: Lose its fat, you mean. But a nation of pigs should be destroyed. It doesn't deserve to live at the cost of the whole world's suffering. Then maybe we'd have a resurrection of lean and hungry men — spirited — with the light of heaven in their eyes.

(*Enter Father Murphy, Great-Grandfather and Grandmother.*)

CHARLES: Michael . . . Michael . . . our position is . . .

MICHAEL: Your position, Uncle Charles, is built on a lie.

CHARLES: I think I understand you, Michael. When I was your age, I felt as you do. Then, little by little, I came to see the world for what it was. You're in a dream, Michael, a lovely dream, but you can't expect these things to happen overnight. You can't change human nature all at once, son. You must learn patience.

MICHAEL: Overnight? For ten thousand years men of your persuasion have been saying "Patience, patience! You can't change people! That's the way the world is. Little by little . . . It's always been this way. The world will never change." Until, little by little, we've drifted to the edge of chaos; and unless something is done now, immediately and all at once, there won't be anyone around to say "patience" anymore. But our generation is going to change all that.

GREAT-GRANDFATHER: That's telling him, me boy.

CHARLES: You insist on going on this march then?

MICHAEL: Yes, now and forever. All the way 'til victory.

CHARLES: Michael, you mustn't go. There'll be violence, perhaps even bloodshed.

MICHAEL: Anything that isn't worth dying for isn't worth living for. Father Murphy, give me your blessing.

GREAT-GRANDFATHER: Hooray! You're going; I knew you wouldn't let anyone stop you.

CHARLES: What a beautiful boy!

PADRAIC: That's what I like about you, Charles — that you can recognize that. You weren't born to be a second-rater.

MARY: Does he remind you of someone, Charles? You were just like him, when you were his age.

GREAT-GRANDFATHER: For the love of God, make it a short blessing, Father. We've got work to do.

GRANDMOTHER: Father, stay out of this.

GREAT-GRANDFATHER: Not on your life. Daughter, bring me my coat and hat and high-stepping boots.

GRANDMOTHER: Father, please!

GREAT-GRANDFATHER: Not another word, Daughter. (*Exit Grandmother.*)

PADRAIC: Grandfather, you're not going out there in all that ruckus.

GREAT-GRANDFATHER: I am! And if you had any brains, you'd go out too.

(*As he reaches for his walking stick, Mars hands it to him.*)

PADRAIC: You're mad.

GREAT-GRANDFATHER: We'll see who's mad. I'm going to march with my great-grandson. And who's to stop me? And if you weren't too lazy to get off your fat backside, you'd be marching with us. That's how it should be — the three of us together, shoulder to shoulder.

PADRAIC: I'll not march today or any other day.

GREAT-GRANDFATHER: No! Padraic Clancy . . . you'd rather talk your life away. Now remember what I tell you, Michael . . . When you're going out to fight dragons, you've got to keep your wits about you, you're the leader. You've got to have eyes in back of your head. Don't trust anyone. Here's something to keep you on your guard.

(*Great-Grandfather removes his cross and gives it to Michael.*)

MICHAEL: Great-Grandfather, your cross!

GREAT-GRANDFATHER: I've been saving it for you. Remember now, watch out, for you don't know what's apt to happen. Don't forget my words now. Listen to what an old man has to teach you. I've lived a long time on this earth, Michael. You're young; you don't know people.

MICHAEL: People are people, Great-Grandfather.

GREAT-GRANDFATHER: Shh! Now listen! People are no damn good. They only pretend to be human. They'll betray a man every damn time. Did I ever tell you about the time I was with my leader

Parnell . . . ?[5]

MICHAEL: (*As he leads Great-Grandfather out into the garden.*)
Yes, Great-Grandfather . . .

CHARLES: I must get to a phone!

MARY: Charles, what is it? I've never seen you like this. It's only a march.

CHARLES: Yes, only a march.

MARY: Is there something you're not telling us?

CHARLES: No . . . it's just that I have this terrible foreboding . . .

MARY: Another headache?

CHARLES: *Oui, un peu.*

MARY: *Charles, tu devrais t'occuper mieux de toi.*
(*Pluto and Neptune come down and surround Charles.*)

CHARLES: *Ce n'est rien. Ca va s'en aller.*

MARY: *Excuse-moi. Je te cherche quelque chose à prendre.*

CHARLES: *Je dois trouver un téléphone.*

MARY: *Par ici, Charles, ca fait plus privé.*
(*Pluto and Neptune accompany Mary as she leads Charles offstage.*)

PADRAIC: Do you ever wonder what we're living for, Father?

FATHER MURPHY: Why, to be good Christians! For the immortality of the soul.

PADRAIC: I wish I could call myself a Christian, but I'm not. I'm no more Christian than the church is.

FATHER MURPHY: Well, if the church ain't Christian, I'll be damned for a pagan.

PADRAIC: Aye, pagans all. It's so hard to love your neighbor. I can't even love myself properly. (*Padraic goes to window.*) Michael, Katie, where are you? You're out there somewhere in all that mess. Our grandfathers and fathers were in it, and now our sons and daughters, fighting blindly in a dark world for the eternal revolution that never comes.

FATHER MURPHY: I have many a spiritual son and daughter struggling alongside of them, Paddy.

PADRAIC: That's right, you do. I'm tempted to go out there looking for them, but what good would it do? There I go, weeping my eyes out in the midst of a riot. Has anyone seen my children? I can't help worrying a bit, though.

FATHER MURPHY: You can't lie in bed forever, Paddy.

PADRAIC: Ah, Father . . . This age wished to deceive itself. I've set my face against it. I'll hide myself between the sheets and pray for sweet oblivion. Do you think the gods, from jealousy, placed some organ in our ancestors to make them not quite right in the head? We must be upside down the way we clearly miss reality and take fantasy for the sober light of day.

FATHER MURPHY: Patience, Padraic. Humanity is still in swaddling clothes.

PADRAIC: Ah, Father, this world's an insubstantial dream. We're shipwrecked on a speck of dirt revolving 'round a spark of light somewhere on the wheel of time.

FATHER MURPHY: Shipwrecks all.

PADRAIC: I'm in exile.

FATHER MURPHY: We're all exiled here — exiles from heaven.

PADRAIC: We fell from the sky, Father?

FATHER MURPHY: Something like that.

PADRAIC: "Humpty Dumpty sat on a wall.
Humpty Dumpty took a great fall.
All the King's horses and all the King's men
Couldn't put Humpty Dumpty together again."
How in hell do we find the way back together again?

FATHER MURPHY: The world's sins are knocking at my door, waiting for that answer — the misery of the world pouring in my ear. Oh, to pour the misery in an ocean — in one ear and out the other.

PADRAIC: Stop your blubbering, Father.

FATHER MURPHY: Wretched sins, hardly worth a good confessional.

PADRAIC: I see you haven't kept up with the evil of the world. You're behind the times, Father.

FATHER MURPHY: Oh, but *I have*, Padraic. I have. People have just forgotten themselves. All they need is a little tenderness, a bit of encouraging kindness to remember themselves.

PADRAIC: If I'm to hear this heavenly gush, have the decency to provide me with a drink. (*Father Murphy takes a bottle of whiskey out from under his frock.*) I'm glad to see you haven't lost all your bad habits.

FATHER MURPHY: A wee nip now and then does the fighting soul some good.

PADRAIC: What a heavenly ascent! There's spirit in you yet. I thought you were a man of peace.

FATHER MURPHY: I'm naturally ill-tempered. I put on the cloth to mortify the flesh and, in Christ's sweet name, subjugate old Adam.

PADRAIC: Aye, you were a hellion when we were kids. Remember Peggy Clancy, Father?

FATHER MURPHY: Peggy *Curran*! How could I forget her!

PADRAIC: The devil's in you yet. There's hope for you still. And here I was, thinking you might be a lost soul.

FATHER MURPHY: Not yet.

PADRAIC: Ah, you were a sweet lover in those days. You had all the lovelies in a swoon 'til you started teaching them their Christian duty. You've gotten a bit crusty since.

FATHER MURPHY: The old Adam's bobbling yet, if that's what you mean. But I've no time for that.

PADRAIC: Your piety's misplaced. You priests are walking cauldrons of desire.

FATHER MURPHY: The church has taught us well. We're alchemical retorts. And since I've learned to transform the star stuff that makes babes into higher matter, I've got a rage to love.

PADRAIC: It's true. Divine love's the balm will heal all wounds. Ah, for one drop of that healing fluid — ambrosial fire!

FATHER MURPHY: Amen!

PADRAIC: Well, you're a Christian. That's for sure. And I? What am I? I'm nothing.

FATHER MURPHY: You're a man.

PADRAIC: A man? Well, that's nothing. A piece of nakedness shivering in the dark.

FATHER MURPHY: We've all got to fight.

PADRAIC: Even you, Father?

FATHER MURPHY: Yes, even me. I've got to fight to keep my faith and belief. Sometimes I think a demon created the race. It's a test of faith. But I've got no time for minor temptations; there's too much work to be done. I've got to fight the precinct captain who expects his daily dole. I've got to fight the ward boss, the Fire Department, the police, City Hall. That's the trouble — the whole world wants to go on the dole. They think the government has taken the place of the Lord. There's a limit to greed, you know. These sinners would try the patience of God, much less me. I wasn't cut out for a priestly life.

PADRAIC: To misery, misery knows no bounds. The earth's in upheaval, Satan's loose, and humanity's vomiting up its age-old crimes. Now comes the bursting of the boil of accumulated evil.

FATHER MURPHY: It's the fever of the age. God's in hiding. It's his favorite pastime.

PADRAIC: Is it hide and seek we're playing with Him in this lunatic asylum?

FATHER MURPHY: Aye, and finders keepers!

PADRAIC: Then I'll play hide and seek with God. The bubble's soon to burst. I'll build a Noah's Ark and ride the tide of evil. I'm sick and tired of living this stupid, senseless life.

FATHER MURPHY: We must go on, Paddy.

PADRAIC: Go on? To what? For what? Why are we living? What is life? Come on now, Killian. I've got to know!

FATHER MURPHY: What is it then?

PADRAIC: My skull is cracking. I feel like a man about to go mad! I don't see the sense in living.

FATHER MURPHY: There's God.

PADRAIC: Aye, there's God. But where is He? When you call Him, He never comes.

FATHER MURPHY: One thing's for sure; He'll come in a way and time when you least expect Him.

PADRAIC: I'd love to get my hands on Him. He's a slippery bastard, though.

FATHER MURPHY: Let me know when you find Him. I've been chasing Him all my life. And when I find Him, I'll tell Him a thing or two.

PADRAIC: What would you say to Him?

FATHER MURPHY: I'd say: Lord, help this poor lost soul, Padraic Clancy Muldoon, to get out of bed. He doesn't mean to be a sinner. He's just a poor ignorant man that's lost his way.

PADRAIC: And what's the Lord saying?

FATHER MURPHY: He says He never heard of you.

PADRAIC: Never heard of me? Isn't there an angel up there in paradise can put in a good word for me?

(Father Murphy shakes his head.)

Step aside, and let me have a crack at Him myself.

FATHER MURPHY: Just a second.

PADRAIC: Lord, it's me, Your faithful servant. Padraic Clancy. Can You hear me?

FATHER MURPHY: He's a proudful, vain, melancholy, gluttonous lout, Lord, wishing to repent and in need of forgiveness like the rest of us.

PADRAIC: Tone it down a bit. I'm not that bad.

FATHER MURPHY: You're worse.

PADRAIC: Ah, you're drunk. I'll have a sober judge.

FATHER MURPHY: PADRAIC!!

PADRAIC: You're a spy for God — sending reports up to heaven.

FATHER MURPHY: Yes, I'm that. And the Lord is saying: "Now, Killian, bring him back to the fold."

PADRAIC: The church's a comfort station on the road to Calvary for men too cowardly to go the distance. I want no part of the Church — black dungeons of despair, where men go to worship their sadness. Let in the light, Father, let in the light! The truth! I want the truth.

FATHER MURPHY: The devil eats souls, you know. I'd hate to think of Beelzebub[6] regally dining on your immortal parts.

PADRAIC: I'm crippled now; I'm about to hang myself from the nearest tree. I've nothing to lose. I must go on. There must be something greater than this life.

FATHER MURPHY: And you think you're right in your quarrel with humanity?

PADRAIC: Positive!

FATHER MURPHY: And if divine debate proves you're wrong?

PADRAIC: Then I'll creep back to your church. And if I'm right . . . ?

FATHER MURPHY: Then I'll keep you stocked with Irish whiskey for a month.

PADRAIC: Done! Go on, Father, do your worst.

(By this time, both Father Murphy and Padraic are tipsy.)

FATHER MURPHY: Lord, this man says he can't stand humanity; and he's brazen enough to say he's right — that You agree with him — that You can't stand them any more than he.

PADRAIC: (Winces.) What does He say to that?

FATHER MURPHY: The Lord says: "Then you can't stand Me for I'm the One that made them."

PADRAIC: Not true, Lord, not true. I'm being slandered. This priest of Yours wants to damn me straight to hell.

FATHER MURPHY: You've damned yourself, you loveless creature you. Answer the charge: Is it true or not?

PADRAIC: What? Is what true?

FATHER MURPHY: Stop equivocating!

PADRAIC: I love the herb, the grass, the flowers . . . I love Creation.

FATHER MURPHY: But you don't love men! (Pause.) Answer, in the name of your Creator!

PADRAIC: Aye, it's true. I love not men.

FATHER MURPHY: Will not!

PADRAIC: Cannot!

FATHER MURPHY: Why not?

PADRAIC: What is this? The Holy Inquisition?

FATHER MURPHY: Stop squirming, you heathen, and answer.

PADRAIC: You've done a bad job, Lord. Man's an ill-begotten race. You've botched it.

FATHER MURPHY: The proof! Prove man's misbegotten, if you can.

PADRAIC: He's a liar, a cheat, a swindler, a slanderer, an envious belly-aching rogue; a pompous self-conceited braggart. He loves not God and doesn't deserve the gift of life from his Creator.

FATHER MURPHY: True, only too true.

PADRAIC: Ah, ha! And now I've won. That's the proof!

FATHER MURPHY: Not at all. The Lord says: "You're to love them anyway."

(*Enter Mary.*)

MARY: You've worked a miracle, Father. You've got him to take a stand.

PADRAIC: I'm taking a stand all right — right here on my bed! And not you or anyone else is going to get me out of it.

MARY: Have you not heard, Padraic Clancy Muldoon, the sun is shining. It's a beautiful day. On a day like this, God must still be in His heaven.

PADRAIC: Then pity the poor devils like me who must still be in purgatory.

MARY: It's twelve o'clock. And now for your promise.

PADRAIC: What promise?

MARY: Oh come on, sweetheart, rise and shine.

PADRAIC: Oh, for a little peace and quiet.

MARY: Peace and quiet?

PADRAIC: There must be an awful pounding in God's ears in this year of our Lord, 1971. Have a heart and give the Great Man some peace, and me too, I say.

MARY: You rascal you . . . Get out of bed!

PADRAIC: Woman, do you take me for a fool? Life's a bad dream. An intelligent man will have none of it. I'll to bed; wake me up when it's all over and it's curtains for the world.

MARY: It'll be too late then. We'll all be dead.

PADRAIC: And won't it be a good thing, too? The universe will be rid of its experiment gone astray. And then we'll all get some peace and quiet.

MARY: The universe will only have to try again.

PADRAIC: What are you blabbing about now? Try again for what? What are you talking about?

MARY: You told me so yourself.

PADRAIC: Told you what?

MARY: That man is a great experiment conducted by great Nature herself, the servant of the Soul of the world, to see if she could produce a being capable of reaching the stars.

PADRAIC: Sweet Jesus! I never said any such thing.

MARY: You did, Paddy. You swore it was true — as true as you loved me.

PADRAIC: It was true and still is. Unfortunately the experiment has failed, and man has gone awry. They've even announced it in the *Daily News*: "God is dead!" And then only a short leap to man is dead. And now they're putting these gorgeous sentiments into practice. I've seen enough! It's the end of the world. I'll close my eyes on this nightmare and sleep it off — sleep 'til the end of time. (*Enter Katie, Great-Grandfather, then Grandmother.*)

GRANDMOTHER: Oh my God! What's happened to him?

KATIE: Help me with him, Grandmother!

GRANDMOTHER: I told you not to go out there, Father. Why won't you ever listen to me?

GREAT-GRANDFATHER: Oh, leave off. Leave off!

MARY: Katie! Grandfather! What's happened?

KATIE: Oh, Mother, Great-Grandfather collapsed when the riot broke out.

MARY: Riot! Padraic . . .

GREAT-GRANDFATHER: Collapsed, my eye. I was pushed.

KATIE: Now . . . Great-Grandfather.

MARY: Katie . . . You're trembling . . .

GREAT-GRANDFATHER: I was pushed, I tell you. Some rascals pushed me.

GRANDMOTHER: A man your age going on a march, cavorting with children.

GREAT-GRANDFATHER: What the hell did you expect me to do — lie in me bed?

MARY: What happened, Katie?

KATIE: Oh Mama, it was awful. They used tear gas.

MARY: Tear gas!

KATIE: And then the shooting broke out.
FATHER MURPHY: Shooting! Who was shooting?
KATIE: The militia.
FATHER MURPHY: Why?
KATIE: I don't know! I don't know!
MARY: Oh my God! . . . Padraic. Where's Michael?
KATIE: Great-Grandaddy and I got separated from Michael and Nat when they started shooting. We lost them.
MARY: If anything happens to . . . Paddy . . . Paddy . . .
PADRAIC: What is it?
MARY: There's been trouble. You've got to find Michael; he's in danger.
PADRAIC: Nothing to worry about. Michael can handle himself in a battle. Hello, Katie!
KATIE: Oh, Daddy, you're drunk.
PADRAIC: Who's drunk? I've never been drunk in my life.
KATIE: Oh, Daddy!
MARY: Paddy, he needs you. (*Starts shaking him.*)
FATHER MURPHY: It's serious, Padraic. We've got to go find him.
PADRAIC: Go where? There's nowhere to go . . .
   (*Starts to go and passes out.*)
MARY: Father, help me.
FATHER MURPHY: He's in no condition to do anything; I'll go.
GRANDMOTHER: You can't go without your coat, Father.
FATHER MURPHY: No, I suppose not.
MARY: Oh Killian, don't let anything happen to my boy.
KATIE: I'll go with you, Father.
MARY: You stay here!
KATIE: But Mother, Nat's with Michael. He needs me. What if . . .
   It's not just Michael, Mother. It's Nat.
FATHER MURPHY: It's best you do what your mother says, Katie.
KATIE: But . . .
FATHER MURPHY: Please, Katie, stay with your mother. She needs you too.
MARY: Hurry, Killian.
FATHER MURPHY: Yes.
   (*Exit Father Murphy.*)
KATIE: Oh, Mama, I'm scared, Mama.
MARY: Shhh, honey.
KATIE: I'm so scared.

MARY: It's all right, baby.

KATIE: What are we going to do, Mama?

MARY: Pray . . . Pray . . .

GRANDMOTHER: Put this around you, darling. You're shivering to death. And come into the kitchen. I'll give you a nice hot bowl of soup to warm your bones.

KATIE: Oh, Grandmother.

(*Exit Katie and Grandmother.*)

(*Mary throws water on Padraic.*)

MARY: Oh, the pity of it, Paddy Muldoon!

PADRAIC: What the blazes! You blasted female! You're destroying my life!

MARY: You haven't got a life, Paddy.

PADRAIC: Don't say that, Mary!

MARY: I married a proud man.

PADRAIC: And still am!

MARY: Not a man too timid to get out of bed and help his own son.

PADRAIC: I can't help anyone. I can't save humanity; I can't even save myself.

MARY: You can't turn your back on the world and walk away from it all. It's your world; you're a part of it.

PADRAIC: I want no part of it. Who asked to be born?

MARY: But you agreed to live in it. You can't call it quits now, just because the going's getting rough.

PADRAIC: It's a smooth ride for me.

MARY: And what about Michael? He needs you now. God knows what's happened to him! Don't betray your humanity, Paddy, or I'll have to leave you.

PADRAIC: I can't find it! The world's taken all but a few shreds and patches.

MARY: Get it back then, man! Get it back, as you love me.

PADRAIC: Ah, if only I could!

MARY: You can.

PADRAIC: Do you think I could? Is it possible yet?

MARY: The man I married could. If you're anything like him, you can.

PADRAIC: And do you see in me the faint promise of such a man?

MARY: I see in you what I've always seen. More than the faint promise — the hushed expectation. I've not chosen you all these years to blind myself to what you are.

PADRAIC: I'll for it then.

MARY: Hurry then, while there's light enough.

PADRAIC: I'll just gather myself together now. Yes, before the world is plunged in darkness. I better get a move on.

MARY: There's my darling man. Well, what are you waiting for? Hurry up, honey boy!

PADRAIC: I'm going! I'm going!

MARY: You can't be going if you're sitting. What's the matter with you, Paddy? What's ailing you, darling?

PADRAIC: If only you could understand . . . I wish . . . Mary . . .

MARY: Understand! I understand enough, too much.

PADRAIC: Give me time. I need time.

(*Enter Sean, Molly and Grandmother.*)

MARY: Sean, what are you doing home from school so early?

MOLLY: Sean lied.

SEAN: I did not.

MOLLY: He said Christ was a leprechaun.

GRANDMOTHER: A leprechaun?

MOLLY: And he wouldn't take it back.

SEAN: It's true.

MOLLY: You lied, Sean.

SEAN: I did not. Ask Great-Grandfather.

GRANDMOTHER: What kind of tall tales are you filling his head with now, Father?

SEAN: Great-Grandfather, didn't you tell me Ireland's downfall came when she forsook the fairy's world for Christianity?

GREAT-GRANDFATHER: That's right, lad, and that only because St. Patrick convinced the Gaelic Christ was a leprechaun pretending to be a man.

PADRAIC: Sweet Jesus! St. Patrick was the greatest liar Ireland ever produced. No wonder the Church made him a saint.

GREAT-GRANDFATHER: No, it's true. Christ was the greatest leprechaun of all.

SEAN: You see, Molly?

MOLLY: Yes, Sean.

GREAT-GRANDFATHER: Only a leprechaun could die, rise from the dead and be reborn.

PADRAIC: I'd like to follow him in that!

GREAT-GRANDFATHER: Once I went into the garden and dug for elves. I found one too, but he was so forlorn that I scared him and he ran away. But tell me, children, have you found Him yet? Have you found Him yet?

MOLLY: Found who?

SEAN: Found who?

GREAT-GRANDFATHER: Found who? You know who! You know who!

SEAN: I know who!

MOLLY: I know who!

GREAT-GRANDFATHER: God! God! God!

SEAN: But where is God, Great-Grandfather?

GREAT-GRANDFATHER: Well, in your Easter egg. That's what you're going on the Easter hunt for. Don't you know that God is in everything, from the littlest to the biggest? I'm gonna tell you a secret now. Can you keep a secret?

MOLLY AND SEAN: Yes . . . Yes.

GREAT-GRANDFATHER: Do you know that you are sitting on God? (*Molly jumps up and looks.*)
(*Dancing.*) Look quick now. He's in that post and in that flower. Why, do you know that He's right inside of you?

MOLLY: Inside of me? Then why doesn't He come out?

GREAT-GRANDFATHER: I'm sorry to say God is in prison.

SEAN: What do you mean He's in prison?

GREAT-GRANDFATHER: He's locked up in people and rocks, and trees and flowers, and oceans and butterflies, and everything we can see.

SEAN: Even dirt?

GREAT-GRANDFATHER: Yes, even dirt.

MOLLY: Why doesn't He get out?

GREAT-GRANDFATHER: He can't. This is God's problem; because if He could, the moon would grow up and become like the earth; the earth would burst into a sun; and the sun would spin a web like all the stars in heaven. God keeps crying out for help, but no one hears Him. You see, children, the Lord needs man to help Him do this. But man doesn't want to help.

MOLLY: Why not?

GREAT-GRANDFATHER: Because man's thrown away the key to his heart . . . And he can't see God.

SEAN: But, Great-Grandfather, you said God's inside everyone.

GREAT-GRANDFATHER: Yes, Sean, everyone's got a speck of God in him, even your father.

SEAN: Then, how come we're not all in heaven?

MOLLY: Now, that's a good question.

(*In answer to question, Great-Grandfather does a little jig.*)

GREAT-GRANDFATHER: And that's the answer!

MOLLY: That's no answer, Great-Grandfather.

SEAN: Tell us the truth.

PADRAIC: The truth! The boy wants to know the truth.

GRANDMOTHER: For Christ's sake, tell 'em. Go ahead. Tell 'em the truth, Father.

GREAT-GRANDFATHER: All right, then. Sit down everyone, and be quiet. I'll tell you what my good friend Hans Christian Andersen said.[7] Once upon a time the devil made a diabolical mirror . . . Is that right? Am I making a mistake?

GRANDMOTHER: By Jesus, Father, you're always making a mistake! Get on with it, Father! Go on!

GREAT-GRANDFATHER: And whenever anybody on earth looked into this distorted mirror, they saw themselves as ugly. And then do you know what the devil did? The devil took the images up to heaven. And because no thing in heaven can be other than beautiful, the closer everyone came to God, the more they saw their ugliness. Until everyone burst out laughing, and the immensity of the laughter shattered the mirror into a million pieces. And when all the pieces fell to earth, a little piece of glass entered each man's eye and blinded him to the beauty of life. And that's why since that day only the few who get that little piece of glass out of their eye see that they're in heaven already and that this earth is heaven now, while all the rest of us see life as ugly.

(*The children sit in astonishment, then break out gleefully in applause. The rest of the family join in their mirth. Enter Nat wounded, with Pluto at his side.*)

KATIE: Nat . . . Oh, you're bleeding.

MARY: Where's Michael . . . Where's Michael?

KATIE: Nat!

MARY: Don't say it.

NAT: He's dead.

(*Mary is held invisibly in the arms of Jupiter, god of compassion.*)

PADRAIC: Dead! No!

NAT: There was shooting . . . We broke through their lines. As the rifle came down they were crying: "Get the nigger, get the nigger." Michael threw himself in front of me. He . . . died . . . for me.

(*Quiet consternation as family moves to comfort and console one another.*)

MARY: Oh, no! Oh, no! . . . No! No!

(*Mary runs across the room towards the door. Nat grabs her.*)
Michael! Michael!
NAT: (*Holding her.*) You don't want to go out there, Mrs. Muldoon.
You don't want to go out there!
(*Mary and Nat are held invisibly in Jupiter's arms.*)
MARY: Let me go! Let me go! (*Starts lashing out, beating on his chest.*)
NAT: You don't want to go out there!
(*Mary collapses in Nat's arms.*)
MARY: Oh, my boy . . . my boy!!

ACT II

(*The scene opens in the dining room of the Muldoon home. Everyone in the family from the children to Great-Grandfather is seated around the dining table, a large meal before them. Utter and oppressive silence in the room. Each member registers the shock, disbelief, sorrow of Michael's death.*)

GREAT-GRANDFATHER: I know how you feel, Padraic. It's how I felt the day your father died — that bloody Easter Sunday when my brave boy was murdered — shot from behind . . . The dirty English swine . . . they came with their thick black boots trampling our faces in the mud, squeezing our blood and breaking our backs 'til a million whispers became a mighty roar, and we struck back. It was a day like any other, a day never to be forgot, that day we made our minds up to throw the dirty bastards out. I found him there in the gutter, choking and spitting blood. My bonnie lad . . . he smiled and cried, "Dad" as I held him to my heart. I prayed with all my might as I carried him in my arms, the long way back . . . but when we got home my son was dead. Then I went mad. A black rage drove me out on the street cursing and screaming, my hands aching to strangle the butchers who killed my fair lad. Then I felt something tugging at my boots. It was your mother, poor lass; she was wild, grabbing hold of me legs, not letting go, 'til we both fell into the mud, sobbing out our grief. After a while, we went into our house and closed the door. There we sat for three days and nights with our dead boy and our grief. (*Silence. Great-Grandfather reaches for the bottle of wine, pours, and takes a long drink.*)

Eight months later, you were born, Paddy. Something died in me that day, the day they killed your dad. (*Drinks again.*)

And now it's come again, that bloody Easter Sunday so many years ago. For Michael's dead. Ah, Paddy, Paddy, always the same old tune: the sons of light must fight the sons of darkness; the living against the dead.

(*Silence. Great-Grandfather takes another drink. Mars and Jupiter surround and isolate Padraic in his grief.*)

PADRAIC: Still want to go a'soldiering, lad?

SEAN: No, Dad, my fighting days are done. Oh, Daddy! (*Begins to weep.*) I miss Michael so much. (*Sits on Padraic's lap.*)

PADRAIC: So do I, my boy. So do I.

SEAN: It hurts so much; I want to go with him.

PADRAIC: Oh, my son, my son, would to God I had died instead of you.

GRANDMOTHER: Oh Michael, all your promise washed away.

MARY: I trembled when I conceived you. And when you quickened in my womb, I felt blessed. The day you were born, it was as if the angels danced about your head. When you hungered at my breast I knew a peace I can't forget. I cried with joy that God had sent me a boy, a manchild that would be a blessing to the world. But now you're dead. Oh God, never to see your face again! Never to hold you in my arms once more. Gone . . . all gone. Ohhhh Michael, I loved you so.

PADRAIC: Mary . . . (*rises and holds her in his arms*) Mary . . .

MARY: Shhh . . . it's all right. I never even had a chance to say goodbye. He was so young. Oh, Michael, there was so much I had to tell you. It's so unfair. Why?! Why?! Oh, where was I the day my son died? I should have been at his side. Where was I when he needed me! I keep hearing Michael as he lay dying, "Mother, where are you?" Was he afraid, Paddy, was he afraid as he lay dying? So all alone, vulnerable and lost. Oh, I can't bear to think he was . . . my tender lamb. I hate this world, this poor godforsaken world that slaughters our flesh and blood before our eyes. Must we give our sons as blood offerings forever so that it can go on and on in its pitiable madness? Let the world perish, but give me back my son! Give him back . . . please God . . . give him back to me.

CHARLES: Mary!

MARY: Oh Charles, remember how it used to be? You and he were inseparable. Besides his dad, in all the world, he loved you as he did no other man.

CHARLES: And I loved him as the son I never had.

MARY: Life was so simple then. Why, oh why can't it come again?

GREAT-GRANDFATHER: For the love of sweet Jesus, Father, don't sit around like the bloody church and make official mourners of us all. Take a drink.

FATHER MURPHY: I will, Grandfather. I will.

(*The cup is passed around the table. As it reaches the last person . . .*)

GREAT-GRANDFATHER: Aye, that's the spirit! Now let's break bread. (*Everyone, except Molly, begins eating.*)

It's as good as always, Mary.

ALL: Aye.

GREAT-GRANDFATHER: Molly, why aren't you eatin'?

MOLLY: I don't feel like eating, Great-Grandfather.

GREAT-GRANDFATHER: (*Rising and banging fist on table.*) Well, you damn well better eat! It's the Lord's day. On a day like this we should be glad. And here we are, sitting around, crying our eyes out . . . Waste no tears on those that are leaving, I say. It's those that are coming in that are in trouble.

GRANDMOTHER: Some must go up.

SEAN: And some must go down.

FATHER MURPHY: Some must come back again.

MOLLY: And some go all around.

GREAT-GRANDFATHER: We should mourn those being born and give joy to those who die. All hail death, the great liberator! Give the Virgin Mary a bloody good kiss for me when you see her, Michael! Now why so sad! He'll not come back again in the form of a dog.

SEAN: Nay . . .

GREAT-GRANDFATHER: Or a lizard.

MOLLY: Nay.

GREAT-GRANDFATHER: Or an ant.

KATIE: If he came again he would come with vision. He would come as an eagle soaring high — the boldest bird in the sky — the one he loved so much.

NAT: Or with the wild strength of a tiger.

SEAN: Lionhearted.

FATHER MURPHY: Or as a dove with peace in his heart.

GRANDMOTHER: Or with the great power of a bull.

MOLLY: As a unicorn — so beautiful.

MARY: He'd come with all of these and more, for he'd come with love. He was a loving boy.

MOLLY: A precious boy.

PADRAIC: A goodly lad.

GRANDMOTHER: He had a pure heart.

GREAT-GRANDFATHER: Aye, that's me great-grandson. The spitting image of him. You've described him to a "T". Now you're waking up to the glory of it all. The trouble with you is you're all too young to know how to have a good time at a wake. I don't know what's come over this younger generation! You act like a bunch of ignorant savages. You think when you bury a man you have to crawl underground with him to keep him company. His body's below; his soul's above. You've got to learn how to kick up your heels at a wake. There, right now, he's dancing a jig on his coffin!

MOLLY: Where, Great-Grandfather?

GREAT-GRANDFATHER: There! Are you blind? Can't you see him? Hello, Michael.

SEAN: I see him, Great-Grandfather; I see him.

GREAT-GRANDFATHER: I'll do a dance with you. (*To Molly.*) Come, my darling girl, we'll dance a jig with your sweet brother.

MOLLY: Is Michael in heaven?

GREAT-GRANDFATHER: Not yet. We've got to dance him up there.

(*Great-Grandfather and Molly, accompanied by Mercury, begin to dance.*)

Dance harder, lass.

MOLLY: Now, Great-Grandfather?

GREAT-GRANDFATHER: Almost. Keep it up now.

(*They dance harder and harder, faster and faster. All join in the rhythm by beating their spoons on the table.*)

MOLLY: Now?

GREAT-GRANDFATHER: Now! Hooray!

(*Everyone cheers. Sean runs to Mercury. Out of sight of the family, Mercury lifts him to his shoulder and carries him up to heaven.*)

Remember me in paradise to all those saints and virtuous people, Michael! I'll handle the Lord myself.

MOLLY: You're not worried about God, Great-Grandfather?

GREAT-GRANDFATHER: Hell no! He's an understanding fellah.

PADRAIC: My son was shot down like a dog in the street — in cold blood — and they're calling it an accident?

FATHER MURPHY: We must forgive and forget, Padraic.

PADRAIC: (*As Venus and Mars struggle around him.*) I'll not forget. I'll never forgive myself. I want to remember!

FATHER MURPHY: But no one is responsible.

PADRAIC: The innocent blood of my son is crying out and you say no one is responsible? My son marched for peace. He was slain for that. He wanted a decent world where all men could be brothers.

His blood was shed for that. There was no provocation, no provocation at all. You'll allow innocent blood to be shed?

FATHER MURPHY: Once, a long time ago, innocent blood was shed . . . for many.

PADRAIC: You don't help people with that kind of talk, Father. Your confessional just makes babies out of them.

FATHER MURPHY: But they are children!

PADRAIC: When will they understand? When all our sons are murdered?

FATHER MURPHY: God will stop them.

PADRAIC: When?

FATHER MURPHY: In His good time.

PADRAIC: Sorry, Father, I can't wait.

CHARLES: (*Influenced by a touch from Saturn.*) Father Murphy's right, Padraic. If there is any responsibility, it is a collective one. No one person is to blame. Or if there is blame then it must be for a society that creates the atmosphere for such violence and bloodshed. And we are all part of that.

PADRAIC: (*Applauds.*) A speech at a time like this. You're clever, I must say, Charles. A blood bath of collective repentance where all are responsible and therefore no one is responsible. A world without individuals. That's what you'd like to make us believe. So evil can have a clear day. That's as much as to say there are lies but no liars, betrayals but no betrayers, evil but no evildoers, killings but no killers. A lying creed right out of hell that justifies and condones the killer. No wonder you endow the churches so heavily, Charles. You're both in cahoots with the devil. The devil's favorite trick. If evil doesn't exist, then you can't fight it.

GRANDMOTHER: You must forgive my son, Charles. He's not himself.

CHARLES: I understand, Mother. But come now, Padraic, who are we to accuse? The governor who sent out the militia, the soldiers themselves, or the poor pimply-faced kid who pulled the trigger?

PADRAIC: Or yourself for allowing those hired killers on campus!

MARY: What are you saying? Charles tried to stop them.

PADRAIC: Did he?

MARY: It's the truth. He did everything in his power once he knew he couldn't prevent Michael from going on the march.

CHARLES: Believe me, Padraic. I know how you feel. But there is no way on earth to assess who fired that shot.

PADRAIC: I don't want the robot who pulled the trigger; I want the man who gave the order.

CHARLES: You presume a great deal. What makes you think it was intentional? Why can't you call it an accident and let it go at that?

PADRAIC: There are no accidents of that kind in your system, Charles.

CHARLES: My system! Now you're being ridiculous!

NAT: In the entire history of America, no student has ever been fired on. Those soldiers never would have fired a shot unless someone higher up, someone powerful enough, had told them to.

CHARLES: I don't see what business this is of yours, young man.

NAT: Michael died in my arms, Mr. Bordelaise.

CHARLES: Well . . . it's just that . . . this is a family matter. I'll thank you to stay out of it.

KATIE: But Nat is family, Uncle Charles.

CHARLES: Not yet, he isn't.

GREAT-GRANDFATHER: I guess the lass can marry who she wants, Charles.

GRANDMOTHER: Stay out of this, Father.

GREAT-GRANDFATHER: I sired this whole goddamned family! How am I to stay out of it?

NAT: (*To Charles.*) You don't like me, do you?

CHARLES: I have nothing against you personally, but frankly . . . it's just that . . .

NAT: I'm black.

CHARLES: Since you put it that way . . .

NAT: Well, that's my cue to go.

KATIE: Nat! Uncle Charles, please . . . Daddy!

PADRAIC: You'll do nothing of the kind, Nat. Sit down.

NAT: I'm afraid you feel pretty much the same way, Professor.

PADRAIC: Nat, I . . .

CHARLES: I didn't want this discussion to occur now, at this time, but it has. I have nothing against your race, young man.

MARY: Charles, don't . . .

CHARLES: What is to be gained by putting it off, Mary? Sooner or later it has to be faced. I know this is unpleasant for you, for all of us. I don't wish to hurt your feelings, but my niece is very precious to me, and I don't want to see her hurt.

KATIE: Oh Uncle Charles, please . . .

CHARLES: And I don't think you do either . . . A marriage to someone who is . . .

NAT: Black.

CHARLES: . . . Yes, black, would only cause pain and it would end tragically for you both. Not to mention your families.

KATIE: That's not true, Uncle Charles. Nat and I are very happy, and we always will be.

CHARLES: Yes, now. But later you both must face a brutal, cruel world. You don't know what devils men can be, Katie. And what of your children? You must think of them. What place will there be for them? Isn't there enough misery in the world without bringing more into it?

KATIE: But I love Nat!

CHARLES: Love is not loved in this world, Katie.

KATIE: Mother, say something. Tell him!

MARY: Your Uncle Charles knows I'm for this marriage. But I think it's important that you hear what he says.

KATIE: No!

CHARLES: Katie, I wouldn't hurt you for the world. It's just that . . .

KATIE: No!!

CHARLES: What about your father? He's against it too. Have you thought of the unhappiness you'd be causing him?

PADRAIC: I'll speak for myself, Charles.

KATIE: I won't listen to you!

GREAT-GRANDFATHER: That's right, lass! Don't listen to any of them. Follow the song in your heart.

CHARLES: You're not helping matters, Grandfather.

GREAT-GRANDFATHER: That's what you think, my fine bucko! You ain't gonna hurt my great-granddaughter just because she's chosen a man who ain't elegant enough to fit into your grand notions of high society.

GRANDMOTHER: Calm down, Father.

GREAT-GRANDFATHER: Calm down, my ass! No harm's gonna come to my Katie in this household. Not as long as I can breathe.

CHARLES: Can't you see the damage such a marriage would cause — is causing already? Dissension in our own family. You don't want that, do you?

NAT: I'd better be going.

KATIE: Nat! (She starts to go after him)

GREAT-GRANDFATHER: Why you must be the dumbest man alive, Charles. What the hell do you think Michael marched and died for? It was over this very issue! Hold your ground and fight, Nat. Don't go!

NAT: It's no use, Great-Grandfather.

GREAT-GRANDFATHER: Is this the way to celebrate Michael's death?

NAT: It's no use.

KATIE: Come into the garden with me, Nat.

(*In the garden.*)

Don't quit on me now, Nat.

NAT: Oh, what's the use.

KATIE: We'll run away from this whole sorry mess.

NAT: Run! Where? Can't you understand Michael's blood is between us?

KATIE: I only understand I love you.

NAT: Oh God, he'd be alive if it weren't for me. That bullet had my name on it.

KATIE: I lost my brother; I won't lose my lover.

NAT: How can we live with Michael dead? He'll always be between us.

KATIE: If Michael had to die, I'm glad he died for us.

NAT: Katie!

KATIE: He did, Nat. And our lives must give meaning to his death.

NAT: It's unbearable. Every time you look into my eyes, you'd see him.

KATIE: And honor him in you.

NAT: To have his shadow between us forever.

KATIE: Not his shadow. Michael is the bond that binds us together forever.

NAT: It's true.

KATIE: Oh, hold me in your arms, Nat. Let the world pass by and nothing else will matter. We'll lay upon the earth and pluck wild berries from the trees and dine on nectar and ambrosia.

NAT: Where? On this planet of unfulfilled desire? This hell of four billion souls on fire.

KATIE: Yes, 'til heaven comes with fulfilled desire. Remember when we found the forest of paradise?

NAT: Our secret grove.

KATIE: The air was honeyed. We lay upon the river bank and knew it was true — all the ancient stories. That the gods lived there. Oh, to have a life like that. A fine life by the sea and woods.

NAT: I've spent too many seasons in hell and seen too many souls on fire to walk away when my friends need me.

KATIE: You can't slake the hunger of the world.

NAT: Your brother died for me. What's my life worth if I run now? I couldn't take another step, breathe another breath if my life doesn't give meaning to his. I can't ignore the world. I just can't. You taught me that, Katie.

KATIE: Yes.

NAT: I was born to be a man and shape the world to my purpose. I won't be bent and broken.

KATIE: Oh Nat . . .

NAT: I'll take a hammer to the world and shatter it to pieces, and rebuild it closer to the heart's desire.

KATIE: What will you do?

NAT: I'll be the hammer and not the anvil. I'll be the spark that sets the world aflame. I'll strike and not be struck. Oh Katie, I think I've found my way. Are you with me?

KATIE: Oh my love, forever and a day.

NAT: Let's go.

KATIE: Wherever you go, I will go with you.
  (*Back to wake scene.*)

PADRAIC: (*To Charles.*) Get out of here!

GRANDMOTHER: Padraic!

PADRAIC: I'm to let this man come into my home and destroy my daughter? I'm to see my son killed and say nothing? No, not for a son who was as fine a lad as any man could have. I'll roast in hell before that day comes!

FATHER MURPHY: You're making things worse.

PADRAIC: So you're siding with him?

FATHER MURPHY: I'm siding with the truth.

PADRAIC: And the truth says that I'm wrong; is that it? (*Father Murphy says nothing.*) Why don't you leave with him, Father? I'm sure you've nothing further to do here. Don't let me keep you.

MARY: Padraic, Killian's your best friend!

PADRAIC: Was. (*To Charles.*) I told you to get the hell out of here! What are you waiting for?!

CHARLES: You can't talk that way to me!

PADRAIC: Oh, can't I? We'll see about that. Get the hell out of my way, Father!

FATHER MURPHY: Paddy, we've been friends since youth.

PADRAIC: I'm warning you, Killian. Get out of my way! I want him out. Out of my house!

CHARLES: Someone should teach you manners. Why, you're no more than a violent animal! I'll have you arrested.

PADRAIC: In my own home?

CHARLES: And my sister's.

PADRAIC: That does it. You rotten son-of-a-bitch.

(*Goes for his throat and starts choking him across the table.*)

CHARLES: Help! He's choking me!

MARY: Killian, stop him.

FATHER MURPHY: Peace! Peace! You've got to stop this, Padraic!

PADRAIC: Get out of here you bloodsucking bastard, or I'll kill you!

CHARLES: Mary! Mary! He's murdering me.

MARY: Paddy, Paddy, you're killing him! Please, for my sake.

PADRAIC: Get away from me! (*He throws her off against the wall. She slumps to the floor.*)

GRANDMOTHER: Mary! Oh, my God! Mary!

MOLLY: Daddy, you hurt Mommy.

PADRAIC: What!

GRANDMOTHER: Now you've done it, you fool!

PADRAIC: No! No! Mary!

CHARLES: Someone call the doctor. Mary dear . . . it's Charles.

PADRAIC: Get away from her. You're not her husband.

CHARLES: If anything happens to her, I'll see you put behind bars and have the key thrown away.

PADRAIC: Mary! Oh, my God, what have I done?!

MARY: (*Regaining consciousness.*) Paddy . . .

GRANDMOTHER: Mary, listen to me. Are you all right?

MARY: Yes . . . I'm fine.

CHARLES: Mary . . .

MARY: Charles . . .

GRANDMOTHER: Oh Lord, you gave us such a scare. No bones broken?

MARY: No, Mother, I'm fine.

GRANDMOTHER: Thank God.

CHARLES: Get your coat, Mary, I'm taking you with me.

PADRAIC: You're not taking her anywhere.

CHARLES: I won't allow you to treat my sister this way.

MARY: Charles . . . Padraic, don't you touch him! Haven't you done enough damage?

PADRAIC: What about him?

MARY: Charles cares for me; he's only concerned that I'll be all right.

PADRAIC: Charles! Charles! Must I always hear that bloody name?

Must you always defend him?

MARY: Yes, when he needs defending.

PADRAIC: From the likes of me, huh?

MARY: He's my brother.

CHARLES: It's all right, Mary. I won't be coming to this house again.

PADRAIC: That's good, for the door will be barred to you forever.

MARY: You've no right to say that, Padraic.

PADRAIC: Well, if you're so mad to be in his company, why don't you go with him?

MARY: You're my husband.

PADRAIC: Am I? Well, you're no wife to me. Go on . . . I don't want you.

MARY: Paddy!

GRANDMOTHER: Are you crazy, you lunatic? Hold your tongue. You've got the finest woman a man can have.

PADRAIC: Get away from me, old lady.

GRANDMOTHER: I will not!

PADRAIC: Stop poking your nose into other people's business.

GRANDMOTHER: This is my business.

PADRAIC: Clear away! All of you! I don't want any part of you! Any of you! I've had enough!

GRANDMOTHER: Why the man's gone bongo!

CHARLES: You're not safe here, Mary, You'd better come with me.

GRANDMOTHER: Do that child. I don't recognize my own son. He's possessed.

PADRAIC: Where are you going?

MARY: I'm leaving you.

PADRAIC: Leaving me, is it? After twenty years, the first time I'm in trouble, you're sure to be gone.

MARY: I can't live with a man like you. I can't live with you another moment.

PADRAIC: Get your hands off her, or I'll break every bone in your body!

CHARLES: Why you . . .

MARY: Charles, please . . .

CHARLES: *L'homme est insensé alors!*

PADRAIC: Crazy am I! We'll see who's crazy.

MARY: I want to talk to Padraic alone.

CHARLES: *Mais, je ne peux pas te laisser avec lui . . . Il est . . .*

MARY: *Charles, fais ce que je supplie!*

CHARLES: *Je t'attendrai.* If you lay a finger on her, I'll see you black-balled in every university in the country. You'll never teach again!

PADRAIC: That'll suit me fine. I'll never be one of your obsequious ass-licking clowns!

(*Exit Charles.*)

MARY: Oh Paddy, Paddy, Paddy . . .

PADRAIC: You were the last to leave my side when the sun was shining and I was riding high and the good times were flowing, and now when I'm fighting for my very life, you're the first to duck out the door. Is that it?

MARY: It was good between us. It can't be good anymore.

PADRAIC: Why not?

MARY: You're not the man you were.

PADRAIC: I am! I will be again!

MARY: When? You're a coward, Paddy. You're not a man at all.

PADRAIC: Don't say that, Mary.

MARY: And why not? It's true enough. I'll say it again. Coward!

PADRAIC: Get the hell out of here then, you tormenting bitch straight out of hell! Good riddance to you! And don't come back again! . . . Where the hell do you think you're going?

MARY: Let me pass.

PADRAIC: You're not going anywhere!

MARY: Oh, yes I am.

PADRAIC: This is your home. You're my wife! You belong here . . .

MARY: Not anymore.

PADRAIC: You can't walk out on me!

MARY: Oh can't I, Mister Big Shot? Try and stop me!

PADRAIC: Mary, you made a promise — a promise to the death. You can't betray that!

MARY: Yes, to the death. And you're dead now. And so I'm free — free to go my way.

PADRAIC: My way is your way. You said that our marriage day. Don't cry, my love, my heart . . . don't cry. I love you.

MARY: Your love is a killing love.

PADRAIC: The deepest love.

MARY: A love that wounds — that sears the heart.

PADRAIC: You wouldn't have it any other way.

MARY: I'll go my way, Muldoon.

PADRAIC: You'll not.

MARY: I will, I won't be hurt anymore.

PADRAIC: I'll not hurt you again, ever, sweetheart; there'll be no more hurting from this day forth.

MARY: You will. You're that kind of man; you can't help it, you love nobody but yourself.

PADRAIC: I'll change, me darling.

MARY: Don't touch me! I can't bear any more pain.

PADRAIC: Mary! Mary!

MARY: You're killing me.

PADRAIC: Then kill you I will — you belong to me — you're mine!

MARY: I belong to no one but myself; first, last and always. You'll not destroy me. I'm your equal. I'm as strong as you, when it comes to that. And I'll find my own way, alone. Get out of my way or I'll kill *you*!

(*Padraic strikes her. Mary starts sobbing.*)

PADRAIC: (*Falls on his knees.*) Forgive me! Mary, don't go! I need you . . .

(*Exit Mary, sobbing down hallway. She enters bedroom, Charles following.*)

MARY: To be leaving . . . this home I've loved so much. So many memories!

CHARLES: In a few moments, Mary, you'll be down the stairs and have put all of this behind forever.

MARY: Forever? Did you say forever? Forever is such a long time.

CHARLES: This time tomorrow, you'll be at the family estate. You need a long rest, my dear. That brute has worn you out.

MARY: My family . . . yes. But *this* is my family! The children . . .

CHARLES: We will make arrangements for the children later. The important thing is to leave this house, and at once.

MARY: Yes, at once.

CHARLES: (*Guided by Saturn.*) Well, what is it Mary?

MARY: (*Restrained invisibly by Venus.*) I don't know . . . You must give me a few moments to say goodbye.

CHARLES: One would think you had time enough for that.

MARY: It's all happening so suddenly.

CHARLES: Mary, you must consider me. After the way that ruffian treated me, I would have never stayed — save to get you out of here as quickly as possible.

MARY: How does one say goodbye to twenty years of living?

CHARLES: The past is lined with bitterness; you must forget it.

MARY: Yes, with bitterness, but with good things too. With fun and laughter — and love. It's not so easy to forget the past. I've only known one man my whole life. How does one start again, Mrs Padraic Clancy Muldoon?

CHARLES: The past of which you were robbed. You're still young — in your prime. Think of the future, and of the life that should have been yours, *will* be yours. You're a Bordelaise!

MARY: Bordelaise . . . It's so strange. No longer to be Mrs. Padraic Clancy Muldoon . . .

CHARLES: The strangeness is that you could ever have departed from it. You had such promise. You were always father's favorite — everyone's favorite. The whole world that wealth and culture could provide — yours to command. You could have had your choice of any man to marry. And to think you gave it all up for . . . for . . .

MARY: The man I loved.

CHARLES: Love! Don't speak of love! The man was an unconscionable upstart — an opportunist. You were young, impressionable, unacquainted with the world. You were stolen. He stole you from your family, your friends . . . from me.

MARY: You mustn't speak unkindly of him. He's not a bad man.

CHARLES: A black Irishman! He smells of the gutter. He's a rascal, a braggart, a liar, a cheat! He filled your head with cheap romances.

MARY: He filled my heart with joy; he was strong in those days. He knew where he was going. He had purpose. All the other men seemed so effete — so ineffectual.

CHARLES: And where did he lead you? I tried to warn you, Mary. But you wouldn't listen to me. And to have run off with the scoundrel without getting father's permission. He would never have approved.

MARY: Yes, I ran off with him. Father feigned anger, but inside he was secretly glad. And father *would* have approved. But it wasn't Padraic's idea, it was mine. I couldn't wait.

CHARLES: Mary!

MARY: It's true, Charles.

CHARLES: Don't say that. You're my sister. I won't believe it.

MARY: He surely was the man of all men who knew where he was going. And with joy and with charm and the strength of his purpose, he knew how to play on a young girl's heart. My knees would buckle at his coming. And all the meaning of life was in his eyes.

CHARLES: You're defending him.

MARY: Why should I do that now? It's over. All over. Never to be again. And now my world is in a thousand pieces — and I must pick them up and start from scratch. I've loved a thousand loves in this bed. This room is filled with perfume from all my loves. And now farewell — the love knot bound in love now unloosed. This house has bound me in so many ways: all the sad recriminations, subtle pains, stolen glances, mad romances. My first born — here in this very bed. I was happy then . . . tokens . . . wild with joy. And then the second came tumbling out, wilder than the dance. A house to make, and building pains, 'til every nook and cranny filled to bursting. My own house, my very own! Seventeen — Katie's age. Good morning, Mrs. Muldoon, and will you be expecting shortly? Mrs. Padraic Clancy Muldoon! Oh, how proud I was! And the days filled with expectations — and nights of love; oh, the love nights of soft gaiety — indescribable whisperings of love, the sweetness of his flesh against mine, and the soft dawn as we woke from our love slumberings, winging our way through the misty morning air. The plans and ambitions, the trips, the thousand and one unexpected things — his body — the imprint of a million meetings. Oh, take me out of here, away from this house, Charles!

CHARLES: I will.

MARY: Oh, what is this pain that keeps me from leaving? Is it just my flesh unwilling? Do I lack resolve or is there something that holds my spirit, too? I want to go, but something wild within me says *stay*.

CHARLES: *Ce qui est fini est fini. Il n'y a plus de raison de le prolonger.*

MARY: *Oui . . . fini.* I'll get my things. (*She begins to pack.*)

(*Back to the wake scene.*)

PADRAIC: Oh God! What have I done? I've killed my son! I've killed my son. How can I go on? Oh Lord, God, help me, help me!

(*During Padraic's speech, Sean descends on a ladder from heaven. Enter Great-Grandfather.*)

GREAT-GRANDFATHER: Fight for what you believe, Paddy. Don't let them get you down.

SEAN: Daddy, Daddy! I've found them. I've found them. Hurry! Come with me.

PADRAIC: What?

SEAN: They said it's all right. They want to meet you!

PADRAIC: Not now, Sean.

SEAN: Yes, now!

(*He leads his father by the hand and they ascend the ladder to heaven, while Great-Grandfather is left below in freeze.*)

Look Daddy, the spheres! Aren't they pretty?!

PADRAIC: Beautiful!

SEAN: Every one's a different color. And listen to the music! Each one a different song! These are my friends . . . Mercury, Venus, Mars, Saturn, Jupiter, Uranus, Neptune, and . . .

PLUTO: (*Whispering.*) Pluto.

SEAN: Pluto. (*Whispering back to Pluto.*) Sorry. And this is my daddy, the one I told you about.

JUPITER: Welcome.

PADRAIC: Am I dreaming?

JUPITER: All that you lived before was but a dream. Now you must awaken and live in reality what you only dreamed before.

PADRAIC: I didn't know that you really are.

JUPITER: You've always known . . . You were born knowing it. You knew it when your mother cradled you in her arms. There is an ancient tale whispered in your ears that you sons of Adam were sent from the starry world above to govern the Earth, but that you forgot yourselves in time because of the great din and violence of your world. And so it will remain until each man overcomes the violence in himself and rises a son of heaven. Only then will you fulfill your promise and do your duty to your Mother Earth.

PADRAIC: I remember . . . now . . . but why do I always forget? Life cuts me in a thousand pieces. I keep losing myself and finding the world instead.

SATURN: The outer world is finite — a changeling victimized by time — the kingdom of shadows; any fool can conquer it, only to grasp at nothingness. The inner world is infinite and unchangeable, the kingdom of the wise — the land of certainty. Conquering this, the wise man rides infinity to endlessness.

PADRAIC: I am dizzy, I cannot follow you.

SATURN: Follow your self and you will arrive!

PADRAIC: What is the way?

PLUTO: You are the way.

PADRAIC: Is it a secret?

PLUTO: The great secret; he who seeks it will find great treasure — the answer to all his questions and all his dreams fulfilled. For he will find the voice of God whispering in his ear. Your dark Earth is the place of strife where men must struggle to create their souls, until each man and woman becomes a self-creator, transcending himself on each occasion — each one as different, as unique as every star in heaven. The only riches — the souls you make; the greatest riches — your greatest souls. Each man who finds his conscience, one jewel on the necklace of God, each man who helps his neighbors to find theirs, a diamond on the crown of God.

PADRAIC: That will take forever.

SATURN: What does it matter? Do you think man is a creature for a day? Man is an eternal principle in the mind of God, made in the image of our Creator.

PADRAIC: The universe is so great, and man is so small. I see there is nothing any one man can do.

MERCURY: No! On Earth, God's work must be done by you. Every man is responsible to play his part in the Great Work — the regeneration of the Earth. Only then will the Earth be a fit habitation for God and His associates.

PADRAIC: But that is so hard, there is so much dissension down below. What can I do?

NEPTUNE: Prepare yourself in silence until the day comes. This dark time will pass. Nothing lasts forever. Even God will not last forever. Even He must die and be reborn. After winter comes spring. After hard comes easy. This is the night-time of the world — soon a bright new time will be shimmering in.

PADRAIC: But why is it so difficult?

MARS: It must be difficult. Humanity is on the forge. The hammer of God is pounding you to pieces.

PADRAIC: Why must we be tortured this way? Why is humanity on the rack?

NEPTUNE: How do you test for gold? You put it in a blast furnace and burn out all the dross. God is heat and pressure, and things are getting hot and heavy.

PADRAIC: And heavier and heavier.

URANUS: God will have His way. Do you think He created this endless universe only to settle for men of brass and lead? Oh no. He'll play His tune with all stops out.

PADRAIC: Tell Him to stop playing. He's making a terrible din.

MARS: That din is the music of His holy orchestra. His players: Jupiter, Pluto, Neptune, Uranus, Mercury, Saturn, Venus.

VENUS: And Mars.

MARS: And all the rest circling in their spheres. We're calling you to arms, for the theme is holy warfare, against the Great Beast that lurks within you. Can you hear that terrible tune that calls you into existence against the infidel within you? You mustn't shirk. You must be brave and open wide your ears to that terrifying insistent melody that engages you in divine warfare against all your ancient enemies: cowardice, sloth, envy, fear, 'til overcoming your lower natures, you raise yourselves as men.

JUPITER: We're on a holy pilgrimage, here for only a moment; sooner or later we all must die. If we do not participate in that divine warfare, existence will be the poorer for our absence. But perhaps you don't wish to pay the price for becoming a real man.

PADRAIC: More than anything else, I want to be a man.

VENUS: Then you must inquire of the nightingale why he sings for love of the rose. Arm yourself in his knowledge, and you will forge the weapon that conquers the world.

PADRAIC: Love's not a weapon.

MARS: Oh, no?

VENUS: The most powerful weapon of all. In a sense, more powerful than God. Listen to this story. Once there was a contest in heaven, and Justice arose and said, "I am the most powerful of all, for I bring harmony to all that is." Then Truth arose and said, "No, I am, for I am a sword that separates the true from the false." Then Goodness arose and said, "No, I am, for I am the Meaning of all creation." But Love who said nothing was awarded the prize. For Love will dare what none of the others could. He is so brazen, impudent and shameless, he will go to hell and change it. Love fills nonexistence. God does not. There's only one law God is under — Love — that ever leads Him on, and He must submit. For it's Love that bows before Him and illuminates His path.

PADRAIC: The God of Love! Oh, when will all men pray to Him?

VENUS: God has many names: Truth, Justice, Courage, Beauty. Each man prays to the god he loves. God is the ultimate meaning. Pray for the meaning . . . that the meaning may come to us on wings of love.

PADRAIC: Oh, what would I not give to be worthy of Him.

MARS: Then you must will it.

PLUTO: You and all men must arise and take your places — as teachers, poets, orators, statesmen, and sing out the new age . . .

bring a new world into existence.

MERCURY: One man with God on his side can lift humanity and be the spark that ignites the world.

PADRAIC: Until he falls into the mire.

URANUS: Each of you is a spark of fire caked with mud, but ignite those sparks to spirits of fire and you'll illuminate the earth.

PADRAIC: Vessels of clay that live a day and expire in the mud?

NEPTUNE: Vessels of clay contain sparks of fire. Could you but learn to pray, you'd harness the energy of love and lift humanity on the wings of the dove, and release those sparks back to the primordial fire that is our source.

PADRAIC: If I could dare to remember this glorious vision . . . but I am weak.

URANUS: We are all weak. Each and every one of us. Even the best of us have something wrong, some flaw, some mole that streaks our disposition. See how the world goes; there's nothing perfect. It's this intractable stuff of clay, our own creaturehood we must master.

PADRAIC: Only a hero can do that.

URANUS: Only a hero . . .

PADRAIC: I am so little.

MERCURY: He who follows what is little in himself becomes a little man. He who follows what is great in himself becomes a great man.

PADRAIC: Yes. Oh Uranus, Pluto, Mercury, Venus, and all of you, help me to remember this. Don't let me forget! If only I could stay with you. I've been lost for so long, I'm afraid I'll lose my way without you. I need your guidance. Help me!

JUPITER: As you wish. Come look! See our sister the Earth, in her raiment of glory. How many aeons we watched her. We watched her when those great black kings — a noble race — built the pyramids to the sun. You were there — each one of you sons of Adam carrying the burden of the race, the great flow of blood circulating through all humanity: black, red, white, yellow, and brown blood — all mixed together in each of your veins making the whole greater and more glorious than any of its parts.

PADRAIC: Oh God!

JUPITER: Tell what you see.

PADRAIC: I see each man a carrier of the whole, a tiny particle in the bloodstream of time — the great flow of blood transmitting all the thoughts, feelings, sensations of every man that ever lived; each one of us stretching ourselves to contain all humanity and carry it forward, uphill, against the river of time, leaving death far behind.

JUPITER: That is your burden; you must pick it up.

PADRAIC: We are all one paste and I am a part of all that.

SATURN: (*Turning from Sean momentarily.*) And as you are a man you must be responsible to all of that. There is your place. You must put your shoulder to the wheel and not turn back.

PADRAIC: I see at last!

MERCURY: Will you live for it? Will you stake your life on it? That's the only thing that counts; what you'll never swerve from or betray though men try to stop you, even though they kill you for it.

PADRAIC: Yes, Mercury, I will try. But will we never meet again? (*All the gods laugh.*)

PLUTO: How can we not? Atoms, galaxies, suns, planets, men, we're all on the same journey — and have been since the beginning of time. Somewhere beyond space and time, beyond all contradiction, beyond anything we can sense or think or feel or know, lies the Whole. To be able to take our stand in that, and say yes forever. To be in the Presence of that Unknowable, Unnameable Knower of us all — that Quickener of life that makes each passing moment so fair, and all creation new. What would a man not pay for that great privilege? What cost would be too great?

PADRAIC: I would give my life.

JUPITER: Let it be then, as you have said. Look!!

(*Scene shifts back to Mary and Charles in bedroom. Mary has finished packing, and is about to leave with Charles, when Katie and Nat enter.*)

KATIE: Mother, where are you going?

MARY: I'm leaving, Katie.

KATIE: Leaving! What are you talking about? You can't leave. What about Daddy?

MARY: I can't stay with your father any longer, darling.

KATIE: You can't stay with my . . . What is going on here? Will someone please tell me?!

MARY: I . . . I can't talk about it now.

KATIE: Mother!

MARY: Let me go, dear. I'll speak to you in a few days.

KATIE: I won't let you go. Uncle Charles, stop her!

MARY: I'm not leaving you, my darling. I just need to get away for a while.

KATIE: But you can't leave Daddy. It would kill him; he needs you.

MARY: I've got to get out of this house, or I'll die.

KATIE: Mother, what's happened?

MARY: Your father and I . . . Oh, how can I explain . . . Charles.

CHARLES: It's best this way, Katie.

KATIE: How can it be best? They love each other. People who love each other belong together.

CHARLES: Your father's very sick. And it's better that your mother be alone for a while.

KATIE: He's not sick.

CHARLES: Katie . . .

KATIE: He's upset. There's a difference. But he will be sick if you go.

MARY: I must go, I'll get sick too if I don't. You don't want that, baby.

KATIE: You've just had a fight. It will pass. That's no reason to . . . Mother, we've been together all our lives.

CHARLES: Your mother has been through a terrible ordeal. Her nerves are . . . Please, Katie . . . She can't take any more of this . . .

KATIE: Where's Dad? I'll get him; we'll patch everything up.

MARY: It can't be patched up.

KATIE: What are you saying?

MARY: I . . . (*Breaks down crying.*)

KATIE: Mother, please don't cry. I love you. Everything will be all right.

MARY: Nothing will ever be the same again.

CHARLES: Come, Mary. (*Takes her to door.*)

KATIE: (*Barring door.*) No . . . I won't let you do this to my father.

CHARLES: Katie, I've never seen you this way. What's got into you? You want your mother to have a nervous breakdown?

KATIE: She'll have a nervous breakdown if she goes.

CHARLES: You mean if she stays! Can't you understand what we're telling you? Your father's behaved unconscionably toward her.

KATIE: What happened between my father and mother? I want to know.

CHARLES: I'll tell you what . . .

MARY: Charles . . . Please don't . . .

CHARLES: No! I am going to tell her. She's old enough to know how he's abused you.

KATIE: That's a lie! My father's loved my mother every moment of his life.

CHARLES: Is that why he struck her?!

KATIE: He couldn't have!

CHARLES: Why don't you ask your mother?

MARY: Charles . . .

CHARLES: Ask her . . .

MARY: He didn't mean it, Katie.

KATIE: Why are you doing this, Uncle Charles?

(*Enter Father Murphy. He stands quietly in the background unseen.*)

CHARLES: Your father . . .

KATIE: My father's wild with grief. If he did anything to hurt Mother, he didn't mean it. You know he blames himself for Michael's death.

CHARLES: Precisely.

KATIE: And you blame him too?

CHARLES: I don't have to. The facts speak for themselves.

KATIE: The facts?

CHARLES: And now that your mother knows the truth, she can't bear to stay in this house a moment longer. Every time she looks into your father's eyes, it's a reminder of why Michael died.

KATIE: You don't believe that, Mother?

MARY: Oh Katie, I don't know what to believe.

KATIE: And you'd desert him now?

CHARLES: Your mother is not deserting him; she's fighting for her health and sanity.

KATIE: But why should my father be made to bear the guilt? What's he got to do with my brother's death?!

CHARLES: Everything. Michael would be alive now if your father had been by his side.

FATHER MURPHY: Would he, Mr. Bordelaise! Would he?

CHARLES: What . . .

FATHER MURPHY: I think you better tell the truth.

CHARLES: What did you say?

FATHER MURPHY: I said, I think you better tell the truth.

CHARLES: I don't know what you're talking about.

FATHER MURPHY: I think you do. Suppose you tell them what really happened that day.

CHARLES: That day . . .

FATHER MURPHY: The day Michael died.

(*He starts to take off his collar.*)

MARY: Killian, what are you doing?

KATIE: Father Murphy, you're taking off your collar.

FATHER MURPHY: Yes.

MARY: Why?

FATHER MURPHY: A priest cannot reveal what he's heard in confessional.

MARY: But Killian, it's your life . . . your whole life.

FATHER MURPHY: My life isn't worth much if I can't help my friends when they need me most.

MARY: No, Killian.

FATHER MURPHY: Yes, Mary. I must.

CHARLES: Father Murphy . . .

FATHER MURPHY: I have broken my vow. I am no longer a priest. Shall I tell them, Mr. Bordelaise, or will you?

MARY: Tell them . . . what? What does he want you to tell us, Charles?

CHARLES: Mary, I . . . This is ridiculous.

MARY: What does he want you to tell me, Charles?

CHARLES: It was an accident! We all know it was an accident! No one is responsible. I tried my best to stop it. You know that. You said so yourself, Mary. I did everything in my power. I tried to call off the shooting. I tried to stop them. I tried! God knows, I tried. But no one is responsible, don't you see that? No one. I tried to tell Paddy that, but he wouldn't listen. I can't be held responsible for what a bunch of fools have done. I tried to get through to them, but it was too late . . . too late . . . I would have never given the order if I had thought Michael would be on that march. You must believe that, you must! I loved him . . .

MARY: Oh God!

NAT: Three other students died that day. One of them was a girl. She was only sixteen. Yet you wouldn't have given the order if you knew about Michael.

CHARLES: They weren't supposed to hurt anyone. Just give a warning if necessary.

NAT: They were ordered to kill. They shot straight at us.

CHARLES: No! No! It's not true. It's not true. You must believe me. You must! . . . What was I to do? The students were going wild. Everything was out of hand. I couldn't let them destroy the university.

NAT: So you destroyed four lives instead; Michael's was one of them.

CHARLES: I tried to stop them. Can't you hear me? It wasn't meant to be . . . the way it turned out. Only to stop them from going too far. It was an accident . . . an accident. Why are you all looking at me that way? Don't look at me that way.

MARY: (*Mars, god of war pressing her forward.*) My son is dead . . . and you killed him.

CHARLES: No.

MARY: One word from you and he'd be alive.

CHARLES: Mary, don't look at me that way . . .

MARY: One word . . .

CHARLES: I can't bear it.

MARY: One little word . . . and you couldn't say it.
(*Breaks down crying.*)

CHARLES: I'd give anything . . . anything . . . to undo what's been done! (*Falls at her feet.*)

MARY: Why didn't you tell us they would open fire?

CHARLES: I did tell you; I told you the governor had called out the militia.

MARY: If he had known in time, Paddy would have risen like a tiger to protect Michael — all his students. He would have killed anyone who tried to harm our son. Oh why, Charles, why didn't you speak?!

CHARLES: I told you there would be violence and bloodshed. I begged you not to let him go!

MARY: Those boys and girls were unarmed . . . innocent children shot down in cold blood without warning . . . And you gave that order . . .

CHARLES: You think I wanted Michael to die?!

MARY: Yes!

CHARLES: Mary!

MARY: I do!

CHARLES: I loved Michael.

MARY: And you murdered him . . . my own brother.

CHARLES: Mary, you don't know what you're saying!

MARY: Oh my God, what have I done! All these years . . . Paddy has known what you are . . . all these years . . . And I couldn't hear him. This terrible sickness he's fallen into . . . he's ashamed because he doesn't know how to fight men like you . . . ashamed and demoralized, like the whole country. And to think I almost betrayed him . . . I'm so ashamed. I never want to see you again.

CHARLES: *Impossible. Nous sommes famille . . . nous sommes de la même souche . . .*

MARY: Speak English! I'm going to fight you, Charles, as Michael did. I'll be true to my son, and if I ever get another chance, to Padraic.

CHARLES: Forgive me, forgive me! You must forgive me, I beg of you!

MARY: What can I forgive you? You're all alone now, Charles.

CHARLES: Mary . . . when father died, I tried to carry on the family tradition as he would have wanted . . .

MARY: Charles, don't you know what you've done? You've betrayed father. You're no longer his son.

CHARLES: Betrayed him . . .

MARY: Oh Charles, I feel so sorry for you, I could cry. You've become the very thing you hated! You lead the mob! You throw good men to them when they clamor for blood! You give them the lies they cry for in your newspapers and television! You had them slaughter Michael! That's what you've given your life for — to kill the very thing you love.

CHARLES: You can't hold me responsible for everything!

MARY: But you are responsible; we all are.

CHARLES: My destiny . . .

MARY: Was to stand against the madness and fight it!

CHARLES: I tried, Mary, I tried . . . but fate hasn't been kind to me.

MARY: You were born to change your fate.

CHARLES: I had to make some concessions, or I would have lost everything.

MARY: They broke you. You belong to the mob now.

CHARLES: Don't we all?

MARY: I know a man who doesn't. I married him.

CHARLES: He doesn't seem to be doing so well.

MARY: No, because you and men of your ilk are trying to kill him, just as you killed my boy. But I know Paddy. He's been down before, but he won't stay down. One day he'll rise up, and I pray to God that I'll be at his side to help him do it.

CHARLES: You think a lot of your Paddy, don't you?

MARY: I think the world of him.

CHARLES: There doesn't seem to be anything further to say.

MARY: No, there isn't.

(*Easter bells begin to ring. Mary and Charles freeze.*)

(*Back with the gods in heaven.*)

SEAN: Come on, Daddy; we'll be late for dinner.

JUPITER: Your son is calling you.

PADRAIC: Yes . . .

SEAN: You don't want to get Mommy mad at me.

PADRAIC: I'm coming, Sean.

SEAN: Hurry, Daddy!

PADRAIC: I'll be right down, son. (*Pause.*) I must be on my way.

JUPITER: Yes.

PADRAIC: Goodbye.

GODS: Goodbye.

PADRAIC: I'll never forget you. How shall I find you again?

JUPITER: We'll always be with you.

MERCURY: When you sense your limbs bursting with motion and song, know it is I, Mercury.

VENUS: When your flesh rings with fellow feeling, it is I, Venus.

MARS: When your blood is fired with passion, know it is I, Mars.

SATURN: Ponder and find me in your thoughts.

JUPITER: Compassion's mine to give.

GODS: We are your limbs, your flesh, your blood, your mind.

URANUS: Your sex.

NEPTUNE: Your heart.

PLUTO: Your higher mind.

PADRAIC: All this and heaven too! And He who is without form or name, where shall I find Him?

MERCURY: (*Calling to him as Padraic descends the ladder toward earth.*) That is not for us to say; but when you earn Him, you shall find Him.

PADRAIC: Is that a promise?

GODS: By the living gods, a promise.

(*As the last bell sounds.*)

MARY: It's Easter.

CHARLES: Yes.

MARY: "Christ is risen from the dead. He hath conquered Death with death, giving life to those in tombs." [8] Oh, Charles, give it all up. Get out now, while you still have a chance.

CHARLES: I don't know that I can.

MARY: In the name of all that's holy, in the name of everything you've ever loved, don't let Michael have died in vain.

CHARLES: Michael . . . Michael . . . (*He starts to weep.*)

MARY: Oh, Charles!

CHARLES: Will I ever know what I've lost . . . Michael . . . Michael
. . . what you could have been . . . what I could have been. If only
I could ask for his forgiveness.

MARY: I'm sure somewhere in heaven Michael hears you.

CHARLES: I'm afraid heaven doesn't exist.

MARY: We must believe that it does, Charles, or there's no sense in
living.

CHARLES: Mary, I can't!

MARY: Then may God have mercy on your soul. Oh Charles, you're
deep in bondage.

CHARLES: As all men are.

MARY: Not all.

CHARLES: We all can't be as lucky as your Padraic.

MARY: Men make their own luck.

CHARLES: Yes, if they've been kissed by the gods.

MARY: Oh, for a Moses to deliver you!
   (*Padraic gets off ladder, kisses Great-Grandfather on head,
   releasing him from freeze.*)

GREAT-GRANDFATHER: Well, I see my words have gotten to you!
   (*Padraic laughs and enters bedroom.*)

PADRAIC: I'm no Moses, but will I do?

MARY: Oh Paddy, I needed you so. Where have you been?

PADRAIC: With all women and yet one woman: you. She instructed
me in the art of love; a goddess of a woman! I passed the time with
her . . . I know not — an hour, a day, a year, a century or a
millennium were all the same with her. Time stood still. There was
no time inside or beyond.

MARY: Are you feeling all right, Paddy?

PADRAIC: I never felt better in my life!

MARY: I think you're clear out of your mind.

PADRAIC: I think at last I've found my mind, for at last I've come to
myself, and found the secret of all creation. It's a mystery I'd soon
be talking about, but I think you've found a mystery or two
yourself. And now for you, brother. I hold no grudge against you.
I forgive you as I must forgive myself. *Il te faudra vivre avec cette
situation tout le reste de la vie, Charles, comme moi, je le devrai.
Garde-la dans le coeur comme une flamme sacrée. Ca te servira.*

MOLLY: Oh, Daddy, Daddy, I missed you. Sean said you were in
paradise with the gods but he lied, didn't he, Daddy? Here, Uncle

Charles.

CHARLES: But Molly, it's your dolly. I gave it to you.

MOLLY: Take it back.

CHARLES: But you loved it so.

MOLLY: I can't keep it.

CHARLES: Mary!

MARY: Goodbye, Charles.

(*Exit Charles.*)

GREAT-GRANDFATHER: Well, I don't suppose we'll be hearing any more French around here. She's got a lot of spirit, your woman. I think she'll make you a good wife.

GRANDMOTHER: And you, my son, I think you're ready to get married at last.

PADRAIC: Where are you going, Nat?

NAT: Well, I didn't want to intrude in your family.

PADRAIC: Didn't you know *you're* family, Nat?

NAT: I . . . I . . .

PADRAIC: Hold on; you're not getting away so fast. I lost a son. I've found him again in you.

NAT: Professor Muldoon, I don't know what . . .

PADRAIC: Paddy's my name, son, or Dad.

NAT: I better start with Paddy. It'll take me a while to get used to Dad.

KATIE: Oh Daddy, I love you.

PADRAIC: And I, you.

KATIE: Oh Mommy, I'm so happy I could burst.

MARY: Oh darling, that makes two of us; my man is back at last.

PADRAIC: You thought you lost your honey boy.

MARY: I did, but I found my honey man. And since when does honey man speak such perfect French?

PADRAIC: Well, I've had to keep up with it, in order to understand you, my love. The gods must be smiling on us, huh, Sean?

SEAN: They sure are, Dad.

MOLLY: You're lying, Sean.

SEAN: I am not. Ask D . . . (*He gets a wink from Padraic.*) Oh never mind; you'll never understand.

KATIE: Oh Nat, we made it.

NAT: Yes baby, we made it.

MARY: We've come through the rye.

GREAT-GRANDFATHER: Well, there's nothing for it but to give both couples our blessing. Hot diggity, a double wedding! I've been waiting for this all my life. Well, get on with it, Killian. It's not every day a man has a double-header to perform.

FATHER MURPHY: But I'm no longer a priest, Grandfather.

GREAT-GRANDFATHER: What the hell difference does that make? The church doesn't know that yet. It'll be your last official act.

KATIE: Oh Father Murphy, I've dreamed of this all my life; I wouldn't have anyone else but you.

PADRAIC: No longer a priest, Killian. It seems hard to believe. What will you do?

FATHER MURPHY: I'll go out into the world. There are many ways of serving God.

PADRAIC: Killian . . . for everything, thanks.

FATHER MURPHY: If blessings count, then you have mine. Let me be a witness to the truth before God and all assembled, that this man and woman are meant for each other. (*Uranus brings them together.*) And what God hath joined together, let no man put asunder.

MARY: For every unkind word . . . for every act of unwomanliness . . . I'm sorry. I . . .

PADRAIC: Shh . . . Hush. (*They unite in a kiss.*) My soul . . . The mirror of myself . . . My soul's delight.

GREAT-GRANDFATHER: She's your booster rocket to glory. She'll fan your fire.

PADRAIC: She'll light my way to paradise.

GREAT-GRANDFATHER: With a woman like that on your tail, you'll soon be champion of the world.

MARY: Oh Mother, your wedding ring!

GRANDMOTHER: I'd say I could die in peace now. My crazy son has finally got a woman with sense. You're a Muldoon at last.

GREAT-GRANDFATHER: Die? You're terribly selfish. And who'd take care of me?

GRANDMOTHER: Don't worry, Father. I've no time to die. I've too much work to do.

GREAT-GRANDFATHER: Oh, you almost scared the life out of me. Well, son of my best beloved son, I see you're ready to inherit the earth at last. She reminds me of your mother, Daughter. Now, there was a woman could get a rise out of any man! Did I ever tell you the time when I . . . well, never mind. It's a long story. Now for Nat and Katie. Well, get on with it, Killian. Get on with it!

(*Uranus and Killian open the Bible.*)

FATHER MURPHY: Do you, Nathaniel, take Kathryn to be your lawful wedded wife, to have and to hold from this day forward, for better for worse, for richer for poorer, in sickness and in health, to love and to cherish, 'til death do you part?

NAT: I do.

FATHER MURPHY: Do you, Kathryn take Nathaniel to be your lawful wedded husband, to have and to hold from this day forward, for better for worse, for richer for poorer, in sickness and in health, to love and to cherish, 'til death do you part?

KATIE: I do.

NAT: With this ring, I thee wed.

KATIE: And thereto I plight thee my troth.

FATHER MURPHY: If any man knows why these two should not be joined together in holy wedlock, let him step forth, or forever hold his peace. In the name of the Father, and of the Son and in the name of the Holy Ghost, I now pronounce you man and wife.

GRANDMOTHER: Amen.

KATIE: Oh, if only Michael were here to see this.

PADRAIC: He's here with us.

KATIE: Oh, if I could only see his face once more.

PADRAIC: You can, if you wish.

KATIE: Oh Daddy, if only I could . . .

MOLLY: Can we really see him, Daddy?

PADRAIC: Yes honey, we can.

MOLLY: Oh, Michael, Michael, Michael!

GREAT-GRANDFATHER: What are we waiting for! Let's go!

PADRAIC: That's what I want to hear! Come on then, lads and lasses, Grandfather, Mother, all. I'm taking the Muldoon family on one final voyage. You too, Killian, hop aboard.

MARY: Oh, Padraic Clancy — here we go again!

PADRAIC: Let's get on our chariots of fire. We'll travel fast as heart's desire and off we go through the Fourth Dimension! What mankind needs is a reconciling vision, past all division, that harmonizes instinct, mind and heart. We need a mighty vision that unifies the world. We've got to stretch to reach that.

MARY: The dance has begun.

PADRAIC: Can you see?

KATIE: Yes, here comes India with Krishna and the Song of God.

MARY: The celestial Middle Kingdom, China, spins its golden thread. Confucius brings the law of reciprocity, and the spirit of family is bred.

PADRAIC: We're standing tiptoe on the shoulders of time. What comes next?

FATHER MURPHY: Mars is in ascendancy. Europe spawns its first civilization, the fighting men of ancient Greece.

KATIE: Next comes Venus, stargazer, medieval cathedrals — the Holy Roman Empire which sires all the Hapsburgs,[9] France, England, Germany.

NAT: Arabia and medicine, alchemy, and the stars, the poets of Provence,[10] the Grand Inquisition — the Reformation.

PADRAIC: What a history lesson! The conquest of time and space.

SEAN: Yippee! We're going through time.

(*The planetary gods begin in cosmic dance as Padraic takes the Muldoon family and Father Murphy on one final voyage through the Fourth Dimension.*)

PADRAIC: And the journey's just begun. Fasten your safety belts, for here we come! Look out now! We've broken through to the Fourth Dimension and we're going backward toward the source of life itself. And now, as far as the eye can see, forward or backward turning, new nations being born and old ones dying, civilizations rising and perishing, new races coming into existence and old ones dying out like waves in the sea of time; constant, incessant change, perpetual turmoil. But still, Man goes on and on, leaving the bloody trail of crime . . . and it's almost all crime . . . in his tracks. We're not angels yet, you know, you young rascals. But look! Here come a gothic steeple and look! A temple to the sun!

SEAN: I see it, Daddy! It's the Taj Mahal!

KATIE: And there's a Socrates!

NAT: And a Lao-tzu!

MARY: How can they arise through all that death and destruction . . . but they are, they are!

PADRAIC: For we're watching the making of the human race. Out of the primordial slime, out of the raw material, the mass of men crawling on the face of the earth, from time to time, a man arises.

NAT: Oh, look! It's Pythagoras!

KATIE: And here comes Buddha!

GRANDMOTHER: And right beside him, Saint Lama![11]

NAT: There's Mohammed!

FATHER MURPHY: Here comes Moses with the Ten Commandments! And walking hand in hand with him is Christ!

MARY: All the world's great leaders, beckoning us on.

PADRAIC: Here's another — one with no name, but just as great. Here they come, through the corridors of time, one after another. And now we can't be stopped, for out of the primordial dust this one Great Man has arisen and shaking off the mud and dust of his long journey, he's stretching his limbs to the rising sun; and his name's Humanity. And all the men and women that we saw before are simply cells within him that have now blended into One. Do you see it?!

MOLLY: Oh yes! Daddy. Oh yes, yes, yes . . .

PADRAIC: We've gone backward and forward, sluicing through time, and finally we've arrived at Now. And now, look who's coming!

MOLLY: Who, Daddy? Who?

PADRAIC: Don't you see?

MOLLY: No.

PADRAIC: Can't you see?

SEAN: No, no, Who?

PADRAIC: Why, it's Michael.

MOLLY: (*She starts laughing.*) Oh my. (*She covers her face with her hands.*)

SEAN: It's him! It's him!

MOLLY: Oh my, it is Michael!

SEAN: Michael! Michael! Can he see us, Daddy?

PADRAIC: Of course he can. And right behind him, all his friends; millions of boys and girls of all descriptions, millions of them locked arm in arm; and billions and billions more waiting to be born, laughing and singing and crying, coming from all directions — from all the valleys and mountains, and countries and continents and races of the world.

MARY: Oh Paddy, I dreamed I gave birth to Michael again.

PADRAIC: Is it possible . . .

MARY: Oh Paddy.

PADRAIC: We've turned a corner of time. And here come Sean and Molly.

SEAN AND MOLLY: Oh boy, it's us! It is us!

PADRAIC: And Great-Grandfather and Grandmother.

GRANDMOTHER: Why, Father, it's you.

GREAT-GRANDFATHER: Of course it's me! I can see that, Daughter. And you're right beside me.

GRANDMOTHER: So I am.

SEAN: And there's Nat and Katie — making love.

KATIE: Sean!

SEAN: It's true! Look for yourself.

PADRAIC: And here's Killian.

SEAN: And you and Mom.

PADRAIC: Here we come, from all the points in time and space, making up all together one solid mass — the time body of humanity on its triumphant march!

ALL: It *is* us! It *is* us!

PADRAIC: Can we do it, Molly? Can we do it?

MOLLY: Can we do it? Daddy, we're doing it! Look! Look! (*She shakes him.*)

PADRAIC: So we are.

KATIE: (*Jumping up and down.*) We're doing it! We're doing it! Hurrah for us! Hurrah for us! Three cheers for humanity.

GREAT-GRANDFATHER: Here's to the human race. Long may we live!

ALL: Up the world! Up the earth!

PADRAIC: Up the Ancient of Days! He must be very lonely up there all by Himself.

KATIE: Not at all, Dad. He's got us traveling with Him.

PADRAIC: Well then, how about a standing ovation to God for carrying the whole created universe and us on His back?

ALL: To the Ancient of Days! Hurrah! Hurrah!

NAT: Well, if He can do that, we can do our tiny little part. *Adios!* To God!

ALL: *Adios! Adios! Adios!*

MARY: Oh Lord! Here we come!

PADRAIC: That's the spirit! Now I know we're on our way. Come on, let's go! We'll travel to the Sun in search of buried treasure. Once upon a time old Adam . . .

MARY: And his Eve . . .

PADRAIC: Ate the fruit of knowledge but failed to keep their conscience. They fell, and all humanity came tumbling down. Once more up the Tree of Life we'll go. With resurrected conscience we'll eat again old Adam's and his Eve's knowledge. And then we'll reach and reach again, and keep on reaching 'til we reach the root of Heaven.

(*During Padraic's last speech, the gods come down and dance with the family as the play ends.*)

MUSIC

BY MACK SCHLEFER

LYRICS BY ARTHUR GELLER

MARY'S SONG

(The Brightest Day and Sweetest Night)

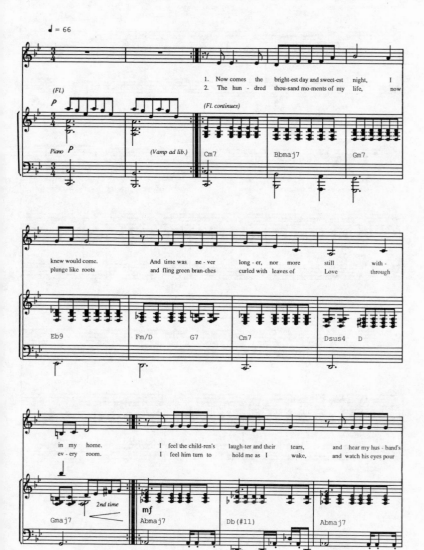

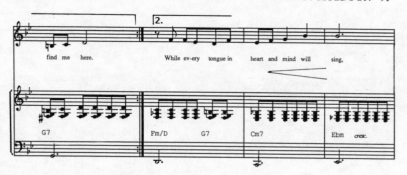

This is the theme music to the play.
It may be used before, during, or after the performance
at the director's discretion.

THE LEGEND OF
SHARON SHASHANOVAH

A Play in Three Acts

1979

For Constantin Stanislavsky

All the world's a stage
And all the men and women merely players;
They have their exits and their entrances;
And one man in his time plays many parts . . .

As You Like It

CHARACTERS

The Producer, Joseph Ravensky

The Teacher, Madame Natasha Ilyichna Ravenskaya

The Playwright, Julio Adolpho Raoul Castillo

The Actor, Billy Brenner

The Actress, Sharon Shashanovah

The Critic, Otto Schechler

The Script Girl, Elene

The Singer, Andrea

PROLOGUE

(Greek masks line the walls of the theatre. Life-size puppets are found in various postures on stage. Lights darken. Sharon, a woman of about 37, appears in spotlight.)

SHARON: Somewhere you'll find me, like jetsam washed up from the sea; shipwrecked, cast adrift, floating from town to town, a stranger to land and sea, and stranger still — a stranger to myself. But, whenever at sound of churchbells ringing, the bird of paradise within begins wildly singing and flapping her wings, begins beating and clutching at my heart, and against my will, I enter chapels, praying at long-deserted altars to long-departed gods; whenever I wend my solitary way in this new Atlantis, searching every cove and inlet for the self that I have lost; or whenever the imperious eagle that sits upon my brow begins pecking at my head, urging me to flights of fancy in hopes of newfound castles in the sky; or whenever in winter's falling, I trudge the snow-clogged streets, one foot in the grave and one foot out, gazing attentively at each man and woman as they pass me by for some faint promise of that original stuff that made us one, that primordial Adam that fathered our race, of which we are but the dim and forgotten fragments; well then, I know it's time to cast anchor deep in my own dark earth. For I'm of an outcast race, one of the deserters of Eden, who turned her back on Deity to carve out her destiny on her own good earth. This is my story. *(A message flutters down from the sky. She begins to read.)* "Good news — Puppet Theatre now casting. All roles available. Leading lady urgently needed. If you are in search of identity, welcome . . . only for the foolish and young in heart. Must be able to sing and dance. Experience not necessary, but simplicity and capacity to listen, essential. Those with souls need not apply." *(To audience.)* That is good news. I don't . . . think I have a soul. I don't even know who I am. I'm changing all the time. This must be meant for me. *(Continues to read.)* "Follow your vision." What vision? *(She sees her vision.)* Oh, how beautiful. Wait . . . wait for me! *(Blackout.)*

ACT I

(*Lights come up. The puppets have disappeared. In their place are human beings, frozen in the postures of puppets. At all times the characters remain in sight of the audience. When they are not participating directly in the action, they can be found frozen in various puppet postures around the stage. They begin to come to life during Sharon's speech.*)

SHARON: I beg your pardon. Am I in the right place? Hello, I'm sorry to disturb you, but I don't know if I'm in the right place. I was told there was an audition here. You see, I'm an actress. You're looking at me so strangely, I'm sure I must be in the wrong place. I wish you would say something. I don't want to babble on. (*Silence.*) I brought the message with me. It says right here, "Puppet Theatre now casting. Leading lady urgently needed."

JOSEPH: (*A man of about 58, rises from puppet freeze. A moment of shocked recognition.*) Ah . . . you've come at last. I am Joseph Ravensky, the impresario. Perhaps you've heard of me, producer, director, manager. Welcome to the theatre. For me, the theatre is a passion and a prayer: the only sacrament. It's a temple where the Holy Ghost descends revealing the soul of humanity in all its majesty and folly. Is there anything like the hushed expectation before the curtain opens? The actors wait in the wings. (*The Critic, as if remembering his cue, breaks from puppet freeze and takes his seat in the audience. Sharon, entranced, comes downstage.*) They enter — eternity descends. A speech, a gesture, and now one character steps forward. Suddenly the audience is caught, and now all are actors are in the play. The miracle has occurred — the magic of communion and its mystery. The holy ritual has begun and, for those two brief hours on the stage, our illusory consciousness is gone. We are pierced to the heart, revealed to ourselves in an eternity that can never be forgotten. That is the theatre.

JULIO: (*A man of about 36, breaks out of puppet freeze and addresses the audience.*) I am Julio Adolpho Raoul Castillo, the playwright. I am filled with revolutionary fury. I want to shake the world to its foundations. Right now, I am angry with this man and have a bone to pick. (*To Joseph.*) Yes, the stage . . . where a new image of man is presented. But you forget to mention all this happens only in a real theatre.

JOSEPH: Always you say this and always I tell you, it is only in a real theatre that I am interested.

JULIO: Oh, if only I could believe you.

JOSEPH: You can say this to me, Julio. A man who lost his own country, who kissed the earth when he came to these shores. For forty years, I have labored to create a great theatre, and I shall go on laboring to the day I die. Do not forget that it was I who started the first People's Theatre here in this country.

JULIO: A strange thing for an aristocrat to do.

JOSEPH: After the Revolution, I was no longer an aristocrat. When I left Russia, I was freed from the past. Now I am one of the people.

JULIO: Do you expect me to believe this? A man who has betrayed his own comrades.

JOSEPH: You see. What did I tell you? I am surrounded by philistines, sycophants, commercial hacks, who despise art and seek to destroy me. But I hardly expected you to repeat this slander. It is beneath you, Julio . . . beneath you.

JULIO: But evidently not beneath you.

JOSEPH: Betrayal . . . what does it signify? It is meaningless. It has nothing to do with the present reality under which we live. This is the twentieth century and we must survive. All this talk is simply old-fashioned rhetoric. Castillian morality. It's time you've outgrown it.

JULIO: You cannot keep politics out of the theatre.

JOSEPH: One's first duty is to art.

JULIO: One's first duty is to be a man.

JOSEPH: Oh, all this is nonsense, Julio. I love this country as I love the theatre, as you do, as we all do. Was I to see it all go down, murdered before my eyes because of a political squabble? No, I fought for it. I did what was necessary and I won. Perhaps I acted hastily. Am I to blame for it?

JULIO: Your character is . . .

JOSEPH: My own affair! Alright, it's not without blemish. But whose is? I've made mistakes. I admit it. But am I to be judged for it? Let bygones be bygones. The past is done. Can't you accept that, Julio? Remember, to err is human, to forgive, divine.

JULIO: You know what this play means to me.

SHARON: You both appear to want the same thing, a beautiful play and a real theatre. Why are you arguing?

JOSEPH: You see. You must listen to her, Julio.

JULIO: I want to awaken men's conscience. A new world is coming and the old won't do.

JOSEPH: Why are we in the theatre if not for that? As artists, we have the same struggle and the same goal. Man at his highest. We have the same aim. That is why the idea of Puppet Theatre is so intriguing.

JULIO: Yes, but will the audience accept it? That's what worries me.

JOSEPH: Leave that to me. As producer and artistic director, it is my business to see that they do. I have not spent my life in art for nothing.

JULIO: I can rely on you then.

JOSEPH: Absolutely. Your play will be in good hands. For me it is a sacred trust.

JULIO: Shall I?

SHARON: Yes, do.

JULIO: Alright then. If you say so.

JOSEPH: You will see. You won't regret it.

JULIO: I hope not.

JOSEPH: The contract, if you please, Elene.

SHARON: Elene, what are you doing here?

ELENE: (*A woman of about 40.*) I'm the script girl.

SHARON: The script girl? I can't believe it! I was so excited when I got the message, I followed the instructions: you go out your door, and turn to the right.

ELENE: . . . then turn to the left . . .

SHARON and ELENE: . . . then come back to the centre . . .

ELENE: . . . and then don't turn back . . .

SHARON: . . . but go straight ahead till you come to yourself. And then follow your heart and you're sure to get there. So you're the script girl.

ELENE: Well, someone has to prompt you. That's my job. Go on. Don't be nervous. Give 'em hell!

SHARON: You mean you have a part in the play, too?

ELENE: Of course.

SHARON: But . . .

JOSEPH: Let us begin. Where are the actors?

SHARON: Right here. I can do all sorts of roles. I've played old

women, young girls, teenagers and even inanimate objects. I've studied Stanislavsky. I've read all his books, but I don't have to be a method actress if it isn't necessary. I can work externally just as well as internally. I can do a flower, a tree, a cat, a bee, an old shoe. I can do fifty different faces, moods, and emotions. I'm very good at plastic, if you would rather have that kind of actress. Actually, I've had a great deal of experience. (*They all stare at her in silence.*) I'm very sorry for disturbing you. Really, you're making me feel awfully foolish. Excuse me for having taken your time. (*Exits; re-enters immediately.*) I can even sing and dance a little. I'm not very good at it, but I can do it in a pinch. (*Singing.*)
You're the cream in my coffee,
You're the ice in my tea.
I would rather be your necessity.
I'd be lost without you. (*She faints.*)

JULIO: Oh, my God. Is she dead?

JOSEPH: Don't be ridiculous.

JULIO: This is the one, Joseph!

JOSEPH: Yes, this is she. I think she's perfect. Don't you?

JULIO: Perfect.

JOSEPH: Of course it is up to Madame.

JULIO: Of course.

SHARON: Madame who?

JOSEPH: Allow me to introduce myself. Joseph Ravensky.

SHARON: You seem strangely familiar and very comfortable to be with.

JULIO: Julio Adolpho Raoul Castillo at your service.

SHARON: Charmed.

JULIO: *Señorita, usted tiene una presencia maravillosa, una personalidad irresistible. Una poesia en movimiento que es un primor.*

SHARON: Actually, I'm taller than I look.

(*Elene and Julio open curtain revealing numerous pictures, among which are Sharon Shashanovah, Cleopatra and Joan of Arc.*)

JOSEPH: You shall play the Legend of Sharon Shashanovah.

SHARON: Sharon Shashanovah . . . oh no!

JOSEPH: What is the matter, my dear?

SHARON: You don't understand. I can't. That's who I am. That's me!

JOSEPH: Of course it's you. Who else should it be?

SHARON: Can't I play the role of Cleopatra?

JOSEPH: That is not your part.

SHARON: Or Joan of Arc?

JOSEPH: Impossible.

SHARON: Then this one. (*Points to a picture. Joseph shakes his head, no.*) Oh, I'm so tired of being me. Can't I be someone else?

JOSEPH: Out of the question. Your own life. Always your own life.

SHARON: But my life is so boring.

JOSEPH: That's what they all say. But it's far better to play your own life, my dear, than someone else's. I assure you. That's why you've been cast. You're perfect for the part.

SHARON: Please . . .

JOSEPH: Sorry. Those are the rules of Puppet Theatre. There are no exceptions.

SHARON: Why must there be rules?

ELENE: Listen!

JOSEPH: How else could we get on without them?

SHARON: I hate them.

JOSEPH: You must abide by them, nevertheless. It's Sharon Shashanovah or nothing. There is no other part for you in the play. Choose!

SHARON: Very well. (*Lights darken. Lights come up revealing a scroll which has unfolded from the ceiling. The scroll remains hanging in front of the audience throughout the entire course of the play. Sharon reads aloud in increasing excitement as Joseph prompts and encourages her.*)

THE LEGEND OF SHARON SHASHANOVAH
A Life in Three Acts

THE BEGINNING

0. She ponders the meaning of her life.
1. The message falls from the sky. She sees her vision and rejoices.
2. She seeks to find a role in Puppet Theatre, is tested, and accepted.
3. Her history is revealed.
4. She understands this is the real beginning of her life.
5. She falls in love with her leading man.

6. The Producer and Teacher discuss her future.
7. She tries to run away, is persuaded by the Playwright to stay, and they make a pact of friendship.
8. She begins rehearsals for the play within the play.

THE MIDDLE

9. The Critic introduces himself and expounds on the meaninglessness of our life in Puppet Theatre.
10. All assembled toast her dizzying success, but Sharon falls into distress when the Playwright questions her motives.
11. An argument about art and its relationship to life ensues.
12. The reality of her vision is questioned and the disillusionment of Sharon Shashanovah begins.
13. The party's over. At the parting of the ways Sharon is forced to choose.

THE END

14. She throws her life away for the man she loves.
15. Caught in a labyrinth, she runs for her life, determined to find the exit.
16. She laments her lost love.
17. She sleeps with her father.
18. The Legend is fulfilled.
19. The mystery of her life is revealed.
20. She is transformed from a make-believe character into a real human being.
21. She leaves Puppet Theatre.

JOSEPH: Come.

SHARON: Where am I going?

JOSEPH: To fulfill your destiny.

SHARON: There's been some mistake. That's not my destiny. You've given me the wrong life. Besides, my father is dead. I'd never live such a . . . what's that?!

JOSEPH: That . . . is the Maestro.

SHARON: The Maestro . . . ?

JULIO: The Master of the Puppet Theatre.

SHARON: The vision that I saw . . . that led me here. Will I see it again?

JOSEPH: That depends . . .

JULIO: On how you play your role.

NATASHA: (*From offstage.*) Joseph!

JOSEPH: Coming, Mama.

NATASHA: Joseph!

JOSEPH: Coming, Natasha.

(*Enter Natasha, a woman of about 80, dressed in the old Russian fashion with shawl and walking stick.*)

NATASHA: Why do you bring me these creatures, Joseph? Take it away.

JOSEPH: Now, Mama . . .

NATASHA: Mama, Mama, no "Mama." I am Natalya Ilyichna Ravenskaya, student of Constantin Sergeivich Stanislavsky, friend of Michael Chekhov[1] and Eugene Vakhtangov,[2] member of the first and second studio of the Moscow Art Theatre.[3]

(*Julio moves to kiss her hand, which she extends graciously.*)

JOSEPH: Yes.

NATASHA: Yes, what?

SHARON: I don't think she likes me.

JOSEPH: She's very sweet. She just has to get to know you.

NATASHA: You! Yes, you. Sit down. Well! Are you an idiot? Say something. Can't you talk?

SHARON: I . . .

NATASHA: This is ridiculous. The woman has no force, no verve, no presence. I can't go on with the scene. The woman's an imbecile!

SHARON: I am not.

NATASHA: Oh, the creature can talk, can it? And what does it have to say?

SHARON: You can't treat me this way.

NATASHA: Oh, and why not?

SHARON: Because I'm a human being.

NATASHA: A human being? Quite interesting. Can you prove it?

SHARON: I don't have to prove it. I just am.

NATASHA: We do have illusions, don't we? You think, because you are Jacob Shashanov's daughter, that makes you human.

SHARON: No, no.

NATASHA: That you can just barge in here and play the prima donna. Your father was a great human being and a great artist. Such an actor comes only once, perhaps twice, in a generation.

SHARON: I know that, Madame.

NATASHA: And do you also know what he went through to become the man he was? No, you do not. Because you are spoiled and weak like all the members of your generation. I will tell you about your father. I remember the first time I saw him. He found his way to us shocked and dazed. He was looking for a crust of bread. Wherever he could hide — that is what he called home. For the rest . . . for years he wandered across Europe hiding and fighting, starving. It was madness. That is what the Great War had done to him, to all of us. Then he found his way to me . . . to us . . . to the theatre. We fed him and washed him. And the theatre became his home. Jacob . . . naturally, you would wish to follow in his footsteps. You don't look like him.

SHARON: Is that important?

NATASHA: You have not his bearing nor his carriage, nor his talent, I dare say.

SHARON: I'm not my father, Madame. I'm myself.

NATASHA: Impudence!

SHARON: Which is just what he wanted me to be.

NATASHA: We are very proud, aren't we? We shall remedy that at once. Well and good. *Attencion!* (*Bangs her stick.*) Juliet. Act II, Scene 2. You know it?

SHARON: I know it.

NATASHA: Present yourself.

SHARON: "But to be frank, and give it thee again.
And yet I wish for but the thing I have.
My bounty is as boundless as the sea,
My love as deep; the more I give to thee,
The more I have, for both are infinite . . ."

NATASHA: (*Muttering in disdain and banging her stick.*) *Attencion!*

SHARON: (*Glaring at her.*) ". . . Dear love, *adieu!*"

NATASHA: (*Bangs her stick again.*) *Attencion!!* Electra. Act I, Scene 1.

SHARON: ". . . But my mother and the man who shared her bed, Aegisthus, split my father's head with a murderous ax, like woodsmen with an oak tree. For all this, no pity was given him. For my part, I shall never cease my dirges or sorrowful laments, as long as I have eyes to see the twinkling lights of the stars or this day . . ."

NATASHA: (*Bangs her stick.*) *Attencion!!!* Nina, Act IV, Scene 2, the seagull scene.

SHARON: "Why do you say you kissed the ground I walked on? I ought to have been killed. I'm so tired! If I could rest . . . rest! I am a seagull . . . No, that's not it . . . I'm an actress. Ah, well! So, he's here too . . . Well, it doesn't matter . . . He didn't believe in the theatre, he always laughed at my dreams, and gradually I too ceased believing and lost heart. And then there was the anxiety of love, jealousy, the constant fears for my baby . . . I grew petty, trivial, my acting was insipid . . . I didn't know what to do with my hands, I didn't know how to stand on the stage, I couldn't control my voice. You can't imagine what it's like to feel that you are acting abominably. I am a seagull. No, that's not it . . . Do you remember, you shot a seagull? A man came along by chance, saw it, and having nothing better to do, destroyed it . . . A subject for a short story . . ."

NATASHA: Well and good, Shashi.

SHARON: Shashi?

ELENE: A term of endearment, used by members of the family and old acquaintances.

(*The Company surrounds and welcomes Sharon.*)

NATASHA: (*To Sharon*). Will you take tea? Sugar?

SHARON: Please.

NATASHA: How many lumps?

SHARON: Four.

NATASHA: One will be sufficient. (*She waves everyone away. As they leave, they go into various puppet freezes.*) Too much sugar is not good for an actress. Do you understand?

SHARON: I understand.

NATASHA: Why do you wish to act?

SHARON: Because I must.

NATASHA: But why?

SHARON: It's my life.

NATASHA: They all say that. Until some rich man comes along and tells them he can't live without them. Then they become fat, raise two brats and settle down to a sordid life in the suburbs. And all the training, all the life's blood I've poured into these ungrateful girls goes for naught. They betray me and the theatre.

SHARON: That will never happen to me.

NATASHA: Why not?

SHARON: Because I already have two children, became fat, settled down to a sordid life in the suburbs with a rich man, and found it was not enough.

JOSEPH: (*Breaks from freeze.*) No! Remember your role. You're Sharon Shashanovah. Say that with more feeling!

SHARON: Because I already have two children, became fat, settled down to a sordid life in the suburbs with a rich man, and found it was not enough.

(*Joseph, with a nod of approval, returns to puppet freeze.*)

NATASHA: You're married? Why have I not heard of this?

SHARON: Divorced.

NATASHA: And you have . . .

SHARON: Two children. A boy and a girl.

NATASHA: How old are they?

SHARON: Nine and ten.

NATASHA: Their names?

SHARON: John and Rebecca.

NATASHA: Where are they now?

SHARON: With me.

NATASHA: You raise them?

SHARON: Yes.

NATASHA: Incredible. And why do you come to us now?

SHARON: I tried to run away but it was useless. All those years when my father suffered so, and toward the end when I nursed him, I swore that never, never would I allow anyone or anything to hurt me in that way. Until one day, passing by a little theatre, something made me enter. (*The Company breaks from their puppet postures and imperceptibly stir to life.*) And then I knew my father's soul had come for me . . . possessing me.

NATASHA: Jacob Shashanov . . . yes, yes, you are his daughter!

SHARON: It was like being in the presence of . . .

NATASHA: Yes, my child, I know.

SHARON: What is this sacred feeling whenever I go on stage? This passion for understanding that night or day gives me no rest?

NATASHA: It is your calling.

SHARON: Sometimes I feel that it will utterly break me. (*Natasha turns away.*) What is it, Madame? Have I offended you?

NATASHA: Offended? Come here, my child. I am crying for you.

SHARON: For me? Why?

NATASHA: (*Looking through window with Sharon.*) There is the world, waiting for you. It will seek to destroy and break your heart. People will not always love you for your talent, your beauty, your strength, your courage. They will envy and crucify you for it. There is no place in that world for you. If only you could . . .

SHARON: Would you have me live a sordid life in the suburbs with some rich man?

NATASHA: Never! Never! I would strangle you with my bare hands if . . . the thought that such a talent . . .

(*Sharon begins laughing. They embrace.*)

And you are willing to go through the fire?

SHARON: If I must . . . yes.

NATASHA: That is what I wanted to hear. My daughter, for all the dark days and nights ahead, when you wake in terror, trembling, in the middle of the night, cursing yourself and the thing you love, don't let them take what you love from you. In that dark hour, don't let them break you. Spit in their eye.

SHARON: Madame! (*Natasha kisses her.*) Ohhh . . . !

NATASHA: Go now, or I shall make a fool of myself and begin to cry. I despise sentimentality. (*Exits to puppet freeze.*)

SHARON: Now, in the middle of my life, is this the beginning . . . the real beginning of my life? Who can tell me? At that single thought the world goes silent and all grow incoherent. When I see how distressful it is to be a woman, all the pain and strangeness of it, and the sadness too, I'd rather change places with brute creation. But there's no way back. I've been that way before. Slept for unknown ages in my Mother's womb, suckled honey at her star-spangled breast. Rumor has it we were once encased in bodies of light, flew the Galaxies, the Universe our playground 'til we alighted on this star which wrapped us in a bubble — this solar system in which we've pranced for endless ages. Could it be true, or is it just an old wives' tale?

BILLY: (*A man of about 38, breaks out of puppet freeze and addresses the audience.*) I'm the actor, Billy Brenner, and I'm the greatest thing that ever hit this country, and I'm going to live forever. Sharon Shashanovah . . . what a vision. The moment I saw her, I had to have her. Here goes.

ELENE: Scene Five. Places. The Legend of Sharon Shashanovah.

BILLY: (*To Sharon.*) You were very good.

SHARON: Oh, do you think so?

BILLY: Yes.

SHARON: I want so badly to be an actress. To play my part well.

BILLY: The part was made for you. And you were born to play it.

SHARON: You're kind. Excuse me, but don't I know you?

BILLY: I'm your young man.

SHARON: Excuse me, but there must be some mistake. I don't . . . have a young man.

BILLY: You do now. (*Kisses her.*)

SHARON: Oh, oh . . . oh . . . !

JULIO: (*Breaks from puppet freeze.*) This is Billy Brenner. Your leading man. (*Freezes.*)

SHARON: Oh, I didn't understand. And do I love you very much?

BILLY: Very much.

SHARON: Is that because you need me so badly?

BILLY: Very badly.

SHARON: And you're vulnerable and shy and lonely?

(*He nods.*)

And you'd be lost without me?

(*He nods.*)

Don't cry, Billy. I won't ever leave you.

(*He reaches out and touches her hair.*)

Oh, Billy, I think I'm falling in love with you.

(*She faints. As Billy catches her, they freeze in postures of puppets.*)

JULIO: (*Coming out of freeze.*) Oh, no, not again.

ELENE: Places.

(*Billy remains in freeze.*)

SHARON: Was it an earthquake?

JULIO: No, it was Billy Brenner.

SHARON: I feel the world shaking under my feet. I better run.

JULIO: Now's your chance. It's only Act I. You can still get out.

SHARON: My legs are paralyzed. I'm trembling.

JULIO: When the comedy unfolds, it'll be too late.

SHARON: I can't move.

JULIO: Tough luck. You like him too much.

SHARON: Oh, yes, I like him, I like him very much. I'm wild about him. He's so alive, it's intoxicating just to be in his presence.

JULIO: You can't help loving Billy. Everybody does.

SHARON: Tell me about him.

JULIO: He's a devil.

SHARON: He's the saddest man I've ever known.

JULIO: He's a wild man from Barnum and Bailey, a natural rogue and clown, the eternal boy running between Heaven and Earth. A high flyer — the original young man on the flying trapeze doing triple somersaults from here to eternity, flirting with death, daring God to break his neck.

SHARON: And if he falls, I'll be his net.

JULIO: Careful, Sharon, he'll break your heart.

SHARON: A woman has to have her heart broken once in a lifetime.

JULIO: Sure, but Billy won't be around to pick up the pieces. Want to hear his history?

SHARON: You know I do.

JULIO: Billy was conceived in a movie during the first feature of the last great dance of death, as the world went mad and began pounding itself to pieces. His father, a pilot, dropped into the local cinemas on his way to Hiroshima. Though he was a total stranger, it was dark enough and his mother didn't seem to care. Billy was born during the intermission. As his father took off, his mother went into a frenzy and danced herself to death in a discotheque. Billy tried to follow but he couldn't find the exit. The usher found him crying because his picture wasn't on the screen. But when the manager promised he could become a moving picture star, Billy became so enthralled, he stayed for the double feature, and almost laughed himself to death. He's been searching for his image ever since. Thus began Billy's long love affair with himself. It's never ended.

SHARON: The theatre is your home, Billy. You don't want to live among shadows.

BILLY: (*Breaking out of freeze.*) You don't understand, Sunshine. The movies are the brotherhood of man, where all are equal, losing themselves in an orgy of togetherness.

SHARON: Plato's cave where men sit chained in darkness, doomed to watch images of themselves on the screen of life. Oh, Billy, you're too real to be chasing insubstantial dreams. Come out into the world of light.

BILLY: With you, Sunshine?

SHARON: Yes, with me, into the sunlight. Past all pictures to reality.

BILLY: Not until I become master of the world of dreams. I'll be a legend. The movies shall become my epitaph and my tomb.

SHARON: Where you'll endlessly be playing and replaying, fixated to all eternity?

BILLY: My image projected, unreeling on spools forever.

SHARON: Oh, Billy, you're mad.

BILLY: And you'd like to cure me.

SHARON: Oh, yes, if you'd let me.

BILLY: I'll haunt the imagination of the world.

SHARON: My demon lover. Part god, part devil.

BILLY: Life's my mirror.

SHARON: That's what Narcissus thought until he drowned.

BILLY: I'm going to live forever.

SHARON: Until the mirror breaks.

BILLY: I'm going right through that mirror and come out the other side.

SHARON: You're a mortal creature. You're bound to die.

BILLY: Not on your life. I'll be immortal. I'll send my double out to screw the world. I'll embalm myself in fantastic images that caress and stroke the non-existent egos of my generation, while the children of darkness jerk off in self-annihilation, and I, presiding at every mental fornication, squeeze the milk-wet tit of the world. I'll penetrate and sodomize the empty cavity of their minds, breeding children of despair to infect the world.

SHARON: That's a prescription for madness. You'll die of rage.

BILLY: The sooner the better.

SHARON: How can you live with so much hate?

BILLY: How can I live without it? Conceived in a dark time, of the devil's root, a child of chaos, I was born in the age of fire, orphaned at an early age in the iron womb of my mother. I drank bitter gall at her breast while humanity went to an all-night movie. I'm uncouth and ill-mannered because I have no past. And I'm insolent and impudent because I have no future. And what's more, I don't want one. You better stay away from me.

SHARON: If only I could. Oh, Billy, what do you really want?

BILLY: To tell our story.

SHARON: And then?

BILLY: Nothing. Finis. The end. I'm going to beat humanity to the punch. It's on self-destruct, on the road to oblivion. But I'm going to get there first.

SHARON: Not if I can keep my hands on you.

BILLY: Besides, how else could I show my contempt for the whole rotten mess? I can't imagine myself becoming a middle-aged man. Who would love me?

SHARON: I would.

BILLY: You, Sunshine? You're not enough.

SHARON: I am, Billy, only you don't know it. But that's because you're just a little sick in the head. I used to feel the way you do. My life was such a burden I wanted to throw it away. But that's all changed now! I'm happy. Now, do you suppose you can stop posing and tell me what you really want?

BILLY: That's it. I said it.

SHARON: I want to live and you want to die. We can't make it.

BILLY: Who says?

SHARON: I do.

BILLY: Where do you think you're going?

SHARON: To wipe you out of my life.

BILLY: Fat chance. When love comes, that dark tyrant, ego, disappears.

SHARON: Don't flatter yourself. There's plenty of fish in the sea.

BILLY: Are there? Then why so quick to run?

SHARON: I want you to bring sanity into my life. Not madness.

BILLY: If you can keep your hands off me.

SHARON: You bastard! This is goodbye!

BILLY: Goodbye? This is the fastest romance I've ever had.

SHARON: Well . . .

BILLY: Well . . . ?

SHARON: There's something in your eye that promises more than one-night-stands in cheap hotels. But don't expect too much. I'm damaged goods.

BILLY: I know a remedy that cures all ills.

SHARON: Platitudes! Platitudes!

BILLY: There's nothing love can't cure.

SHARON: Tell me more. Can it cure the gout . . . hunger, old age, disease? Can it cure the human heart?

BILLY: I can see you're a woman who'll never let love interfere with ambition.

SHARON: That's not true. I'd give it all up for a man that's mine. All mine.

BILLY: Like hell you would. Who's posing now?

SHARON: (*Laughing.*) He'd have to be the right man.

BILLY: And there's no such animal. Is there? But, we'll change all that.

SHARON: You're so conceited you'd try to force your way into my heart.

(*He kisses her.*)

Oh, God. (*Looking at Legend.*) This is terrible. I've fallen in love with my leading man. I'm on fire! Tell me that you love me. No, don't. You'd only be lying. No, tell me anyway. Hold me in your arms and say . . .

BILLY: I love you.

SHARON: (*Puts hand over his mouth.*) Shhh . . . that it will never end; that it will be like this forever. Even though it's all illusion.

BILLY: Sharon . . . I . . .

SHARON: Oh, Billy, I'm stuck. I'll never be able to leave you now. Whatever little time we have together, let it be good. A maiden had a golden ball. She threw it out, but held the string. For you to find your way back to me.

(*Andrea sings "The Song of the Golden Ball."* * *Sharon hands Billy a golden thread which he unravels from locket she wears around her neck.*)

BILLY: What's this?

SHARON: A token of remembrance. So you can never lose me.

(*Music ends.*)

BILLY: Did you ever think there was something splendid about throwing your life away when all eyes were upon you?

SHARON: Oh, Billy, what am I going to do with you?

(*Sharon and Billy go into freeze.*)

ELENE: Scene Six. The Legend of Sharon Shashanovah.

(*Andrea sings "The Song of the Golden Ball" reprise.* *)

(*Joseph and Natasha break from puppet freeze. In his private scenes with Natasha, Joseph's light Russian accent becomes heavily accentuated.*)

JOSEPH: Well, Mama, what do you think of her? Isn't she adorable?

NATASHA: Adorable! Is that all you can see? She has greatness.

JOSEPH: Oh, well, yes, of course. That goes without saying.

NATASHA: Ambition has clouded your vision. In your blindness, you have never known the difference between mere talent and great art.

JOSEPH: Not another lecture on art, please, Natasha.

NATASHA: What do you intend to do with her? Make her your protégée?

JOSEPH: Hmmmm . . . well, yes, why not?

NATASHA: Listen to me, Joseph.

JOSEPH: I am always listening to you, Mama.

*Music p. 163

NATASHA: You are not to hurt this woman. You must not hurt her heart. She is not like the others.

JOSEPH: Such a lovely creature.

NATASHA: Do you hear me, Joseph?

JOSEPH: Why are you making a scene over this woman?

NATASHA: Jacob's daughter . . .

JOSEPH: Dead and forgotten.

NATASHA: How dare you speak of him that way. You are not worthy to shine his shoes.

JOSEPH: Strange fatality. Your feelings for him have never changed.

NATASHA: I loved him. I am proud of it.

JOSEPH: Don't worry, Natasha. The woman is in good hands.

NATASHA: The worst of hands. I do not forget what you did to her mother.

JOSEPH: She was a tramp.

NATASHA: Joseph!

JOSEPH: You have my word.

NATASHA: And what does it mean, your word?

JOSEPH: You won't forget the past, will you?

NATASHA: You have fooled the world, my son, but you cannot fool me. I know you for what you are. You have hurt the father enough. You will not hurt his daughter.

JOSEPH: Really, Mama, to hear you talk this way, no one would know how proud you are of me.

NATASHA: You are a poor masquerade of a man, my son. And no one is more sorry for it than I.

JOSEPH: You are in a black mood today. You have never forgiven me because it is I who walked out of Russia and not my brother.

NATASHA: We will not speak of your brother. He stood up to those commissar swine.

JOSEPH: Communist swine, capitalist swine, is there any difference? You blame me because I live! I had to survive. It wasn't just myself. I had you to think of. I got you out of Russia, didn't I? Is that wrong?

NATASHA: Yes, it is wrong, when you hurt others to do so! Wrong — when you use men as stepping stones to your ambition! Wrong! And here, there is no need for it. The people here have been good to us. They have allowed us to practice our art. It is all we have left.

JOSEPH: I have news for you, Natasha. The barbarians are here, too.

NATASHA: And you are the first to accommodate yourself to them. You are their lackey, just as in the past. You haven't changed. You never will.

JOSEPH: I see that we will never understand one another. (*Takes flower from table and puts it in his lapel.*) Let's speak of gayer things.

NATASHA: This much we do understand. (*Catching his arm with the hook of her cane.*) If any harm befalls that woman, you are responsible, before God, and before me.

JOSEPH: I must go. Rehearsals for Puppet Theatre are about to begin.

NATASHA: Remember my words, Joseph.

ELENE: Scene Seven. The Legend of Sharon Shashanovah.

JULIO: Sharon, where are you going?

SHARON: I'm sorry, Julio, but love's just not in my plans. I'm leaving.

JULIO: You can't do that. We've a play to put on. Rehearsals are about to begin.

SHARON: Get yourself another actress.

JULIO: Are you crazy? You're the leading lady. It's your role. No one else can do it.

SHARON: I won't play it.

JULIO: You have to. (*Pointing to the Legend.*)

SHARON: It's my life. I can do what I want with it.

JULIO: To refuse to live your own life — that's cowardly.

SHARON: I never met a man yet who didn't try to reveal me to myself.

JULIO: But, I'm the author.

SHARON: Every woman's the author of her own life.

JULIO: What are you afraid of?

SHARON: You know damn well what I'm afraid of. It'll be a catastrophe if I stay. I just know it.

JULIO: Love is beautiful.

SHARON: Love's a disease, a madness. A man and a woman meet, and what do they do? They try to cover their inadequacies with love. And when they fail, they try to destroy each other. It's obscene.

JULIO: Love tears off all masks.

SHARON: Oh, yeah? And what will I find?

JULIO: That's the mystery you must stay to discover.

SHARON: No, no, no.

JULIO: But you don't even know who you are.

SHARON: Oh, yes I do. I'm Sharon Shashanovah, and I know where I'm going.

JULIO: If you miss your love, you miss your life.

SHARON: If that's life, I don't want any part of it.

JULIO: Then, why did you come to Puppet Theatre?

SHARON: To create something so real, so true, so beautiful . . . to dare to bring something into existence that's never existed before: myself. And to do that, I need a theatre of shock and transformation, where I am forced to meet myself at every turning. Don't you see there's no room for anything personal in any of that? Love is so messy.

JULIO: Then stay for that. For that's what I want, too.

SHARON: A real theatre. Do you think we could be friends for the sake of that?

JULIO: I am sure of it. And for the sake of something else.

SHARON: Something else?

JULIO: We both love the same man.

SHARON: What are . . . you saying, Julio?

JULIO: Just that.

SHARON: Oh . . .

JULIO: You find it difficult to believe a man can love another man?

SHARON: It's so strange.

JULIO: Why strange?

SHARON: Because I feel that Billy is my person . . . mine. And to think that we both feel the . . . it's eerie.

JULIO: Does it change the way you feel toward me?

SHARON: No, it doesn't. And that's the . . . Julio, I have the strangest feeling that we've met before.

JULIO: How do you mean?

SHARON: I don't know. It's just that I feel we've known each other . . . some place before. I can't explain it. A real theatre. Is it possible?

JULIO: It must be possible or why go on living?

(*Andrea sings, "The Song of the Dreamers."**)

If an artist doesn't dare to steal fire from heaven, no one else would. And then what would happen to the race of man?

SHARON: How did you come to be a writer?

JULIO: I wanted to be able to solve the mystery of creation.

SHARON: And so you wrote plays.

JULIO: No, the plays wrote me. (*Music ends.*) It was as if the characters came from a secret world begging for admission into

---

*Music p. 163

life.

SHARON: Yes, that's how it is. All the people inside me, knocking furiously at my heart, crying out to be born. And I have to decide who's going to live and who's going to die. They make a terrible clamor and get furious if I don't give birth to them; tugging and mauling me, giving me no peace 'til I think I'll go mad. Once it got so bad I ran away, but there was no escape and I came back.

JULIO: Came back?

SHARON: To the stage. What's the matter with those people? I can't lend my heart and mind and body to all of them. I'd need a thousand lives. There's one woman . . . she's lewd and depraved. She's vicious. I don't want to know her.

JULIO: But even she must have her chance to live, no?

SHARON: I hope not. I want no part of her. If only I had the courage, I'd follow . . .

JULIO: Who?

SHARON: I'm not sure. She's nameless. She has no mother or father or country. She doesn't know where she comes from or where she's going. I call her my lady.

JULIO: Sharon, you never mention your mother. Why?

SHARON: Oh, my mother . . . she was all right, I guess. I don't like to think about her.

JULIO: Why not?

SHARON: She hurt my father. She betrayed him.

(*Joseph and Natasha tremble in puppet freeze.*)

JULIO: When did this happen?

SHARON: Oh, just before I was . . . oh, it was a long time ago. I . . . I don't want to talk about it.

JOSEPH: (*Coming out of freeze.*) Elene! Elene!

ELENE: (*Straightening her dress.*) Coming, Mr. Ravensky.

JOSEPH: Where have you been?

ELENE: I was going over the script with Billy Brenner.

JOSEPH: Yes, I bet you were. (*Joseph grabs Elene and kisses her.*) Where are the actors? Call, "Places."

ELENE: Yes, sir. Places.

BILLY: Did someone call?

JOSEPH: Billy, before we begin rehearsals, I must have a word with you. Madame tells me you plan to create two characters for the play. Is that true?

BILLY: Why, yes. One for Theseus and the other for Dionysus.

JOSEPH: That's out of the question. You have a lovely quality and people wish to see it. How are they going to recognize you when you're a different person every time?

BILLY: But Mr. Ravensky, you told me to create a different character for Dionysus.

JOSEPH: Yes, as artistic director I told you that. As producer, I am telling you something different. Please pay attention.

JULIO: But by telling him to throw away the character, you will ruin the play.

JOSEPH: I don't believe you're listening, Julio. As the artistic director, I am telling him to keep it. It is only as the producer that I have told him to throw it away.

JULIO: But that is an irreconcilable contradiction.

JOSEPH: Billy gets paid for solving irreconcilable contradictions.

JULIO: But how can he do both things at the same time?

JOSEPH: That's his problem. I see you're not very well acquainted with the theatre. Fortunately, Billy is. We have worked together before and he understands me perfectly. Don't you, Billy?

BILLY: (*Smiling.*) I sure do.

JOSEPH: You must trust me, Julio. That's what you agreed to do. Are you going to back down now?

JULIO: No, of course not . . . but . . .

JOSEPH: You gave me your word. After all, what do you know about directing, Julio? I cannot have an hysterical playwright on my hands. Stay out of rehearsals as you have promised. Leave the production to me.

NATASHA: Julio is right. You are placing an intolerable burden on the actors. Children, you are not to listen to him.

JOSEPH: Mama, I have asked you not to interfere with my rehearsals.

NATASHA: You are botching my work.

JOSEPH: Everyone here knows I seek only to serve you. I am continuing your work.

NATASHA: My work. It is no longer my work. You have stolen it.

JOSEPH: Mama . . . please.

NATASHA: *Thief! Vor! Plat! Ulgun! Podletz!*

JOSEPH: I will not tolerate this abuse. And before the entire company. You will kindly take that back, Natasha.

NATASHA: I will not.

JOSEPH: Very well. Then, I resign. I am an artist. I cannot work in such an uncreative and hostile environment. Ladies and gentlemen, you will forgive me. Come, Elene. (*They exit into puppet freeze.*)

NATASHA: My children, remember what brings us together. It is to create the inner life of a human spirit in a beautiful and artistic form. These are the words of Constantin Stanislavsky. May you always follow what is most holy in your souls. May you never betray it.

JOSEPH: (*Breaks from freeze.*) Are you finished, Natasha?

NATASHA: Quite finished. You may proceed with the rehearsal.

JOSEPH: Well, what are you waiting for? Proceed. Proceed! Can't you hear her? Our production will have the same high values my mother and I have always stood for. I assure you, Julio. (*Julio and Natasha look at each other. Julio throws his hands up and walks away.*)

SHARON: Have faith in him, Julio. I'm sure everything will turn out fine. After all, he has a wonderful reputation. It was he who first saw the beauty in your play.

JULIO: I trust you, Sharon. You will tell me if anything goes wrong in rehearsals.

SHARON: Of course I will.

JOSEPH: Are the actors ready?

ELENE: Yes, Mr. Ravensky.

JOSEPH: Well, begin . . . begin!

ELENE: Where from?

JOSEPH: Where from? From the beginning. Where else, you senseless creature?

ELENE: Yes, sir.

JOSEPH: My God . . . four weeks before we face the critics. Why am I surrounded by senseless pieces of wood, can you tell me that? We'll never make it.

ELENE: Are you ready, Mr. Ravensky?

JOSEPH: Of course I'm ready.

ELENE: May we begin?

JOSEPH: By all means. (*Signals Sharon and Billy to begin. Andrea starts to play "The Song of Plunder"* which continues throughout the scene.*)

SHARON: Take me with you.

BILLY: I must go alone. The god that leads me says I must go to a

*Music p. 164

strange land. There I will found seven-gated Thebes, city to the sun.

SHARON: Would you have conquered the Minotaur without me? Many great heroes before you labored and failed — because they lacked the knowledge. I loved you, Theseus, and I showed you the way. Then it was I, Ariadne, daughter of King Minos, who held the Golden Ball of your destiny as you unraveled its thread through the dreaded Labyrinth. Had I faltered, had I broken the thread, your life would have run out, doomed, a pitiable prey to the Minotaur, who devoured so many others before you.[4]

BILLY: And because of that, must I be tied to you forever?

SHARON: You were bound to me when you accepted my help.

BILLY: You gave it freely.

SHARON: Yes, because I loved you.

BILLY: And now you wish to put a price on it.

SHARON: Only because you wish to betray me.

BILLY: Zeus, is there anything greater than the wiles of women? If there is, I do not know it.

SHARON: Yes. The guile of men.

BILLY: I will not be bound by you or anyone. Must you grudge me this journey?

JOSEPH: (*Directing them with great intensity.*) Archetypes! Archetypes!

(*Song crescendos until the end of the act.*)

SHARON: I do not grudge you anything. Not your cities, your conquests, or the towns you pillage; not your concubines or followers . . .

JOSEPH: (*Gesticulating wildly.*) Bigger! Bigger!

SHARON: . . . Nor your worshippers or adoring crowds, or the death and destruction you leave in your wake . . .

JOSEPH: Bigger!

SHARON: We go our separate ways. Go, Theseus. The hour has come.

BILLY: Ariadne.

SHARON: Go, Theseus, go. Your destiny awaits you. The poets will sing of your fame forever. And I . . . I will go to Dionysus, to be reborn in love.

(*All freeze in puppet postures. Curtain.*)

ACT II

(*One month later. Opening night party in Otto Schechler's home. The stage is set with male and female puppets dressed in evening clothes. Joseph and Elene are discovered in puppet freeze, champagne glasses in one hand and newspaper reviews in the other. The rest of the Company in background in various puppet freezes.*)

OTTO: (*A man of about 75, rises from his seat in the audience.*) I am the critic, Otto Schechler, an old man in a dry season, going toward my death. But do not think I am bitter. I am not bitter. Let us say, I am out of tune. Like an old violin that needs a master's hand to pluck it, but played upon by an inferior musician, produces only harsh and discordant music. Lacking a Maestro's touch, I prefer myself to all others. A season or two in Buchenwald has cured me of all illusion. My world, the old world of Europe, its gaiety and charm, and yes . . . its decadence, has disappeared, and so I find myself upon these shores. What am I now? Quite frankly, a thought peddler, a trend setter, a moulder of public opinion. In the old days when people used to think for themselves, every man was his own critic. But, that was a long time ago, when life was simpler. Today, life has become such an enigma, that I perform a useful function. Consider me a sort of guide. These are my thoughts on Puppet Theatre: what is the final solution to life? I'm afraid there is none.

ELENE: (*Breaks from freeze. Laughing, she hands him a drink.*) But there must be a purpose behind it all?

OTTO: No purpose that I or anyone can fathom. No meaning that the wisest minds can decipher. Life is a headless rider on the merry-go-round of death. An unending jest.

JOSEPH: What are you doing, Schechler? This is a party, not a philosophical discussion. Drink up, my darlings!

OTTO: Come, my dear, let us drink to the joke, "before we two in the dust descend," as the poet says. What better way to entertain ourselves than through the brilliant effervescence of ideas, the last glittering of light, before western civilization descends into the twilight of the gods.

ELENE: (*Mockingly.*) Here's to the twilight.

OTTO: Of the grave. The final resting place of all our dreams.

JOSEPH: You speak of grave matters. For pity's sake. Come now, Schechler, we are here to have a good time. Let us have a lighter note, if you please.

OTTO: Yes, you can well afford that. Your play's a hit.

JOSEPH: A hit, "a hit, a very palpable hit." Money in the pocket . . . money in the pocket!

OTTO: For all your culture, Joseph, you're still a child. (*Enter Billy and Sharon.*) But if you must have a lighter note — here's to our lovers, come to bolster our dying dreams with the myth of love. I shall drink to Love, undying Love, ever dying and ever being reborn, waxing and waning with the phases of the moon.

ELENE: Miss Shashanovah . . . Mr. Schechler.

BILLY: (*To Joseph, aside.*) Does she know about the contract?

JOSEPH: Not yet.

OTTO: The daughter of Jacob Shashanov hardly needs an introduction.

BILLY: When are you going to tell her?

JOSEPH: Everything in due time.

SHARON: It's a privilege to meet you, Mr. Schechler. My father spoke so highly of you.

OTTO: We had many close theatrical ties. Coleridge said, "Watching Edmund Kean act was to see Shakespeare revealed by flashes of lightning." Your father was like that.

SHARON: You have kind eyes.

(*All freeze.*)

ELENE: No, your line is: "You were one of the few men who were with my father at the end."

SHARON: Oh. You were one of the few men who were with my father at the end.

(*All break from freeze.*)

OTTO: Greatness has always moved me. I loved him.

SHARON: And yet you say love is an illusion.

OTTO: The great illusion. It is with that tune the Pied Piper most plays upon us. It is our damnation. Love makes willing slaves of us all.

SHARON: But, Mr. Schechler, there has to be a love that is real. Don't you think so?

OTTO: Yes, to will another's freedom. That is the great love. But few are capable of that.

SHARON: It sounds like a warning.

OTTO: The daughter of my old friend hardly needs a warning.

SHARON: I think you have too low an opinion of humanity.

OTTO: I try to forget what I've seen men do to one another. I only hope the world is kinder to you than it was to him.

SHARON: I have my art. They can't take that from me.

OTTO: My dear, they can take everything from you.

(*Elene dances across stage with puppet in arms.*)

SHARON: For my father . . . I owe you a debt I can never repay.

OTTO: You have already repaid me by your performance tonight when you illuminated the stage.

SHARON: I don't understand.

OTTO: Old men want very little. But there is something about you that touches me. All my life I have lived for beauty. It is so rare, that when it comes, just to be in its presence is enough.

SHARON: I'm not beautiful.

OTTO: A love goddess, not beautiful?

SHARON: Now you're teasing me.

OTTO: I'm afraid you don't know your own power.

JOSEPH: Well, Otto, what do you think of my protégée?

OTTO: I think that she's a rare jewel. And that you are lucky to have found her. But, be careful, my dear. Joseph's a bit of a scoundrel.

JOSEPH: Nothing of the kind.

SHARON: Oh, no, Mr. Ravensky has been like a father to me.

OTTO: Has he?

JOSEPH: You see? You've had her all to yourself long enough. It's my turn to make a fuss over her. (*Leading her out on the terrace.*) Come along my dear. (*While Joseph and Sharon talk, the rest of the Company socializes with the party puppets.*) You were wonderful tonight.

SHARON: If only you knew what it meant to hear you say that. I did it all for you.

JOSEPH: Your Legend will sweep the country . . .

SHARON: My Legend . . . Yes. (*Glancing at her Legend.*) Oh, no. No. Oh, Joseph.

JOSEPH: I'm going to see to it.

SHARON: I don't care what anyone thinks but you.

JOSEPH: Are you happy?

SHARON: Yes. Very happy. If you are.

(*Enter Julio.*)

OTTO: Julio, it's you. Congratulations. A wonderful play.

JULIO: What is wonderful about it?

OTTO: Haven't you read my review? We're all raving. (*Enter Natasha.*) You've brought mystery back into the theatre.

NATASHA: And magic.

OTTO: Natasha, how good of you to come.

NATASHA: I've been thinking of you, Schechler.

JULIO: My play is a failure.

OTTO: Come, come, my boy . . . the whole town is enchanted.

JULIO: No one understands.

OTTO: Now, now, my dear friend.

JULIO: The idea has been lost.

OTTO: There are those of us who do understand. Let me assure you.

JOSEPH: Natasha! You never go to parties. I should feel honored that you've come to celebrate my success.

NATASHA: I have not come for that. I have come to talk to Schechler.

JOSEPH: Oh . . .

NATASHA: Are you having a good time, Joseph?

JOSEPH: Marvelous, marvelous! Otto is a superb host. The caviar is first rate, the wine is exquisite, and the company as delightful as ever.

NATASHA: I am glad to hear it. Go, enjoy yourself, my son. I will talk to our friend for a while.

JOSEPH: As you wish, Mama.

NATASHA: Come, Schechler. Shashi, come here. You look lovely.

SHARON: Thank you, Madame. Did I do well?

NATASHA: Yes, my child, but you must work harder. Your second act was weak.

SHARON: I tried so hard. I didn't want to disappoint you.

NATASHA: You didn't disappoint me. But one can always do better, no? Remember, our way is one of self-perfection.

SHARON: Yes, Madame.

NATASHA: We will work. Rehearsal tomorrow at nine a.m.

SHARON: So early, Madame?

NATASHA: Why? Have you anything better to do?

SHARON: Oh no, but I thought . . . since tonight is a party . . .

NATASHA: Not too much of a party, I hope.

SHARON: As you wish. Nine a.m.

NATASHA: Promptly.

SHARON: Yes, Madame.

NATASHA: Come, Otto.

BILLY: You haven't told me what you think of my performance, Madame.

NATASHA: Great heart, great vulnerability. But you lacked mind. The cure for that is detachment. You were lost in your emotions. As a consequence, so was the audience. As charming as you are, young man, one goes to the theatre to see the play, not the actor. Come Otto, let us go on the terrace.

BILLY: Whew, what a museum piece.

SHARON: Shut up, Billy.

BILLY: She's so old, she creaks.

SHARON: If you want to be my friend, don't ever talk that way.

BILLY: Who does she think she is?

SHARON: She's a great actress and always will be.

(*On the terrace.*)

OTTO: What a beautiful moon.

NATASHA: Just as in olden times.

OTTO: Do you often think of him?

NATASHA: An old woman has only her memories.

OTTO: And now his daughter in his place. The irony . . . Jacob would be proud of her.

NATASHA: He is — very proud of her.

OTTO: Yes, she is brilliant.

(*Sharon, lost in her own thoughts, enters the terrace. She looks up at the stars.*)

SHARON: A perfect night. The stars shine bright and clear. We are more than flesh and blood. What endless aeons were present at the birthing of the human heart. (*Becoming aware of Otto and Natasha, she smiles as Otto applauds her. Joseph beckons her to return to the party.*)

NATASHA: You must not spoil her, Otto.

OTTO: Spoil?

NATASHA: You praise her too much.

OTTO: Oh . . .

NATASHA: No, you must not.

OTTO: Can't an old man indulge himself a little?

NATASHA: Otto, she will get enough of that from everyone else. You must promise to be firm with her.

OTTO: She has divine fire.

NATASHA: She must be reined in and held tightly. I cannot afford to lose this child to the ignorance and stupidity of the world. Jacob would never forgive me.

OTTO: Does she know her true history?

NATASHA: Does anyone?

OTTO: Come, Natasha, you know what I mean.

NATASHA: No. And she must never find out.

OTTO: But why? It seems so unfair to the child.

NATASHA: Do you want her to know where she really comes from?

OTTO: She has a right to reality, no?

NATASHA: Reality breaks. It might break her. Let her rest in illusion.

OTTO: You know I could never refuse you. It shall be as you wish.

NATASHA: Thank you, Otto.

(*Inside the apartment. By this time everyone has been drinking steadily, and is feeling the effects. Joseph and Elene tango.*)

SHARON: Ladies and Gentleman, your attention, please. Here's to someone very special. I propose a toast to Joseph Ravensky, the man who's made our dreams come true.

(*All but Julio toast him. After the toast, Joseph and Elene resume the tango.*)

JULIO: But why did you direct them in such a weepy, stilted, old-fashioned way? They're not wooden blocks.

JOSEPH: Of course not. They are archetypes.

JULIO: Archetypes?

JOSEPH: Archetypes.

JULIO: What are you talking about?

JOSEPH: Don't you understand? They're myths.

JULIO: They are not. They're real human beings.

JOSEPH: To you they're human beings. To me, they're myths.

JULIO: But that doesn't make any sense.

JOSEPH: Reality doesn't make any sense. (*End tango.*)

SHARON: (*A little tipsy.*) But if we're archetypes, how can we be alive?

JOSEPH: Actually, you're not alive. You're dead.

SHARON: I feel alive.

JOSEPH: An illusion. You must overcome it. You belong to that abstract realm of truth beyond life and death. As a poet, you should understand these things, Julio.

JULIO: But you are confusing the audience.

JOSEPH: On the contrary, I am bringing just that touch of mystery that the audience is in search of.

JULIO: But art should be clear.

JOSEPH: Art is a mystery, my boy. And we should not tamper with it.

JULIO: But if I can't understand the play the way you've directed it, how can anyone else?

JOSEPH: The poet is seized by a divine madness. He is the last one to understand what he has written. No one expects you to understand.

SHARON: I understand your play, Julio.

JULIO: You understand nothing! You walk, you talk, you posture, you go through the motions. But what is there inside you to understand?

SHARON: Julio, what are you saying? I promise you, I do understand . . . please.

JULIO: Oh, what is the use.

SHARON: Wait! Let me read the reviews to you.

JULIO: I don't want to hear them.

SHARON: Just listen to Schechler: "Are we nothing more than puppets on a string? To be pulled back and forth by gods, or worse, simply the plaything of accidental forces? This is the question the author insists we must contemplate as we leave the theatre. At last, a serious play that feeds the mind and heart. A metaphysical play on the ontological nature of man that we can ponder, not a social tract that calls us to rude action."

JULIO: I have written the play as a call to action. What have I done? I never should have given him my play. He doesn't understand. No one does.

SHARON: It's not true. He loves you. Where are your ears? We all do. You are loved, Julio.

JULIO: Love! Because of you, I gave him the play. And this is how you repay me. I was a fool to put my faith in you.

SHARON: Julio, what have I done wrong? How have I failed you? I don't understand. Please, tell me.

JULIO: Oh, Sharon, you are naive. These people aren't your friends. You're such a fool.

SHARON: Not my friends? What are you talking about?

JULIO: They are using you as they've used me. And you've joined them . . . against me. You've cheapened yourself.

SHARON: No, no. It's not true.

JULIO: It is true. Why do you act? Why? To serve something greater than yourself, or simply to be admired?

SHARON: I haven't betrayed you, Julio, I haven't.

(*Sharon, in shock, goes into puppet freeze. She strains to break out.*)

JULIO: Is this success?

SHARON: (*In consternation.*) Here is another from . . .

JULIO: Stop it! I have made myself foolish. The critics have slain my play. And now no one will hear it. Can anyone be more ridiculous than I?

SHARON: Oh, Julio . . .

JULIO: I am going back to my own country.

SHARON: Going back . . . ! (*She goes into puppet freeze.*)

JULIO: I will fight for my people. I will put bread in their mouths and a song in their hearts, and one day . . . the next time I write a play it will be with machine gun bullets!

(*On the terrace.*)

OTTO: Natasha, you are trembling.

NATASHA: The moon has made me cold. It is nothing.

OTTO: Natasha!

NATASHA: Take me in, Otto. (*They enter the apartment.*) Julio, why are you weeping?

OTTO: My boy, the way the critics have treated you, I'd think you'd be laughing for joy.

NATASHA: Julio . . .

JULIO: Don't touch me.

NATASHA: Julio . . .

JULIO: You, Mamacita. You and your son. Don't come to rehearsals, you said. Everything is going well.

NATASHA: Try to understand, Julio.

JULIO: Go to your son. He is the one that needs you. Why did you keep me from rehearsals?

NATASHA: I . . . thought it would be better that way.

JULIO: Yes . . . better. For you and your son. Never mind what happens to the play. To think I believed in you.

NATASHA: Try to understand, Julio.

JULIO: I understand — only too well. Away with you!

OTTO: Away with me?

JULIO: Away with you all!

OTTO: What is he saying?

JULIO: I say there shall be no more critics . . . professional assassins. Let each man and woman be judge and jury for himself.

SHARON: Julio, how can you talk that way to Mr. Schechler? He's one of the few men who's kept the theatre going in a real way.

OTTO: My boy, criticism is a function of truth.

JULIO: Is it? Why, you've killed more plays than doctors have patients.

OTTO: But I have given you an excellent review. What cause have you to complain?

JOSEPH: He's raving. Pay no attention to him, Schechler.

JULIO: I have nothing to say to you.

JOSEPH: Do you hear? He has nothing to say to me. Oh, how sharper than a serpent's tooth it is to have a thankless son.

OTTO: "Thankless child."

JOSEPH: What?

OTTO: It was a misquote. "How sharper than a serpent's tooth it is to have a thankless child."

JOSEPH: That's what I said.

NATASHA: This will do no good. I am going.

JULIO: Yes, go!

(*Natasha exits to puppet freeze. Julio turns sharply to Joseph and Otto.*)

Don't you understand? Man must be raised up.

JOSEPH: What if men don't want to be raised up?

OTTO: This is nonsense, Julio. We do the best we can. We accommodate ourselves to the present circumstances.

JULIO: You accommodate yourselves to the box office. You don't try to change anything.

JOSEPH: Since when is it wrong to give the people what they want?

JULIO: You don't care about the people. You enslave them with amusement and comfort.

JOSEPH: You dare say this to me — I who have given the people Shakespeare, Chekhov, Calderon, Ibsen.

JULIO: After you water them down. After you dilute them beyond all recognition.

OTTO: What makes you think the people could understand?

JULIO: What makes you think they can't? (*Shaking Otto vehemently.*) An argument like that is what led you and many others to the concentration camps, to Auschwitz . . . to Buchenwald.

SHARON: (*Intervening.*) That's hitting below the belt. What's the matter with you, Julio?

OTTO: Now, just a moment. Who made you a critic?

JULIO: It's the truth and you know it. You serve the very thing you hate. You're nothing more than an apologist for a dying culture. You know it, Schechler. You've been there. You're responsible.

SHARON: Please . . . It's such a beautiful party and you're destroying it. Oh, what's the matter with you!

OTTO: Yes, it's true. We're living in a dying world. We all know that. But, what is to be done about it?

JULIO: Stand up and fight it.

OTTO: I fought it once and was broken by it. I won't fight again.

JULIO: Then take the gag out of your mouth and speak the truth, so that others can fight.

OTTO: Who would listen?

SHARON: I would.

OTTO: Yes, my dear child, you would. And a few others. A small minority in a barbaric world.

JULIO: Well?!

OTTO: My boy, how long would I have a following, if I didn't consider the others? I must live.

JULIO: Live?!

OTTO: I must put meat and bread on the table for my family.

ELENE: (*Giggling drunkenly.*) "With inflation the way it is."

OTTO: What?

(*All freeze.*)

ELENE: (*Suddenly sober.*) Your line is, "With inflation the way it is."

OTTO: Oh, yes. With inflation the way it is, it's impossible.

(*All break from freeze.*)

JULIO: The same argument as in Nazi Germany.

OTTO: And besides, the apathy is indescribable. Nobody cares. It would all be for nothing. Believe me, Julio, I saw it all happen in Germany.

JULIO: But the same thing is happening here, and all over the world.

OTTO: I know, I know. But what can I do? I'm an old man. I want a little peace before I die.

(*Collapses in Julio's arms. By the time Julio seats him, Otto is frozen in posture of puppet.*)

JOSEPH: Why do you torment him? Is he responsible? Are you? Am I? Is anyone? There are cycles of history. We must obey them.

JULIO: How convenient. Now history is your cop-out.

JOSEPH: You forget that I have presented many wonderful new playwrights. Ask Schechler, he will tell you what I have done. Ask anyone.

JULIO: Artsy-craftsy absurdist dramas, lunatic nightmares, sentimental garbage, incomprehensible gibberish, abortions of the human spirit that would make any sensible man run out of the theatre and vow never to return.

JOSEPH: These are the plays of our time.

JULIO: Like hell they are. They are the plays that do not offend. Garcia Lorca said: "I dread the day when commerce is written across the doors of the theatre." There is a monstrous conflict between art and commerce in this country and all of you are caught up in it.

JOSEPH: I have done your play.

JULIO: It is the Maestro's play. He entrusted it to me as he did the producing and the directing to you. And what have you done?

SHARON: The Maestro!

OTTO: The Maestro, who is he?

JULIO: You know who he is.

OTTO: Upon my word, Julio, I do not.

JULIO: Ask Joseph.

OTTO: Joseph?

JOSEPH: The Maestro . . . he is . . .

OTTO: Who?

JOSEPH: Well, we can't even be sure he exists.

OTTO: A man who doesn't exist? Then why is Julio talking about him?

JOSEPH: Well, he's not exactly a man . . .

OTTO: Well, who or what is he?

SHARON: Mr. Schechler, you of all people should have heard of him.

BILLY: Has anyone here ever seen him? No, of course not.

SHARON: I have. He's beautiful.

BILLY: You can't prove it.

SHARON: Oh, why won't you believe me? I wouldn't lie.

JULIO: I believe you, for I have seen him.

OTTO: This mysticism is beyond me.

JOSEPH: Me, too.

JULIO: You are all accountable to him.

BILLY: I'm not. I'm accountable only to myself.

JOSEPH: Precisely. You're a billion-dollar proposition. And remember, I own you, Billy.

SHARON: He's his own man, Mr. Ravensky. Nobody owns him.

JOSEPH: What are you saying? This is America. Anybody can be bought in America. Isn't that right, Billy?

BILLY: That's right, boss.

JOSEPH: We're going to Hollywood.

SHARON: Hollywood! Why didn't you say anything to me, Billy? Why?

JOSEPH: To make you world famous. I'm taking you both with me.

SHARON: Oh, no you're not. I'm happy right here in the theatre. I'm not going to Hollywood. And you can't take Billy either. He's my leading man.

JOSEPH: I'll get you another one.

SHARON: You don't understand. He's my person. I love him.

JOSEPH: Love? What is this love?

SHARON: And Billy loves me. Don't you, Billy?

BILLY: Sure, Sunshine, but all that money.

SHARON: You'd leave me for money?

BILLY: Never! But I have obligations. I'm a working class boy.

SHARON: Billy, don't play with me at a time like this. Be straight.

BILLY: I can't lie to you, Sunshine. I've decided to sell out.

SHARON: Sell out! But why, Billy? Why?

BILLY: I want to be a large corporation. I'll be more comfortable.

SHARON: Don't you want to be a human being?

JOSEPH: There's no future in it.

SHARON: Be a hero.

BILLY: How?

JOSEPH: There are no heroes. Only celebrities. Do you realize, America's the only country where a man can become a celebrity in 15 minutes and a has-been the next day. That reminds me of a story. I met a man on the street the other day. "Mr. Ravensky," he said, "Don't you recognize me? It's Charlie." "Charlie," I said, "I never would have recognized you. You look wonderful. How are you doing? Are you still in the theatre?" "No," he said, "the theatre was killing me. There was no work. The producers spit on me and I was reduced to a beggar asking for handouts. Now I'm in Hollywood." "Hollywood?" I said. "Sure, Hollywood. There they treat you like a king. First thing they did was take me out of the rags I was wearing and give me a whole new wardrobe. Then, they give me a face lift and make me a blonde. Then, they make me lose thirty pounds. After that, they give me a new car, a new house and a new wife. Then, they give me a new voice, and a new personality. And finally, they change my name. And now my own mother wouldn't recognize me. Until I met you, I forgot who I used to be." "Wonderful," I said, "but how do you know who you are now?" "To tell the truth," he said, "I don't, but with all that money, who can complain."

BILLY: Very funny, but I'm not worried. I know who I am.

SHARON: Do you, Billy?

JULIO: You better watch out, Billy, because that's what he did to me.

BILLY: Take it easy, Julio. It was just a joke.

JULIO: It is not a joke when one man betrays another.

BILLY: Oh, come off it, Julio. Give the man some credit. He made your play work. He's a great showman.

JULIO: Naturally, you agree with him. You're going with him.

BILLY: He brings in the dollars.

JULIO: Money isn't everything.

BILLY: The point is, Julio, the play's a hit. You're a famous man. We're all famous. So relax, drink up!

(*Andrea begins to sing "The Play's a Hit."**)

ANDREA: My God, My God
    The play's a hit
    The play's a smash
    The man's a genius
    Truly a giant
    The theatre lives tonight.

JULIO: (*Incensed with rage, trembling uncontrollably, he goes in and out of puppet freezes in a mounting frenzy.*) Hit! Hit! Is that all you can think of? Hit?!

ANDREA: Drink up, Drink up,
    The theatre lives tonight
    It's in the air
    Excitement everywhere.

JOSEPH: Yes, when our company was on the edge of financial ruin — bankruptcy — what else could we think of?

ANDREA: My God, My God
    The play's a hit
    The critics adored it
    The crowds screamed for more.
    The play's a smash

*Music p. 164

   The play's a hit
   Drink up, Drink up,
   My God, Drink up.

JULIO: Kafka said it. Art should be an ice pick in the skull, not a soporific.

JOSEPH: Why do you talk to me of spirits . . . ghosts? We're not talking about art now. We are talking about money.

ANDREA: A toast to the leading lady,
   A toast to the man who played the god,
   A toast to the one who wrote the play,
   A toast to the pen he held in his hand,
   Direction, just marvelous
   The lighting, sublime
   The casting, magnificent
   The costumes, divine.

JOSEPH: (*Continues speech during song. Pulls Elene down on his lap.*) Where is your sense of values? You are not in Argentina now, my friend. You are in America. Here, you can joke about art, about sex, about politics, about religion, or about anything you goddamn please, but you cannot joke about money.

BILLY: (*Speaks over song.*) They'll shoot you if you do.

ANDREA: My God, My God
   The play's a hit
   The critics adored it
   The crowds screamed for more.
   It went on and on,
   Applause, applause
   My God, My God
   Applause, applause.

JULIO: And for the sake of this money, you have destroyed the truth of the play.

JOSEPH: (*Jumping up.*) What has truth got to do with it? People come to see beautiful people dressed in pretty clothes, doing strange things to one another. Sexy things, funny things, violent things. Or they come to see grotesques, posturing in search of their souls. What am I to do? A pack of hungry animals comes panting into the theatre for amusement. And if they don't get their dinner, they go out snarling. Not to mention the critics who'll tear us apart.

JULIO: What a filthy conception of Mankind.

JOSEPH: It may be filthy, but it's accurate. As my friend, Lee Shubert, has said, "Nobody ever lost money by underestimating the intelligence of the public."

JULIO: And I am to thank you for making Puppet Theatre world famous on these terms?

JOSEPH: That's right. In all modesty, it was I who made your play what it is.

JULIO: As you have so many others.

JOSEPH: Yes, as I have so many others.

JULIO: Then, let me pay you my respect. (*Clicks heels and bows.*)

JOSEPH: With pleasure. (*He bows.*)

JULIO: This is for myself and all the other men you have betrayed. (*Throws glass of wine in his face.*) And until the revolution comes, this is for you. (*Slaps him and throws him down.*)

OTTO: Julio!

JOSEPH: Why you . . .! Is he crazy? He tried to murder me.

OTTO: It's not the first time a playwright has tried to murder a director.

JULIO: Compliments of Julio Raoul Castillo.

JOSEPH: I'm wounded.

OTTO: You are uninjured.

BILLY: (*Drying him off with a handkerchief.*) He didn't mean it, Mr. Ravensky. He didn't know what he was doing.

JULIO: You make a marvelous lackey, Billy.

JOSEPH: How dare you! Am I to be subject to such an indignity in my own home?

OTTO: It is my home, Joseph.

JOSEPH: Your home, my home. Does it matter? I am an artist . . . Well, Otto, what do you intend to do?

OTTO: Apologize.

JOSEPH: I think it is time for me to go. Ladies and gentlemen, you will forgive me. Come, Elene. Are you staying, Billy?

BILLY: No, I'll be along in a while.

JOSEPH: As for you . . . you . . . you, faggot. This finishes things between us. You are finished! Finished!

JULIO: Now it comes out. (*Moves toward him, cursing in Spanish. Joseph darts out with Elene.*)

OTTO: (*Running after him*) Joseph! Joseph! (*They all freeze in puppet postures.*)

BILLY: You idiot. Now you've done it.

JULIO: So it all comes down to money and power. That's all our friendship has meant to you. And I loved you . . .

BILLY: Yes, money. Money! Is that so wrong? Try scrounging like an animal. Try busting your heart going from one producer to another, your hat in your hand, begging for a chance to act. Being kicked out by fat sleek cats, too stupid to recognize real talent, and having to take the sickening looks of pity from their secretaries as you leave their offices and vomit out your life. Eating beans in cold water flats . . . your shoes giving out as you climb fifth-floor walkups to empty rat-infested rooms where the lights are out because sometimes you haven't got the few bucks it costs to keep them on. Try that sickening feeling in your belly, when you duck all your friends because you owe everybody in town. Or all the lonely nights when you look at the lights of a great city, and everybody's doing something and going somewhere and you want to reach out and grab it because you know it belongs to you, but you can't because you haven't got the few pennies it costs to get uptown for an audition. And you think, if you have to buck the wind and the rain and snow one more time, you'll break, and you hide your face in the blanket and cry your eyes out and die a little . . . all the lonely nights. Or the times you get a pass to an uptown show, and you see a no-talent dud murdering a great part, and everything in you wants to cry out "Stop!" And you want to throw the lousy son-of-a-bitch out of the theatre because you know you got it in you to do it ten times better, and you can tear up the stage and do it right, but you can't and you have to stifle the scream in your throat, and bite down your rage, or you'll end up banging your head against the wall, or killing everyone in sight, and they'll call you a maniac and put you in a straightjacket and lock you up and throw away the key. You've never had to walk the streets, Julio, because you're an aristocrat. You're lucky. You'll never know what it is to be in the pits . . . except at second hand. So you'll never know what it means when a guy picks you out of the gutter, and washes you and feeds you and gives you a chance, when nobody else gives a shit if you live or die. That's why I'm sticking with Ravensky, and I'm going with him all the way.

JULIO: Aristocracy is not by birth, but by nature. An artist is naturally an aristocrat, my friend. But, I see you have decided to model yourself on mediocrity. You're hopelessly middle class. You don't want to criticize your age. You want to come to terms with it. Could anything be more debasing?

BILLY: Yes. Never to have taken my shot. You walk alone if you want to. I'm going where the action is.

JULIO: Yes, straight to hell. You have a great talent. It's too bad you use it only to serve yourself.

BILLY: It's my destiny.

JULIO: It's your downfall.

BILLY: *C'est la vie.*

JULIO: The roots of self-love run deep.

BILLY: Oh, can it, Julio! I'm sick and tired of hearing the sound of your voice.

JULIO: So I see.

BILLY: You don't even know who you are. You've lost yourself in a cause. Why don't you dare to stand on your own two feet and be free like me?

(*Julio laughs.*)

BILLY: What's so funny?

JULIO: You are. You're nothing but a slave.

BILLY: A slave?

JULIO: To your own image. You think life's your stage.

BILLY: Doesn't everyone?

JULIO: Yes, but you think you're the main character and everyone else is a bit player.

BILLY: It's the truth.

JULIO: You're absurd.

BILLY: Who the hell do you think you are anyway? If there's anything I hate it's a self-righteous prig. Why don't you tear off that phony idealist mask? You want it all, Julio, the same as the rest of us.

JULIO: Yes, but not at any price.

BILLY: Who are you kidding? You knew what you were doing when you gave the play to Ravensky. You knew exactly how it would turn out. So why whine and bitch about it afterwards. Or haven't you got the guts to face what you really are?

JULIO: (*Pause.*) You're despicable.

BILLY: Naturally. Anyone who told you the truth would be.

JULIO: I'm done with you.

BILLY: That suits me fine.

JULIO: Come with me, Sharon, back to my own country. My people are simple. But, there, we can build a true theatre. Here, it is hopeless.

BILLY: It's hopeless everywhere. Be careful, Sunshine, he wants to seduce you.

JULIO: Here, they make parties and tell bad jokes while the world is perishing. People are starving and they shrug. Everywhere there is war and they laugh. Everywhere, it is a nightmare and they turn their backs. Sharon, help me a little to change this.

BILLY: Don't listen to him. He's crazy.

JULIO: Will you come?

BILLY: Forget it, Julio. She belongs with me.

JULIO: You love no one but yourself. You are a narcissist.

(*Billy starts to go for him. Sharon intercedes.*)

SHARON: I would come with you, but I can't.

JULIO: Why?

SHARON: I . . .

JULIO: He is not worthy of you. He's not a man.

(*Billy grabs him. They begin to fight. Sharon comes between and separates them.*)

SHARON: I feel I belong to him.

JULIO: You will know only pain with him.

SHARON: But, he needs me, Julio. I'm afraid he'll die without me.

BILLY: You see.

JULIO: Remember, I told you, he will break your heart.

SHARON: (*Looking at the Legend.*) Is this the parting of the ways? This can't happen to us.

(*Julio and Billy go into puppet freeze.*)

No, I won't allow it. (*Looking at the Legend, then consulting the audience.*) Oh, Sharon, Sharon, what should you do? It doesn't say. (*Making her decision.*) Goodbye, Julio. And thank you.

JULIO: I have warned you.

SHARON: I will always remember you.

(*Julio exits to puppet freeze.*)

That was a rotten thing to do.

BILLY: Now, you're being a bitch.

SHARON: When a woman tells you the truth, she's a bitch. When she's ambitious, she's ruthless. When she's independent, she's callous. When she's supportive, she wants to smother you. When she's concerned, she's pushy. When she desires, she's greedy. When she's loving, she's devouring; and when she refuses to go along with your madness, she wants to destroy you. Tell me, Billy, do you always leave your friends in the lurch?

BILLY: It was a question of principle.

SHARON: That's funny coming from you.

BILLY: All this talk about art makes me sick. Nobody gives a damn about it. We're in the dark ages.

SHARON: The artist is in eternal warfare against society. He's the corrective of the age. Only he knows how to bring men back to their true selves.

BILLY: In a time like this when no one will listen. What do you want me to do? Bleed my guts out?

SHARON: But you're a creative artist.

BILLY: An extinct animal that used to prowl around the nineteenth century. The stage is dead. I'm going to the coast. The bucks are there and so's the action.

SHARON: Love and applause. Is that all we live for?

BILLY: Let me tell you something. I don't give two raps about western civilization. It's sick to the core. And the sooner it dies, the better.

SHARON: But it's always the few who start a new one. Always.

BILLY: Was it so for your father?

SHARON: You leave my father out of this.

BILLY: You're asking me to follow in his footsteps.

SHARON: I'm asking you to follow in your own. My father was a great-hearted man. Why can't you be the same?

BILLY: I'm not going to bust my heart for some impossible dream.

SHARON: Any man who doesn't fight for what he loves is a coward and a liar, and deserves exactly what he gets.

BILLY: I'm not going to be a sucker! Not for you, not for anyone. If there's any ripping off to do, I'll be the one to do it. I want what's mine, and I want it now.

SHARON: Yes, most people are like that.

BILLY: It's rape or be raped. There's no in-between.

SHARON: If you can live that way. I can't.

BILLY: You love me, Sharon.

SHARON: Yes, I love you. We can't always help who we love.

BILLY: And you'll come with me.

SHARON: No. If I had any brains, I would have gone with Julio.

BILLY: Yes, you will.

SHARON: I'll never come with you. It would be the end of me if I did.

BILLY: And I love you. That's all that counts. The rest is bullshit.

SHARON: You arrogant bastard! You think that all that's in a woman's soul is love, and that she'll come crawling and clinging to you because she can't bear to be alone. Tell me, Billy, what is love?

And what do you love about me? My body, my soul, the truth I stand for?

BILLY: It's a cruel world, baby. It's no good going it alone.

SHARON: Don't worry about me, my love. I'll be fine. I have myself.

BILLY: And your father.

SHARON: Yes, and my father.

BILLY: Is that enough to keep you warm at night?

SHARON: No. But, I have my work.

BILLY: You're crying.

SHARON: So what?

BILLY: You'll come.

SHARON: It's finished.

BILLY: Tough customer.

SHARON: That's the way it has to be. Oh, my love, don't throw your life away. He who hears the siren song never returns.

BILLY: As soon as I get settled, I'll send for you.

SHARON: I told you, I won't come.

BILLY: Oh, yes, you will. You'll see.

(*He kisses her. She breaks away and moves to Natasha. They freeze in an embrace.*)

The trouble with people in this country is, they're shell-shocked. Shell-shocked and jaded. But Billy Brenner . . . he'll light a fire under their ass. Here's to me. (*Toasting himself with champagne.*) Hollywood, here I come! (*He freezes.*)

(*Sharon comes downstage and addresses the audience.*)

SHARON: Whenever I'm at such a crossroads, I wonder which road to take. Then it is, I look in all directions and see infinity spread out before me; and I know it's time for the old serpent within me to shed his skin, in hopes of a star-bright future. But now a strange hankering has come over me to take all roads at once. A holy oracle has whispered in my ear: Fair child, take all ten thousand lives and live them all in one. Impossible, you say? Not at all. For the Book of Life is already written: the sun and moon and stars, and you and I and our star-crossed lives, when we were brothers so very long ago.

(*Curtain.*)

ACT III

(*Hollywood, three years later. Sharon discovered disorientated, disheveled, dressed in a nightgown, a bottle of pills in one hand, a bottle of whiskey in the other. She turns sharply on the audience in a drunken stupor. Behind her is Billy in bed, frozen in puppet posture.*)

SHARON: (*To audience.*) I suppose you'll take me for a liar. What of that? Aren't all men? And women, too? I guess the brotherhood of man exists after all. Liars all. And if I promised to tell the truth, would you believe me? Well then, it would be at your own risk. Or would you say "your" truth — the truth as it appears to you — since the truth is unknowable. Well, as for that, many a man has not been present at his own death, nor at his own life, either. Nor why he should be is not for me to say. Absence and presence is very much a matter of taste, as we moderns say. But I figure the truth is of one piece, and if I dive deep enough into myself, the ore I find there will not differ so much from any other woman, as say, one sparrow from another. I will find the same lead, brass, silver and perhaps, who knows, even a speck or two of gold. Let me but bring it to the surface and I am content. The only problem in deep-sea diving is I may hear some siren song that detains me forever; or meet some monster that will have better use of me than I of him; or crack my skull on some hidden coral reef; or chance upon some mystery better left unsaid; or stumble upon some seductive unworldly beauty that holds me in its grasp forever. Or worse, some grotesque flitting shape that unhinges my mind. Some horror that bursts my mind, and I return demented, raving.

(*Sharon joins Billy in bed. Blackout. During the blackout, Andrea sings "I'm Leaving, Don't Hold Me Back."* At the end of the song there is a scream. Sharon and Billy are having the same nightmare. As the scene unfolds the lights slowly come up. Joseph sits in chair in corner of room, in puppet freeze. The entire company in background watches in puppet freeze.*)

SHARON: Ohhhhhhhh!

*Music p. 166

BILLY: Sharon! What is it? Sharon!

SHARON: I've had a bad dream. I was in the center of the earth and the whole world was applauding, only it wasn't me. It was a monkey . . . a monkey . . . and the monkey was me. And I tried to tell them it wasn't me . . . it was a monkey — but they kept crying, "Sharon Shashanovah, Sharon Shashanovah," and I tried to run away but I was lost in the labyrinth. And the crowd applauded and shouted, "Sing, monkey . . . sing for your supper," and I tried to hide, but the monkey wouldn't let me and I began to sing.

BILLY: And out came sounds . . . horrible and ghastly. And the applause was thunderous, and I began to choke. I tried to stop but I couldn't.

SHARON: It was Joseph . . . Joseph was in the dream.

BILLY: And he wouldn't let me. He was an organ grinder and he held me by a black chain and he made the monkey dance. And the monkey kept singing, and the whole world began petting and caressing me, and Joseph was collecting money . . . money. And I was just a monkey on a string and I bit them, and they began to laugh and fall down and worship me, and Joseph pulled and pulled on the chain, and then, suddenly, it was transformed into a golden thread, and the person who held the thread was you. (*Pause.*) When will this nightmare end?

SHARON: When we dead awaken.

BILLY: What?

SHARON: Nothing.

BILLY: Always the same dream, and always you. Can't you get out of my dreams?

SHARON: I'll get out of your life if you want me to.

BILLY: No! Don't ever do that. Promise me you'll never do that.

SHARON: Why not?

BILLY: I'd go down the tubes without you.

SHARON: (*Singing.*)
       "It's only a paper moon
       Sailing over a cardboard sea.
       But it wouldn't be make-believe
       If you believed in me.
       Without your love,
       It's a honkey-tonk parade. . ."

BILLY: I'd live such a rotten life without you.

SHARON: You've got your starlets to keep you warm.

BILLY: I don't give a damn about them.

SHARON: Don't you? Then come back to New York with me.

BILLY: Just one more picture.

SHARON: It's always one more picture. When will it end? Why don't you wake up and come back to the stage where you belong?

BILLY: I'm just fine here.

JOSEPH: (*Breaks from freeze.*) Of course he is. Here in the South Sea Islands.

(*As if hypnotized, Billy and Sharon in a grotesque ritual begin to make-up and dress for the day's shooting.*)

SHARON: Sure. With the other plastic natives, life's a comfort.

JOSEPH: What's wrong with palm trees? A little decadence goes a long way.

BILLY: You came out, even though you said you wouldn't.

SHARON: Because I was weak and stupid. Give me a pill, will you honey? I guess that's what love does to you. But you . . . you live in a narcotic haze. That's no way to raise my kids. I can't take it.

BILLY: It beats living in a garbage can. New York's awful . . .

SHARON: It was once your city. And you used to love it.

BILLY: Well, if you like dirt . . .

JOSEPH: Tut, tut. Temperament! Temperament! My lovebirds mustn't fight. It's far too early in the morning.

SHARON: I love the dirt and everything that grows from it. (*Joseph begins singing softly "Paper Moon."*) The finest grapes come from the toughest dirt. I want to be where the struggle's most intense, amidst the pace of a great city. It's real, and I'm going back. But now that you're an international celebrity, I guess it's not good enough for you.

BILLY: Why the hell does everyone make me feel good except you? Only you have to make me feel ashamed.

JOSEPH: It's a marvelous scene. But save all that intensity for the camera. We have a full day's shooting schedule ahead of us.

SHARON: Shame, Billy? What's there to be ashamed of? (*Joseph begins singing again.*) Be careful, you'll blow your image. It's show business, life on this earth. A show so immense it would make Barnum and Bailey blush. And we're all in it . . . It won't be long 'til they plug the tube in our heads. Then, we'll never be alone again. We can jet-set our way to celebrity heaven and make commercials with all the beautiful people.

JOSEPH: My, my, what a passionate display. Our Sharon talks as if no one ever made a good picture.

SHARON: There have been some fine movies, even great ones, but that's all over. We don't make movies, movies make us.

JOSEPH: We're talking about money here. We're talking about contribution. We're talking two Academy Awards here. And in such a short time. I mean, really . . .

SHARON: I don't give a damn. What the hell do they know? Look at all the people they've ruined. Griffith, Welles, Von Stroheim, my beautiful Michael Chekhov. And look what they tried to do to Chaplin, Hellman, and so many others. Oh my head, take off my head. Oh, Billy, Billy, take away my pain.

BILLY: You're cruel.

SHARON: Not as cruel as you are to yourself.

BILLY: Who made you a prophetess? Be my lady.

SHARON: I want to live, not die a cardboard figure in a world of papier-mâché. Three years in this wasteland is enough. If you ever want me, you know where to find me.

BILLY: Stay.

SHARON: I won't be used anymore. Julio warned me a long time ago. He told me what Joseph was. Julio told me he'd suck everything out of you.

JOSEPH: Pay no attention to her, Billy. Our darling is just in a bad temper this morning.

BILLY: I want you with me.

SHARON: I can't. Always I hear that poem of Rimbaud, driving me on: "My eternal soul.
Redeem your promise
In spite of the night alone,
And the day on fire."

JOSEPH: That poem was his death cry. He was a comet that flashed across the sky, burned out, and plunged into darkest Africa.

BILLY: He led a terrible life.

SHARON: Oh, Billy, if you only could remember that. (*Pause.*) Billy, are you coming?

BILLY: Maybe she's right, Joseph. Maybe if I went back to the theatre for a while and did some real work . . . I could get a hold of myself.

JOSEPH: And break up the greatest artistic combination this town's ever seen? Are you mad, Billy? The stage is dead. The motion pictures are the art form of the future. And it's only through the movies that you can make a statement that can reach millions of people. It's our responsibility. You'd be a fool to throw all that away. I won't let you.

BILLY: I want Sharon.

JOSEPH: Sure you do. And she wants you. You're good for each other. Haven't I always said that? That's why the three of us are going to stay together. It's our destiny. We have great things to do. Now get yourself together. Both of you! The world's waiting for you. The cameras are about to roll.

SHARON: I can't take it anymore. I'm leaving. And Billy's coming with me.

JOSEPH: Sit down. Relax. Here's a fix so you can give the world a fix. (*Takes out needle.*)

SHARON: Leave us alone.

JOSEPH: Now, how can I do that? I'm responsible for you. I've got to take care of you.

SHARON: Don't take it, Billy!

BILLY: No, no, I don't want it.

JOSEPH: Sure you do.

SHARON: You're killing him.

JOSEPH: The only one who is killing him is you.

SHARON: Me?

JOSEPH: By trying to take him away from here. He belongs here. He's happy here. If you really loved him you'd stay here with him instead of tormenting him.

SHARON: You promised when you brought us out here that we would do something beautiful and good and true. And I believed in you. I trusted you. We both did. And look what we've come to. (*Sharon pulls down motion picture screen and a silent movie begins to play simultaneously with the stage action.*)

(*As the play continues*)	(*The credits flash on the screen as the silent movie begins.*)
SHARON: I can't bear my life a moment longer. I've betrayed everything I ever believed in. I don't know who I am.	TITAN STUDIOS PRESENTS SHARON SHASHANOVAH & BILLY BRENNER IN THE LABYRINTH A JOSEPH RAVENSKY PRODUCTION

JOSEPH: You're Sharon Shashanovah, the face that launched your generation.

SHARON: I'm a whore. I . . . I . . . can't go on this way. And neither can he. There'll be nothing left of me.

JOSEPH: Whataya talking about?

You got everything you ever wanted. The adulation of the world. Why, you're the idols of your generation.

SHARON: We're lost, Joseph. Don't you understand? We're lost.

JOSEPH: You're big business. A multi-million dollar corporation.

SHARON: I don't know where I'm going.

JOSEPH: There's nowhere to go. You're happy here. (*To Billy.*) Feeling better?

BILLY: Oh, yeah.

JOSEPH: Yeah, sure.

BILLY: Joseph, tell me who I am again.

SHARON: Oh, this is ghastly.

JOSEPH: You're Billy Brenner, America's sweetheart.

BILLY: But who am I? (*Slowly running his hands across his face.*) The face behind the face.

(*Joseph deplanes in Hollywood, smiling at reporters, life-size puppets of Sharon Shashanovah and Billy Brenner on each hand.*)

(*Joseph, carrying puppets of Sharon and Billy, enters mouth of gigantic laughing man. The mouth, spasmodically opening and closing in laughter, is the entrance to an amusement park.*)

(*Joseph and puppets Billy and Sharon in Hall of Distorted Mirrors, revealing them as grotesques: giants, midgets, fat, thin, dressed in various costumes.*)

(*Restaurant. Puppets Billy and Sharon sit on either side of Joseph. He pours champagne into their glasses, toasting their success.*)

(*Joseph and puppets Billy and Sharon in opium den in Moroccan dress. They smoke.*)

(*Joseph stands. He presents an Academy Award to puppet Billy.*)

JOSEPH: Nobody.

(*Wild sex orgy. Swarming, naked bodies surround puppets Sharon and Billy, Billy still grasping his Academy Award. Joseph smiles throughout.*)

BILLY: Nobody? (*Goes to mirror.*)
JOSEPH: Just a small-town kid who made it. You should count your blessings, Billy.
SHARON: It's not true. Don't believe him, Billy. It can't be true.
JOSEPH: Isn't it?

(*Clutching and tearing hands reach up, pull puppet Sharon down into midst of orgy.*)
(*Figure dressed in white, stethoscope, black satchel, looms over puppet Sharon.*)

You were nothing when you came to me. And you're nothing now.

(*Closeup of puppet Sharon, mouth agape in silent scream. Figure in white, his hand a black talon, reaches down and rips doll covered in blood from between her thighs. Scene dissolves in blood.*)

It was I who gave you the Part.

(*Puppets Sharon and Billy alone, exhausted, prostrate on floor. A pair of hands reaches down and picks them up.*)

It was I who allowed you to play the Legend of Sharon Shashanovah.
Without me you're nothing.

(*The hands belong to Joseph. He places puppets Sharon and Billy on perches in large cage.*)
(*Pulls down black cover over cage.*)

(*To Billy.*) How does it feel to be caught in a dirty movie with your pants down?

(*Screen is black.*)

SHARON: (*To Joseph.*) You said only I could play it. That it was my life.

(*"The End" flickers on screen.*)

JOSEPH: (*As he pulls up the movie screen.*) It's apparent to me now,

I've wasted my creative energy on an ungrateful bitch.

BILLY: You shouldn't talk to her that way, Joseph.

JOSEPH: Go to the mirror, my dear. What do you see? You're not getting any younger, are you?

SHARON: No, I'm not.

JOSEPH: And what will the future bring? Anyone to care for you? Only I am foolish enough to look out for your best interests.

BILLY: Please, Joseph, don't. You're hurting her.

JOSEPH: (*Pushing him down.*) Sit down, Billy. I'm not going to let her do this to us.

SHARON: I'm getting out of here.

JOSEPH: Go on, run. But you'll be back. You hear — you'll be back.

SHARON: I'm never coming back.

JOSEPH: Where will you work? It's the same everywhere.

SHARON: Then I won't work, unless it's for what I treasure. Billy . . .

(*Billy has picked up the needle for another shot.*)

Billy, please . . . come with me. It's our last . . . it's our only chance. Don't break the thread.

(*Billy looks at her and then at Joseph. He hesitates, then takes the shot.*)

JOSEPH: But Billy stays. Do you understand? He's staying. Aren't you, Billy?

(*Billy looks at Sharon, then turns away. He and Joseph freeze.*)

SHARON: (*To audience.*) Why do all men sell their birthright to nibble at the sickly foliage of Hell, when as babes we could cling to the root of Heaven and suck ambrosia and nectar there? Why these lives of fiction, as if the book of our original creation were not close at hand, as if it had been erased by some degenerate race which had scribbled undecipherable obscenities in our hearts, which we must follow to the end of time? Why these counterfeit lives at every turning, bending our backs to commerce like dumb oxen chained to the wheel of life in a universal procession of pain and misery that will never end? Aren't we Abraham's children that the Divine promised would be as numerous as the stars? Oh Abraham, Abraham, your children are lost in the wilderness and who shall save them? For we have forgotten the music of the spheres and hear only a buzzing in our ears. (*Exits.*)

BILLY: Is she gone?

JOSEPH: Yes, she's gone.

BILLY: I've got to go after her. I've got to find her.

JOSEPH: Don't worry about it. She'll be back.

BILLY: She's never coming back. I know it.

JOSEPH: You're better off without her. She's no good for you.

BILLY: I think I'm going to die.

JOSEPH: Come to bed, baby. (*Pushes Billy towards the bed. Blackout, during which Andrea sings, "Blue."**)

(*Dawn. Billy and Joseph in bed, Joseph in grotesque freeze. The entire company watches in puppet freeze. Billy awakens, sees Joseph and jumps out of bed in horror. He moves wildly around the room, moaning softly. He goes to the makeup table and looks for himself in the mirror. In a daze he discovers a wig and white makeup and puts them on. He looks again. Startled, he strips off the wig and white makeup and grabs the phone.*)

BILLY: Operator, give me New York — 555–8231.

ELENE: (*Playing the role of the telephone operator.*) One moment, please.

SHARON: Hello?

BILLY: Sharon . . .

SHARON: Billy!? Is that you?

BILLY: I love you, Sharon. It's just the two of us now. I'm coming home.

SHARON: Oh, Billy, Billy. I knew you'd come through. Hurry darling, hurry. I'm going crazy. I love you so.

(*Joseph, who has risen from bed, takes the phone and hangs it up.*)

JOSEPH: Why, you little bitch! After all I've done for you. You're not walking out on me.

BILLY: Don't touch me. Keep your hands off me, you dirty, rotten pimp!

SHARON: Billy? Billy! Where are you? What's happened?

JOSEPH: (*To Billy.*) Baby, I love you.

BILLY: You raped me. You pig! You filthy, disgusting freak.

JOSEPH: You wanted it. (*Grabs him and kisses him full on the mouth.*) The whole world wants it.

BILLY: Oh, God, what have I done to myself? (*Exits.*)

SHARON: Operator, we were disconnected.

ELENE: Your party's hung up.

SHARON: No, there must be some mistake. Ring the number again, please.

*Music p. 168

ELENE: One moment.

(*The phone begins ringing. Billy enters with knife.*)

BILLY: You got me. But you won't get Sharon.

JOSEPH: Put down that knife, Billy. (*Billy starts towards him.*) You don't want to do that, Billy. Billy! Billy!

(*Billy wrestles with him on the floor, lashing out at him with knife. Joseph escapes and exits to puppet freeze.*)

BILLY: I've murdered myself!

ELENE: There is no answer on the other end of the line.

SHARON: Keep ringing. Keep ringing. Oh, God, keep ringing.

(*Billy, about to plunge the knife into himself, hears the ringing, hesitates, drops the knife, and picks up the phone.*)

Billy . . . speak to me. Oh, talk to me, sweetheart. What is it? Answer me, Billy. You're frightening me! Hold on to the wire, Billy. I'm on the other end. I'm with you, darling. There was a maiden. She held a golden ball. She let out the string.

BILLY: Sharon . . . where are you?

SHARON: I'm here, darling. I'm with you.

BILLY: Where are you?

SHARON: Hold the wire, Billy. Don't let go. I'm taking the first plane out tonight.

BILLY: Too . . . late. Forget me. Save yourself.

SHARON: Billy!!

(*He drops phone and exits to puppet freeze.*)

Billy! Billy! Where are you!? Come back. Don't leave me! Come back! Oh, God, I've lost him . . .

(*As lights darken, Andrea sings "I'm Leaving, Don't Hold Me Back" reprise.**)

(*Later that night. Lights come up on Sharon's bedroom in New York.*)

OTTO: He died instantly.

SHARON: It's not true.

OTTO: You must believe me, my child. His car went over the cliff at six o'clock this morning. Joseph called me. He's on his way here now.

SHARON: He'll come. You'll see.

OTTO: He's not coming back, ever.

SHARON: He'll come through that door and he'll be smiling. And then

*Music p. 166

he'll call out my name and he'll start laughing. "Hello, Sunshine," he'll say. "Did you miss me?" And then he'll hold me in his arms and I'll start to cry because . . . I'll be so happy.

OTTO: Shashi, he's gone.

SHARON: I know. I was just pretending.

OTTO: I'm so sorry, my child.

SHARON: The only two people I ever loved. My daddy, and now, Billy. And now I've lost them both. Gone, all gone . . . gone . . . my Billy's gone. Oh no. . . oh no. (*Breaks down weeping.*) Oh, somebody help me.

(*Otto goes to her.*)

It's alright. I'm fine. Don't worry about me. I'm a big girl now.

OTTO: If there's anything . . .

SHARON: I want to be alone now . . . please.

(*Otto exits.*)

I must carry a dead man, locked in my heart forever. Oh, Billy, I'm so scared and lonely. I have no one . . . no one. Only my little ones. Where will I go? (*Climbs into bed; Joseph is seen entering silently.*) The moon is mocking me. Oh, I can't breathe, it's so cold. Will I ever be warm again? I'm afraid I'm going to break. Please, don't let me break. And now the stars are rushing down to crush me. If the heavens would only fall on me, then this fever of life would soon be out. And I could rest, yes, rest. I need rest so badly, but there's no place, no place . . . "The foxes have holes, the birds have nests." Why? Why? Oh, Billy, why didn't you wait for me? I didn't know I could miss you so. What will I do? Tomorrow, I'll go to the theatre, and act as if nothing has happened, nothing at all. Oh, please . . . please . . . (*Joseph stirs imperceptibly.*) Billy? Billy? Is that you? I can feel your presence. Why won't you come to me . . . please? (*Joseph sits on bed. She reaches out for him.*) Oh, you're here. You're not Billy. Joseph . . . it's Joseph. Hold me, hold me. Don't leave me. I don't want to be alone. I can't stand it. I'll die if I have to be alone again.

JOSEPH: Shhhh.

SHARON: I don't think I can go on.

JOSEPH: Shhhh.

SHARON: He's dead. Billy's dead.

JOSEPH: Yes . . .

SHARON: We killed him, Joseph. We killed him. It's my fault. Why did you let me go? I should have stayed. Everything would have been different.

JOSEPH: Quiet, my dear. Rest in my arms. We'll make everything all right. We'll build a beautiful new theatre in his name. You and I. You'll see. And I'll protect you. I'll love you. Now you must rest . . . rest. Put your arms around me. Now, give me your lips. (*Blackout.*)

(*A few hours later. Lights come up. Natasha enters.*)

JOSEPH: Mama!

NATASHA: What have you done?

JOSEPH: Mama! What are you doing here? How dare you intrude . . .

NATASHA: You filth! Corrupter! First the mother and now the daughter.

JOSEPH: Get out of here, Natasha.

NATASHA: And you, how could you even let him near you? How could you do it to yourself, to me? See the blood on his hands . . . see? It was he who killed your Billy.

JOSEPH: Mama, be quiet. Hold your tongue.

NATASHA: You sold him for your ambition. Your hands bleed with the blood of that man. You killed him as surely as men like you kill all the Billy Brenners of this world.

JOSEPH: Mama, you're insane. He was a suicide.

NATASHA: We are all suicides unless someone saves us. It was you who drove him to it, and now you want to murder this woman. Are you rich now, my son, from dealing in human flesh?

JOSEPH: You've been in the theatre too long, Natasha. Melodrama has overtaken your sense of reality.

NATASHA: You fool! You don't even know what you've done. She is your daughter!

JOSEPH: You hear what she says, Shashi, this madwoman? Now we are father and daughter it seems.

SHARON: Jacob Shashanov is my father! (*Almost inaudibly.*) The Legend. The Legend. (*Shrieking.*) He's my father!! (*Almost inaudibly.*) The Legend. (*Shrieking.*) Not this man!!

NATASHA: Jacob raised you, but it was this slime who ran off with your mother.

SHARON: (*Silently shrieking, then finding her voice.*) The Legend! Oh God! It's true. (*She faints.*)

JOSEPH: You have an ugly sense of humor, Natasha.

NATASHA: As ugly as yours when you ran off with her mother. She is your child.

JOSEPH: If what you say were true, you would have told me a long time ago.

NATASHA: Jacob swore me to secrecy. He was a proud man. He never wanted anyone to know.

JOSEPH: Liar! Liar!

NATASHA: Truth!

JOSEPH: No! I won't believe it. You want to drive me crazy. You want to destroy me.

NATASHA: There is no need, my son. You have destroyed yourself.

JOSEPH: (*Grabbing Natasha's cane and moving towards her.*) You always hated me. Always envied my success. And now you want to kill me. But you won't.

NATASHA: Go ahead, strike. Strike, why don't you! You are depraved enough to do it. But first, I will teach you a lesson you will never forget. (*Pulls the cane from his hands.*)

JOSEPH: Stay away from me, Natasha! Stay away!

NATASHA: Cringe like the coward you are.

JOSEPH: Mama!

NATASHA: Murderer! Murderer!

(*He falls to the floor covering his head, as she strikes him furiously.*)

Die! Die! In the gutter. Like the dog you are!

(*Goes over to Sharon who is lying in bed, and puts her arm around her.*) Come, my daughter, I will take you home.

SHARON: Oh, Madame! I must . . . must . . . must die. (*Sobs uncontrollably in Natasha's arms as the lights fade out.*)

(*One hundred days later. Lights come up on Sharon in bed. Faintly silhouetted in background is the entire Company. Natasha motions to them. They come down as puppets, and hover in puppet attention around Sharon's bed.*)

NATASHA: Wake up, Sharon. The play is over. The Legend is fulfilled.

SHARON: What is it, where am I? Oh. The sun is hurting my eyes. Can't you close the shades? I want to sleep. Please, let me sleep.

NATASHA: You've been sick for a long time, Sharon. Now it's time to get up.

SHARON: I can't.

NATASHA: You must.

SHARON: (*Getting up to dress.*) Oh, rehearsals are about to begin. Just give me a minute to get dressed. (*Goes behind screen. Natasha motions the puppets back to their former positions. Sharon goes into a role she thinks she has to play.*) It's such a beautiful day. Gosh! I don't want to be late for rehearsals. I've never been late before. I'll be ready in a moment. I'll be right out. Just a few more seconds.

(*Sharon comes out from behind screen.*)

NATASHA: You can stop acting now, Sharon.

SHARON: What! (*She freezes in terror and becomes transformed into an uncontrolled puppet. She plays out all her past roles in a grotesque pantomime.*)

NATASHA: It's all over. La commedia e finita.

SHARON: (*Sits on bed; to Otto.*) Please hold my hand. I'm so grotesque. My life, my life, I've ruined my life. (*Begins weeping.*)

BILLY: Why do you weep? You're not Sharon Shashanovah.

SHARON: Of course, I'm Sharon Shashanovah. What are you talking about?

JULIO: You are, and you are not.

JOSEPH: You forget, she is only a role you play.

SHARON: Who am I then?

ELENE: That is what you must find out.

ANDREA: (*Singing.*) We are the players. Playing the scene.*

SHARON: Does everyone feel like me, or am I just a freak of nature?

NATASHA: (*Stroking her forehead.*) Many feel like you, Shashi, but they forget. Only the pure in heart remember.

SHARON: Julio, Otto, Elene, Andrea, Joseph, Billy, Madame . . . all my friends in Puppet Theatre. Was it a dream or are we . . .

OTTO: Long ago, we have forgotten . . . forgotten who we were. We are the damned, repeating endlessly a role we neither know nor believe in. We know we are not these roles, these fictions we portray. But what we are, in reality, remains a mystery.

BILLY: We're creatures of applause. We die when the applause ends. Only part of the painted scenery.

SHARON: Does everyone have a Legend?

NATASHA: Everyone.

SHARON: What's real then?

JULIO: (Shrugs.) Ask the Maestro.

SHARON: The Maestro's been toying with me all this time. And I'm just a character in a play? What ever made me think I was human? Joseph . . . my own father.

*Music p. 163

NATASHA: Don't you understand you had to live out your Legend in order to know yourself?

SHARON: What good is knowledge when it does the knower no good? It's cut the very ground from under me. I'd like to disappear through a crack in the Universe. Oh, Madame, what should I do?

NATASHA: What do you want to do?

SHARON: If only I knew.

NATASHA: Once, when I was at the crossroads of my life, I had to ask myself the same question.

SHARON: You mean . . . you've known all the time that life is a dream and . . .

NATASHA: Yes, for fifty years, I've stood at my post. I chose to stay with my dreams — only to have them torn from me. Oh, I was so filled with illusions.

SHARON: Do all men betray themselves in Puppet Theatre? Is there no way out?

NATASHA: There is a way. But you must be strong enough to take it and leave your dreams behind.

SHARON: Why haven't you ever told me this, Madame?

NATASHA: You weren't ready. You never asked. No one ever does. They're too filled . . . with themselves. Once, I saw the way out, but I didn't take it. It was only a glimpse. But, it was more real than anything I'd ever known.

SHARON: My vision. It's real.

NATASHA: Yes, my daughter. It's real. The only thing that is real in this unreal world.

SHARON: Oh, madame, thank you, thank you, for giving my vision back to me. Why didn't you follow your vision?

NATASHA: I wanted to. It was singing to me — like angel voices. But I clasped my hands over my ears to drown that music out. That unearthly music that would tear me from my dreams. I had to be a great actress. It was my life. My life . . . my vanity . . . I never saw the vision again.

SHARON: There's something you know that you're not telling me. Who was Jacob Shashanov and who am I? Who is the man who raised me? How did Joseph get to be my father? I must know. Now you must tell me everything.

NATASHA: I knew this day would come.

SHARON: This day?

NATASHA: The day that you would ask. But you must not blame

yourself.

SHARON: No, I did it. The Legend said I would. And something lured me to it. Some fascination. Horrible . . . horrible . . .

NATASHA: We have all committed crimes against ourselves. Mine was not to have told you who your real father was.

SHARON: You've known all this time? You never told me. Why? But then the Legend would not have been fulfilled. And it had to be. Why? Oh, what am I? I've got to find out.

NATASHA: I did it to spare you and Jacob. I loved him.

SHARON: You loved . . . him.

NATASHA: And he loved me. But my damnable ambition kept me from him. Finally, when I went to him, it was too late. He had married your mother.

SHARON: Tell me about my mother.

NATASHA: She ran off with . . .

SHARON: Joseph.

NATASHA: When they were done with each other, she begged Jacob to take her back. That was the sorrow of my life.

SHARON: So that's it.

NATASHA: A few months later you were born. Jacob raised you as his own. (*Pause.*) Oh, it's all been a dream.

SHARON: So she found her way to Joseph, too. It seems we're made of the same cloth, she and I. And all these years I condemned her. Mother, wherever you are, forgive me. Now I understand. I must leave all my dreams behind. Past all dreams and all deceits to a life that should have been mine — will be mine. Break the strings that bind me and go towards my vision. It will lead me to the Maestro. I must go alone, in a solitude like death.

NATASHA: Have you the courage to leave this Puppet Theatre and go into the Unknowable?

SHARON: It's so strange. I feel as if I stood by and watched my whole life unfold. And just when I understand, I must leave it all behind. Never to act the Legend of Sharon Shashanovah again. I've become so attached to her. She's my very self, and yet she's not.

NATASHA: It's only a role, my child. There are others waiting in the wings to take it. Always others.

SHARON: You've said all this to me before. Haven't you?

NATASHA: (*Nods.*) Don't make my mistake. Don't regret your life forever. There's only now. You must seize the moment and go while you can. Otherwise, it will be too late. You don't want your life to repeat endlessly.

SHARON: No. I'll follow my vision wherever it takes me. I won't betray it. But will I never come back to Puppet Theatre?

NATASHA: Always you will come back and always you will forget, unless you are strong enough to remember. And then . . .

SHARON: And then?

NATASHA: You needn't come back. Or if you are strong enough, you can choose to return and help show a few others the way out.

SHARON: (*Pause.*) I must be strong enough.

(*The characters have been listening intently. They suddenly come to attention, waiting to be released.*)

I can't leave Billy and Julio and you, and all the people I love, to perish like shadows. I just can't. I have to come back and play my part.

NATASHA: That is your choice.

SHARON: I know I'm right. The Maestro didn't create me to live in an imaginary paradise while the rest of the world suffers. I'm sure of that. I was created to fight . . . to come back and fight for the ones I love. If I fail, it doesn't matter, but if I succeed, then, I'll be back. I will be back. And then, nothing has to be the same again, does it? If I change, then everyone around me changes. That's the secret, isn't it?

NATASHA: Yes, that's the secret.

SHARON: My life doesn't have to repeat and repeat. The next time around I can change the Legend.

JOSEPH: (*With dawning realization, in wonderment.*) Yes.

(*The other characters, in hope of release, gesture yes, each in their own way.*)

SHARON: Now, awake and in reality, I must do what I only dreamed before. Then, the play can be done right, and Julio's heart doesn't have to be broken. And Billy won't have to die, because the next time, I'd stay by his side. And Joseph wouldn't have to live such a despicable life, because he'd have a daughter who understood him and loved him and oh . . . everything and everyone would be different. The whole world would be different . . . so different. And you could rest. For you'd have a granddaughter and great-grandchildren who loved and adored you and gave you hugs and kisses from morning 'til night, and you'd be so happy. And so would I . . . so would I. Oh, if one day I could come back and do it all again, what would happen on that day? Tell me.

NATASHA: (*Transforming into puppet.*) Then, my child, on that day we would meet in a much greater Theatre, of which this little theatre is but the mirror.

SHARON: And there we shall have stars for light, eternity for our script. The Maestro shall come out to meet us on that day — when all men and women are unmasked, know the truth, and break the bonds that bind them to the Puppet Theatre. Goodbye.

(*Blackout. As the lights come up, the entire cast of Puppet Theatre is assembled onstage. They are frozen in postures of puppets, showing a greater yearning towards Sharon than at the beginning of the play. They begin to come to life during Sharon's speech.*)

SHARON: I beg your pardon. Am I in the right place? Of course, I'm in the right place. I've been here before. Hello, I'm sorry to disturb you, but I don't know if I'm in the right place. At least, I think I've been here before. I was told there was an audition here. You see, I'm an actress. Don't you remember me? You're looking at me so strangely. I know you . . . and you. I . . . I know you. I wish you would say something. I don't want to babble on. Oh, my God, I'm doing it again. How many times do I have to go through this? I've said this all before. But I must go on, and this time, do it right.

(*As the characters come down to the edge of the stage, they begin their opening speeches, one after another, each overlapping the others. In rapid succession they keep repeating their speeches until all are talking simultaneously.*)

JOSEPH: I am Joseph Ravensky, the impresario. Welcome to the theatre . . .

JULIO: I am Julio Adolpho Raoul Castillo, the playwright. I am filled with revolutionary fury . . .

NATASHA: I am Natalya Ilyichna Ravenskaya, student of Constantin Sergeivich Stanislavsky, friend of Michael Chekhov . . .

BILLY: I'm the actor, Billy Brenner, and I'm the greatest thing that ever hit this country, and I'm going to live forever . . .

ELENE: I'm Elene, the script girl. Your line is "With inflation the way it is . . ."

OTTO: I am the critic, Otto Schechler, an old man in a dry season, going toward my death . . .

ANDREA: I'm Andrea, the singer.

SHARON: I'm Sharon Shashanovah, and I pray I know where I'm

going.
(*All freeze. Andrea begins to sing, "Song of the Dreamers."* One by one, the entire company exits singing, leaving a bare stage.*)

*Music p. 163

SONGS

Music for Voice and Guitar

BY JUDI CASTELLI

SONG OF THE GOLDEN BALL

SONG OF THE DREAMERS

SONG OF PLUNDER

Throughout speech develop these themes with increasing intensity.

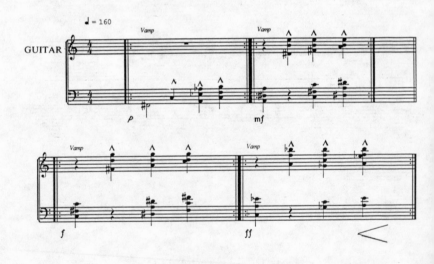

THE PLAY'S A HIT

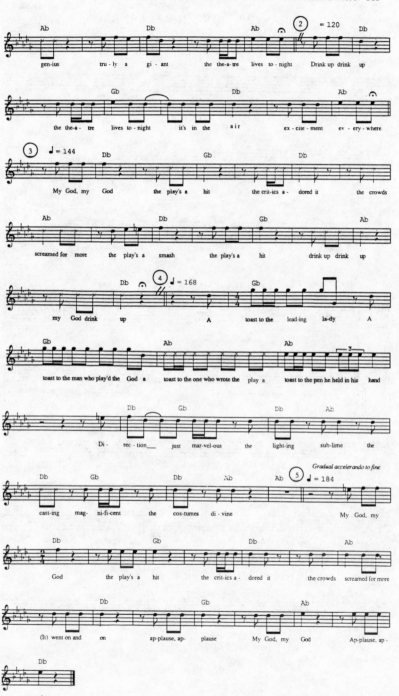

I'M LEAVIN', DON'T HOLD ME BACK

BLUE

JOURNEY
TO JERUSALEM

A Play in Two Acts

1976

The author wishes to pay a debt of love
to one woman, without whom this play could
not have been conceived, sustained or completed.
To Sharon Gans-Horn who led me every step
of the way on my Journey to Jerusalem.

When you make the two one, and
When you make the inner as the outer
And the outer as the inner
And the above as the below,
And when you make the male and the female
        into a single one,
So that the male will not be male
And the female not be female . . .

The Gospel of Thomas

CHARACTERS

Adam as
- a minister
- Baal Shem Tov
- Moslem
- Ikhnaton

Eve as
- Wife of minister
- Wife of Baal Shem Tov
- Lilith
- Bride of Death
- Nefretete
- Madonna of the Stars

Serpent as
- Sammael, The Evil One
- Death
- Lucifer
- Christ
- Hermes Trismegistus

Stage Manager	Lilith
Witness	Azarel ⎫ Angels
Rebbe Gershon	Urael ⎭
Rabbi Zeigler	Dancing Serpent
Rabbi Ciaramitovsky	Death's Double
Rabbi Ozborsky	Servants
Rabbi Roggevitch	Handmaidens
Rabbi Hilsensky	Nathan
Rabbi Koch	James
Rabbi Zalz	Christ's Double
Rabbi Imlavitch	Priests
Jacob Frank	Standard-bearer
Ministering Angels	Queen Mother Tyi
Costumers	Nurse
Hermit	Ayi, a minister to Pharaoh
Watchman of Hell	Harmhab, a general
Satan	Moses
Moloch	Doubles of Adam and Eve
Queen of Folly	Crowds
King Onan/Belial	Tree of Life
King Lucifuge	The Titanic Man

ACT I

SCENE 1: NEW YORK

(*At various times during the play, Serpent breaks from his character and becomes the director. Adam and Eve also break from their characters and become an actor and actress struggling to understand their roles.*)

(*Enter Serpent, wearing tuxedo.*)

SERPENT: Ladies and gentlemen! The actor who plays the role of Adam will be unable to perform this evening. Since he has also disappeared, the author has consented to take his place. As he is unrehearsed, he will be carrying a script.

(*To actors waiting offstage.*) All right, are you ready?

(*Enter Adam and Eve. Eve wears evening gown. Throughout play, Adam wears business suit and carries script.*)

ADAM: Yes. You're playing the Serpent?

SERPENT: Of course.

EVE: You play Adam, I play Eve, he plays Serpent.

SERPENT: Begin then.

EVE: Give me a kiss.

ADAM: Haven't you had enough? You've been messing around all night.

EVE: I never get enough.

ADAM: You lascivious bitch. You'd mate with a snake if you had a chance!

EVE: Why not? It's more than you're offering nowadays.

ADAM: You're disgusting.

SERPENT: No, no, no . . . At this point, Adam, you're supposed to say, "How incredibly vulgar our life is. I can't bear it a moment longer." That's your line.

ADAM: O.K.

EVE: Do you have it?

ADAM: Yeah, O.K. He's rewriting the script as we go along.

SERPENT: No, it's according to the author.

ADAM: Oh . . . sorry.

SERPENT: Take it back, Eve . . . "It's more than you're offering nowadays."

EVE: It's more than you're offering nowadays.

ADAM: How incredibly vulgar our life is.

SERPENT: "I can't bear it another moment."

ADAM: I can't bear it another moment.

EVE: Come on, one little kiss.

ADAM: Watch out, you'll break the lamp!

SERPENT: No, we've cut that. "I said no." is your line.

ADAM: Oh, O.K. I said no.

EVE: Doesn't Adam want to play with his little Eve?

ADAM: For Christ's sake . . .

SERPENT: No! "We've played this scene a thousand times if we've played it once."

EVE: Well, shall we skip this whole next section?

SERPENT: No, that's his cue. After you say, "Doesn't Adam want to play with his little Eve?" (*To Adam*) you say, "We've played this scene a thousand times before."

EVE: You're wasting time, all right?

ADAM: Eve, we've played this scene a thousand times before.

SERPENT: "Must we go on . . ."

ADAM: Must we go on . . . ?

EVE: Give baby a little kiss first.

ADAM: I said no.

EVE: Does my little minister want his theology book . . . hmmm?

ADAM: Eve!

EVE: Give me a kiss.

ADAM: Should I say "slut" here or do you want to cut that line?

SERPENT: No, I think it's all right. It's in the text.

ADAM: Slut.

EVE: Now sugar, don't be naughty.

ADAM: Give me my book.

EVE: Uh, uh.

ADAM: You bitch, I'll kill you!

SERPENT: No, you don't say that here. You say that in the next scene. "You bitch, I'll kill you." You say that in the Lilith scene.

ADAM: Back with the Baal Shem Tov?

SERPENT: No, no. The Baal Shem Tov comes next in the eighteenth century. After that comes the Lilith scene . . . That's when you go to Hell, remember? . . . to find your love.

ADAM: I get all these incarnations mixed up.

SERPENT: Well, Adam, you've got many lives to remember and so do you, Eve. You can't just pretend that you're restricted by this one lifetime in New York . . . You've got to remember all your lifetimes all the way back to the Garden of Eden.

EVE: It's hard.

ADAM: Oh, boy.

SERPENT: O.K. Your line is "Yes."

ADAM: Yes.

EVE: Take it.

ADAM: Don't shout.

SERPENT: "Take it, you impotent son-of-a-bitch."

EVE: I don't like those lines.

SERPENT: Well, it's in the text.

ADAM: It's New York.

SERPENT: It's New York, twentieth century, and Adam is impotent at this point.

ADAM: It's right language . . . later we can get more refined.

SERPENT: Well, later you'll get stronger as you go back to the source of time. Remember . . .?

ADAM: You mean we'll find the reason for all this?

SERPENT: Of course. You know you have to go all the way back through your entire time body in order to find out what went wrong. That's the purpose of the play. The author wrote it. Stick to the text.

EVE: Can't I say, "Take it, you son-of-a-bitch?"

SERPENT: No . . . "impotent!" "You impotent son-of-a-bitch." Because you . . . Look, Adam and Eve are reduced to total impotence . . .

EVE: I understand.

SERPENT: You've lost your way. You've gone the long road down from Paradise. It'll take the rest of the play to go back to Paradise . . . so be true to the transition.

EVE: I got it. Take it, you impotent son-of-a-bitch.

ADAM: Don't shout.

EVE: Ha, ha . . . Who's shouting? Your're the one who's screaming.

ADAM: I am not.

EVE: Oh yes you are.

ADAM: Stop it. You'll wake him up.

EVE: What do I care?

ADAM: Yeah, you'd like that, wouldn't you?

EVE: Maybe.

ADAM: If you're so hot, why don't you go in to him? I don't care.

EVE: Why should you? You're sleeping with him yourself, aren't you?

ADAM: That's different. We have . . . a friendship.

EVE: A friendship? . . . Oh . . . that's what you call it.

ADAM: Well . . . yes.

EVE: Don't make me laugh.

ADAM: What's so funny?

EVE: You are, faggot.

   (*Serpent kisses Adam.*)

ADAM: What did you say?

EVE: I said *faggot*.

ADAM: You take that back.

EVE: Oh . . . (*laughing*) I will not.

ADAM: You take that back.

EVE: You're ridiculous.

SERPENT: Let's stop it now.

ADAM: Yeah.

EVE: Can we skip the next . . . ?

SERPENT: No, just . . .

EVE: Can we get to the death part?

ADAM: Yes, let's get to the death part.

SERPENT: No, you can't.

ADAM: Why?

SERPENT: Because first the Serpent has to awaken.

ADAM: Oh . . .

SERPENT: He's in the next room, you remember?

EVE: But I thought you were playing the role of the Serpent.

SERPENT: I am, but it's not time for my cue yet. I have a few more moments, and if I'm not here to coach you, who knows what you two actors will do, all right?

EVE: O.K.

SERPENT: Now, at this point, Adam, try to change this eternal recurrence. You're in love with Eve.

ADAM: Uh huh.

SERPENT: Try to stop the scene.

EVE: Why don't you say, "We loved each other once."

ADAM: Yes, that's good.

SERPENT: Good.

EVE: We loved each other once.

ADAM: Eve, we loved each other once.

EVE: Yes, yes, a long time ago . . . I was young . . . my hair was beautiful . . . remember?

SERPENT: Yes.

EVE: My skin was so pure . . . the promise . . .

ADAM: Of . . .

EVE: . . . life, I suppose.

ADAM: Life.

SERPENT: No! Say that with even more disgust, because, Adam, you know it will soon be time for you and Eve to die.

ADAM: O.K.

SERPENT: And you're fully disgusted and disillusioned with life. Put all your disillusionment with life . . .

ADAM/SERPENT: Into that one word.

ADAM: Life.

EVE: It's all been a mistake. What does it matter? Calico Pie[1] . . .

SERPENT: You sing this, Eve.

EVE: Yes, I know. I just want to say the first line.

SERPENT: No, it's better to sing it, so you can . . .

EVE: (Singing.)
"Calico Pie,
The little birds fly
Down to the Calico tree.
Their wings were blue
And they sang 'Tilly-loo'
'Til away they all flew,
    And they never came back to me,
        They never came back,
        They never came back,
    They never came back to me."
(Eve begins to cry.)

ADAM: Don't be cruel, Eve.

EVE: It's too late for kindness. It's too late for anything.

ADAM: Then, let's . . . let's end the whole horrible mess; let's end it now.

EVE: Yes, how?

(*Serpent rattles a bottle of pills.*)

ADAM: The sleeping pills. The pact we made.

EVE: Our pact. I forgot about our pact.

ADAM: We discussed it before.

EVE: I know, I just forgot about it. Let's do it . . .

(*Singing.*)
"Calico Pie,
The little birds fly
Down to the Calico tree . . ."

ADAM: You really want to do it?

EVE: Yes, now, now, now.

ADAM: Are you serious?

EVE: Absolutely . . . (*singing softly*) ". . . They never came back to me."

ADAM: Is it time to do it yet?

SERPENT: No, first the Serpent has to come out and have the confrontation. All right, we can cut right to the scene now.

EVE: But can't I get a little bit crazy, like Ophelia?

(*Singing.*)
"Calico Pie,
The little birds fly
Down to the Calico tree . . ."

SERPENT: Yes, then the audience will sympathize with you. Now it's time for the Serpent. Take it from just before the Serpent comes in. "Don't shout, you'll wake him up."

ADAM: Don't shout, you'll wake him up.

SERPENT: I'm going now, but I'm coming right back.

(*Exit Serpent.*)

EVE: O.K. . . . O.K. You don't say anything on that line . . . or maybe you do . . .

ADAM: We're never alone. That's my line.

EVE: Oh, I don't know; you'll have to follow your lines. It doesn't make sense.

SERPENT: (*Calling from offstage.*) Stick to the text!

ADAM: (*Calling to Serpent.*) "We're never alone." That's what it says.

SERPENT: (*Calling from offstage.*) "Well, I don't know. He left the party early tonight."

ADAM: Yeah, O.K.

EVE: I don't know. He left the party early tonight.

ADAM: It's the first time in months.

EVE: So?

ADAM: How can you bear to have him lie between us at night?

EVE: You like it.

ADAM: I loathe it.

EVE: Well, tell him to go.

ADAM: Quiet . . . he'll hear us . . . I can't . . .

EVE: Why not?

ADAM: I feel chained to him.

EVE: That's odd . . . I can take him or leave him.

ADAM: Then why in God's name do you hang all over him?

EVE: You want it that way, Adam.

ADAM: Can't you understand? I want him to leave.

(*Serpent is heard singing offstage.*)

Shhh . . . now you've gone and done it. Act as if nothing has happened.

(*Enter Serpent.*)

SERPENT: You're back early. It's not yet midnight. Did you have a good time?

ADAM: Oh, we had a wonderful time.

EVE: Oh, simply marvelous.

ADAM/SERPENT: I'm glad to . . .

ADAM: Sorry.

SERPENT: That's all right. Glad to hear you weren't bored.

ADAM: Bored? Why should we be bored? Not a bit, not a bit.

EVE: We had a swell time.

SERPENT: A swell time?

ADAM: Yes.

SERPENT: That's fine.

EVE: You left early.

SERPENT: I was bored.

EVE: Oh.

ADAM: Bored?

SERPENT: Yes.

ADAM: Well, it was a little dull.

EVE: To say the least.

SERPENT: You didn't really enjoy it?

ADAM: It was dreadful.

SERPENT: What a shame. Why did you go then?

ADAM: That's a strange question coming from you.

SERPENT: Ohhh?

ADAM: I mean, you arrange these parties.

SERPENT: You must be mistaken. I'm not interested in orgies.

ADAM: But we've only begun going to them since you've come.

SERPENT: You've always gone. You simply called them by different names.

ADAM: What gives you the right to talk to me this way? After all, you're a guest in our house. I should think you owe me some respect. My position in the community entitles me . . .

SERPENT: To what?

ADAM: Well, after all, I am a minister.

EVE: Come off it, dear. You haven't believed a word you've said for years and neither has anyone else.

ADAM: I can't help it if this is a rotten age. It's not my fault if people don't believe in God.

SERPENT: Do you believe in Him?

ADAM: What?

SERPENT: I said, do you believe in God?

ADAM: I fail to see what that has to do with what we're discussing.

SERPENT: Then you don't believe in Him?

ADAM: I didn't say that.

EVE: Hypocrite.

ADAM: I'll thank you to keep out of issues you're too ignorant to understand. It's simply that God is a useful fiction for those who need Him to cement the bonds of brotherhood and good fellowship that make the church. Why, next year in Jerusalem . . . when I . . .

EVE: Jerusalem! Ha! Ha! You'll never get out of New York. Your congregation won't even pay the back taxes. You and your house of prayer.

SERPENT: No, no, "You and your house of prayer" comes in the next scene when Adam plays the Baal Shem Tov and you play his wife.

EVE: Oh, I don't say that now?

SERPENT: No.

EVE: Oh . . . I'm sorry . . . I got confused.

SERPENT: Hurry . . . we have only a minute and a half before . . .

EVE: Let's cut to the death scene.

ADAM: Yeah, let's cut to the exciting part.

EVE: O.K., say "Don't you laugh at me."

ADAM: Don't you laugh at me. Don't you dare.

SERPENT: No, go much further . . . the death is much further on.

EVE: Oh.

ADAM: Oh.

SERPENT: Hurry, we're behind time!! You have to be in Poland in a minute and a half.

ADAM: Oh.

EVE: All right, here . . . I've stayed with a cripple like you out of pity, do you hear? Pity, pity, that's why I've thrown my life away!

ADAM: Then take your life and go. Nobody's asking you to stay.

EVE: Oh, if only I could. There's nowhere to go.

ADAM: You see? I could go.

SERPENT: Could you, Adam?

ADAM: Of course, I . . .

SERPENT: Where would you go?

ADAM: I'd go to . . .

SERPENT: Yes?

ADAM: Ahhh . . . France.

SERPENT: No, France is not in the script.

EVE: (*Laughing*). He's always going to France.

ADAM: Well, I shouldn't want to go back to Jerusalem.

SERPENT: Your line is, Eve, "We tried an open marriage last year."

EVE: We tried an open marriage last year, dear.

ADAM: Well, I don't know where the hell I would go.

SERPENT: You must try to find some way out.

EVE: Hurry up, we only have a minute . . .

ADAM: Let's buy a new summer house somewhere . . . and . . .

EVE: No, it won't work.

ADAM: The Caribbean cruise . . .

EVE: No, it won't work. We've done it all. Let's go. Let's go.

ADAM: You really want to do it now?

SERPENT: Yes, now you play exactly the same scene you were playing before about the contract. Remember, you made the pact before the Serpent came. Now you can play it.

EVE: We made our pact. Let's do it. We'll find in death what we could never find in life. No, you say that line.

ADAM: O.K. We'll find in death what we could never find in life.

EVE: Peace.

ADAM: Yes, peace. Are you frightened?

EVE: I'd rather die than go on this way, destroying each other, destroying ourselves. Give them to me. Give them to me.

ADAM: Are you ready?

EVE: Yes.

ADAM: Oh, thank you.

SERPENT: Now, at the ninth stroke you take them. Yes? . . . O.K. . . . BONG!

(*Stage Manager runs on with glass of water for Adam.*)

EVE: No, no, we don't take them on the ninth stroke.

(*Stage Manager turns and begins to run back with glass of water.*)

ADAM: We start taking them now . . . as it strikes twelve . . . Now!

(*Stage Manager turns again, runs to Adam and hands glass to him, then runs offstage.*)

SERPENT: Correct.

ADAM: It's your line, Eve.

EVE: When I used to think of all the beauty locked within myself that was slowly dying, I used to cry myself to sleep. Now, it doesn't matter.

SERPENT: Hurry, hurry, hurry . . .

EVE: Going to say bye-bye now.

SERPENT: BONG!

ADAM: I'm sorry, Eve.

EVE: There's nothing to be sorry for.

ADAM: No. I . . . I botched it. BONG!

EVE: We both did.

ADAM: Can you forgive me?

EVE: We missed the boat. What's there to forgive?

ADAM: Everything.

EVE: I can't blame you. I was weak.

ADAM: What went wrong? How did we twist our lives so badly? BONG!

EVE: We loved each other in the beginning.

ADAM: Yes, I loved you then.

SERPENT: Break down now and admit how much you love one another. Otherwise, you'll lose the sympathy of the audience for the rest of the play.

ADAM: It's a love story?

SERPENT: Now it's a love story. It always has been. BONG!

EVE: Adam— with all the stars in Heaven, won't one shed a tear for us? It's so sad.

ADAM: Don't cry, Eve.

EVE: I'm not crying!

ADAM: Eve . . .

EVE: Yes . . .

ADAM: I still love you. BONG!

EVE: You hate me.

ADAM: No . . . no, not in these last few moments . . .

SERPENT: Right! You're preparing to return to your past.

EVE: You don't mean that.

ADAM: I mean it, baby . . . I've always loved you . . .

EVE: Oh, Adam.

ADAM: I wanted to tell you a thousand times.

SERPENT: That's it. Better . . .

ADAM: But pride . . . I was a fool. BONG!

SERPENT: Just as it says in the script!

EVE: Oh . . . it didn't have to be this way, did it?

ADAM: No, it didn't have to be . . .

SERPENT: Returning to your origin . . .

ADAM: Yes.

SERPENT: Excellent.

EVE: Oh . . . these last . . . this is yours . . .

SERPENT: Hurry, you have only a few seconds before I take you on your journey.

EVE: These last moments are worth all the rest. Maybe death is the answer for you and me. I love you. I love you, Adam.

SERPENT: BONG!

ADAM: Eve!

EVE: Yes?

ADAM: Say, "All is well."

SERPENT: "Twelve o'clock and all is well."

EVE: Twelve o'clock and all is well.

ADAM: BONG!

SERPENT: That's nine bongs. Save three bongs for the end of the play.

ADAM: What for?

SERPENT: Because the whole play takes place in three moments of time; the crack between life and death.

EVE: Don't leave me . . .

(*Actors playing Adam and Eve slump on couch, throw back their heads, and appear to be unconscious.*)

SERPENT: The prologue to the play is over.

(*Enter Witness in Shoemaker costume. He makes shoes throughout play.*)

Now ladies and gentlemen . . . as we go on our journey with

Adam and Eve back, back to the source of time . . . Next scene: Poland, eighteenth century.

SCENE 2: POLAND

SERPENT: I'm going to take you on a journey. Come with me. What are you waiting for? Come on.

ADAM: O Holy Mother Earth.

SERPENT: No. No. No! What are you waiting for? What are you sitting there for?

ADAM: What do you want me to do? I've got my lines here. It says . . .

SERPENT: No. What lines? What are you sitting there for? What are you acting as if you're dead for?

ADAM: Oh, I understand. I leave the couch, right?

SERPENT: No. Yeah, but do you know why?

ADAM: Because I'm going to be . . .

SERPENT: No, you don't understand. Look, your soul is going on a journey.

ADAM: Yeah.

SERPENT: You don't leave the couch. Your souls leave the couch. Why do you stay on the couch? Your souls leave and come to Poland now.

EVE: Right.

SERPENT: You understand?

ADAM: Yeah . . . but how am I going to act that?

EVE: No. No. You don't understand!

SERPENT: Quit worrying about it. We're going to get two bodies. (*Shouting toward backstage.*) Let's have two bodies, any two bodies in places. All right, come on now.

(*Enter man and woman.*)

EVE: They should look like us.

(*Exit man and woman.*)

SERPENT: What?

(*Enter second man and woman.*)

ADAM: They should look a little like us.

(*Exit second man and woman.*)

(*Enter third man and woman, dressed identically to Adam and Eve.*)

SERPENT: No. Bodies are bodies; it doesn't matter.

EVE: No, no, the bodies should look a little bit like us!

SERPENT: No, the bodies are of the same man: Adam and Eve.

(*Adam and Eve leave the couch. Their doubles take their places on couch and remain motionless throughout play. Enter Costumers who place a rabbi hat on Adam and help Serpent change into Dervish costume and Eve into eighteenth century peasant dress.*)
All right, who's playing Rebbe Gershwin tonight?
(*Enter Rebbe Gershon.²*)

REBBE GERSHON: I am. Gershon, Gershon, not Gershwin!

SERPENT: You're playing it tonight, Gershwin? All right, let's go, let's go, hurry, come on. All right, whose line? Come on. Adam: "We are pledged."

REBBE GERSHON: Pledged! Who pledged you?

SERPENT: No, Adam says the line.

ADAM: I say the line. We are pledged.

SERPENT: No, Rebbe Gershon is there.

ADAM: Oh, sorry.

SERPENT: Hurry!

ADAM: We are pledged.

REBBE GERSHON: Pledged! Who pledged you? By whom? I know nothing of it.

ADAM: Our fathers.

REBBE GERSHON: You come from nowhere. You have no money, no family, no name. I don't know you.

ADAM: Here is the letter.

REBBE GERSHON: I am to believe this?

ADAM: It is written.

EVE: You're not supposed to have an accent.

ADAM: Of course I'm supposed to have an accent.

SERPENT: What for?

ADAM: I'm in Poland now. You told me I was in Poland.

SERPENT: Yes, you're in Poland, but you're the same man you were in New York. You're also in New York now. Don't you understand that? You're in New York and Poland at the same time. Pick it up from the line, "It's a forgery."

REBBE GERSHON: It's a forgery.

EVE: It's true.

REBBE GERSHON: He has nothing. Do you understand? I'm to give my sister to a nothing, a nobody?

EVE: I will go with him.

REBBE GERSHON: You will go with him?

EVE: Yes.

REBBE GERSHON: You will get no help from me.

ADAM: God will help us.

(*Exit Rebbe Gershon.*)

EVE: I am my beloved's.

ADAM: And my beloved is mine.

WITNESS: The bride went forth to meet the groom. In fear and trembling, in happiness and joy, they lay down on the earth as two.

ADAM: O Holy Mother Earth I take you, even as I am taken.

EVE: O Holy Mother Earth as I am taken, so shall I take.

WITNESS: The Shekinah[3] came down and joined them. Shekinah?! What's the Shekinah?

SERPENT: It's in the next line. Say the next line: "Presence of God."

WITNESS: Oh . . . They were in the Presence of God.

EVE: As I am known, so may I know.

ADAM: As I know, so may I be known.

WITNESS: And they entered into the mystery, and they became the mystery, and they were the mystery. And they knew one another.

SERPENT: That's enough. Play the love scene. This is first love.

EVE: Yes, I was just going to say we should be on the ground and rolling around.

SERPENT: Well go ahead . . . do something.

WITNESS: Shall I take that part again?

SERPENT: No, it's not necessary.

WITNESS: This is the tale they tell; as they clung to one another, the waters ran red with their passion.

SERPENT: You're not clinging. Cling! Look, the audience will not understand what's going on here. This is a love scene. It's the first time the Baal Shem Tov makes it with his wife. Do you understand? It's a very ecstatic scene. Play it.

ADAM: You want us to actually play it?

SERPENT: Yes, I want you to be it.

ADAM: O.K. It will be a pleasure.

SERPENT: Well, go ahead.

WITNESS: As they embraced, Heaven and Earth embraced.

EVE: The Earth is shaking.

ADAM: Heaven is trembling.

WITNESS: The Holy One, blessed be His name, descended. In a bright cloud of fire He covered them, His holy fire eating into their thighs, their bellies, feasting on their passion; their love, a burnt offering.

EVE: Oh God, I can't bear it. I'm on fire.

ADAM: The burning, the burning, what is this mystery?

SERPENT: The primordial mystery.

ADAM: You're going to say it like that?

SERPENT: I'll say it the way I say it. Go ahead, don't worry about it. You play your part; I'll play my part.

ADAM: Who art thou?

SERPENT: The brightest angel in Heaven come to lead thy way through Heaven and Hell and all the worlds between. Follow.

EVE: I cannot. Oh, Adam.

SERPENT: Cleave fast to the man and he to thee.

ADAM: I would know who you are.

SERPENT: You'll see.

ADAM: Oh, what a fearful thing.

SERPENT: As is God. Have no fear; I will guide thee and watch over thee.

ADAM: As I consume, let me be consumed.

SERPENT: Faster, faster.

EVE: As I am consumed, let me consume.

WITNESS: The living creatures came to their union and watched and gave up their lives that the man and the woman might know the mystery and be united with all creation.

EVE: Isn't that cut?

SERPENT: Stick to the original script. I don't want any improvements from the actors.

WITNESS: The holy fire severed them from themselves.

SERPENT: What is their personal relationship to each other?

EVE: We're making a personal relationship now.

SERPENT: Go ahead. No! Improvise! Talk to one another! We have to see a love scene here.

WITNESS: The holy fire . . .

SERPENT: (*To Witness.*) Hold it. (*To Adam.*) No, it's enough kissing. Words, words. Can't you say, "I love you very much," and so forth? "I don't know how I lived without you?" In this portion of the script, it says there's a place to improvise. The script calls for it. What does a young man say to a young woman when they first meet? "I love you, I don't know how I lived without you," etcetera, etcetera. Go on.

WITNESS: Well, do you want me to say these things?

SERPENT: You say it while they're talking.

WITNESS: But nobody is going to hear me.

SERPENT: What does that matter? Don't worry about it.

WITNESS: The holy fire severed them from themselves.

SERPENT: Louder . . .

WITNESS: The holy fire severed . . .

ADAM: At last we are one . . .

SERPENT: Now say your line.

WITNESS: The deep fountains opened and bathed them in celestial fires . . .

SERPENT: Now you say something.

WITNESS: Washed them in the heavenly . . .

SERPENT: (To Witness.) That's enough. (To Adam and Eve.) Go on. (To Witness.) The audience hears it. (To Adam and Eve.) Go on. Loud, louder, Eve.

EVE: I love you. I love you. I love you.

WITNESS: Washed them . . .

SERPENT: Wait a second! Let's see how you feel about it! How do you feel about being loved? Talk to her.

ADAM: Your words are like honey.

SERPENT: No! You've got a preconception about how a guy in Poland in the eighteenth century talks.

ADAM: But I am a guy in Poland in the eighteenth century.

SERPENT: No, you're not. You're you. I've told you that before. This play is about you.

EVE: You have a line; you say to him, "Plunge into the fiery waters . . ."

SERPENT: I can't say that until the audience sees how he feels about you.

EVE: Oh, he's mad about me.

SERPENT: No, but it's got to be real.

EVE: If you would only say your line, "Plunge into the fiery waters . . ."

SERPENT: No, not until they see that it's real.

EVE: It is very real.

SERPENT: No, no. Go on.

ADAM: My darling, how long I've had to hide my love for you from the world.

SERPENT: That's better.

ADAM: And now . . .

EVE: And now say your line.

SERPENT: Plunge into the fiery waters, into the ocean of bliss . . .

WITNESS: (*To Serpent.*) "Back, back . . ."

SERPENT: Back, back before time, to the holy whirlings.

WITNESS: The deep fountains . . .

SERPENT: Now you start dancing.

WITNESS: The deep fountains opened and bathed them in the celestial fires.

SERPENT: The dance represents your love for one another.

ADAM: Let's improvise it.

EVE: But when do we say, "I'm dying"? I love that line.

ADAM: He'll tell us.

SERPENT: I'll tell you. Go on.

WITNESS: Washed them in the heavenly waters.

ADAM: Dance with me, my beloved.

WITNESS: Deep called to deep. They floated for endless aeons, cleansed in the heavenly dew.

SERPENT: Faster.

WITNESS: It's their line.

EVE: I would be washed and I would wash.

ADAM: I would be cleansed and I would cleanse.

EVE: I'm dying . . .

ADAM: Dying . . .

WITNESS: Dying . . .

SERPENT: Dying . . .

ALL: Dying, dying, dying . . .

SERPENT: All right, it's clear! Let's go on. Go on to, "I am the first and I am the last." Further on, Adam: "I am the first . . ."

ADAM: I am the first.

EVE: And I am the last.

ADAM: I am the motion.

EVE: And I am the rest.

ADAM: I am the bone.

EVE: I am the flesh.

ADAM: I am the fire.

EVE: And I am the water.

ADAM: I am the air.

EVE: I am the earth.

ADAM: I am the sun.

EVE: And I am the moon.

ADAM: I am the light.

EVE: I am the dark.

WITNESS: The first in the last, the motion in rest, the sun and the moon, the mirror of light.

SERPENT: It is done.

WITNESS: And when they arose they were one.

(*Adam goes to another part of stage.*)

SERPENT: Where is your husband?

EVE: In the Carpathian Mountains[4] in his house of prayer, working the mountain of clay.

SERPENT: And what does he do there?

EVE: He serves his Master.

SERPENT: And . . .

EVE: I serve him.

SERPENT: A simple life.

(*Serpent embraces Eve who cries out. Adam rushes to her.*)

ADAM: You're not going to stage it that way, are you? You're seducing her in front of me.

SERPENT: The way to get to a man is through his wife. It's in the script.

ADAM: It isn't in the script. I'm in the field working.

SERPENT: The play is taking place everywhere simultaneously. I've already told you that. Eve, take it from, "My husband is a simple man."

EVE: My husband is a simple man. (*Eve waves goodbye to Adam.*)

SERPENT: When will he return?

EVE: At Sha . . .

SERPENT: Shabbas.

EVE: What does it mean?

SERPENT: Hebrew for Sabbath.

EVE: Oh.

SERPENT: From morning until dusk he works like an ox and you wait . . . and you wait . . . and you wait for him. (*Serpent grabs Eve.*) No, no Eve. Don't let me seduce you.

EVE: Why not? You're the Serpent. It's part of the story.

SERPENT: That comes later. Here you're to show how loyal and devoted you are.

EVE: Oh, I'm supposed to be faithful to my husband?

SERPENT: Of course! This isn't New York.

EVE: Oh, I'm sorry. I didn't know.

SERPENT: Go on. Pick it up from, "I wait."

EVE: I wait.

SERPENT: From Shabbas to Shabbas to Shabbas he works like an ox and you wait for him.

EVE: He is my husband.

SERPENT: And how do you know what he does in the mountains?

EVE: That is his business.

SERPENT: Such great faithfulness has not been known in all of Israel. Like an ox.

EVE: Yoked to his thoughts.

SERPENT: And what does he think about?

EVE: His thoughts.

SERPENT: No, I mean . . .

EVE: You must ask him!

(*Exit Eve. Serpent joins Adam.*)

SERPENT: Where do you go, Rabbi?

ADAM: To clean the stables.

SERPENT: No! "On my journey."

ADAM: What journey? I'm supposed to be an ignorant peasant.

SERPENT: You only pretend to be ignorant. Actually you're in hiding.

ADAM: What am I hiding from?

SERPENT: The play.

ADAM: No, I'm not. I want to be in the play.

SERPENT: No you don't.

ADAM: I don't?

SERPENT: No.

ADAM: Why not?

SERPENT: Because it's . . . Look, it's too difficult to explain now. It will all be explained in the next scene. Just say the line, "On my journey."

ADAM: On my journey.

SERPENT: And the end of your journey?

ADAM: Jerusalem. Where else? And yours?

SERPENT: Jerusalem. Where else?

ADAM: Ha! Ha!

SERPENT: Ha! Ha! What a coincidence. Perhaps you will permit me to join you.

ADAM: How could I stop you?

SERPENT: (*Laughing.*) And your purpose?

ADAM: To seek God!

SERPENT: I, too, go to seek God. We must become good friends.

ADAM: I hope so.

SERPENT: (*Laughing.*) Don't you notice something strange?

ADAM: Strange?

SERPENT: About me . . . (*Gesturing toward his lame foot.*)

ADAM: Oh, that . . .

SERPENT: You're not afraid?

ADAM: Of what is there to be afraid? From the One we come. To the One we shall return.

SERPENT: You've heard of me?

ADAM: Yes, you're the Serpent.

SERPENT: No, strike "You're the Serpent."

ADAM: But I know you're the Serpent.

SERPENT: No you don't.

ADAM: I remember you from New York.

SERPENT: Yes, in New York you remember, but in Poland you forget. That's what the play is about — remembering and forgetting. Adam and Eve can't remember themselves. That's why you're in so much trouble. That's why you have to take this journey.

ADAM: I see.

SERPENT: All right, let's go on. You've heard of me?

ADAM: Yes.

SERPENT: Men call me Sammael,[5] the Evil One.

ADAM: We should get to know each other better, Sammael . . . Why should we get to know each other better? You're the Evil One. I don't want any part of you.

SERPENT: In everything there's something good. I thought you were a holy man.

(*Enter eight rabbis who remain in background davening.*[6])

ADAM: I think I am.

SERPENT: How can you be holy if you don't know how to live?

ADAM: I don't know how to live? I rejoice in the world every day. Just to go out in the fields and listen to the rocks, the melody of the trees, the whispering of the grasshoppers is a great happiness to me. Just now I was listening to the song of the brook. Come, I'll show you. Do you hear it?

SERPENT: Of course I hear it. Then why don't you teach your people how to live?

ADAM: What?

SERPENT: They're dying. They'll never get to Heaven through the letter of the law.

ADAM: They're trying to do what's right.

SERPENT: How can they know what's right until they know what's wrong?

ADAM: I hadn't thought of that.

SERPENT: I can help you teach your people how to live.

ADAM: Can you?

SERPENT: Yes.

ADAM: Maybe we can work something out.

SERPENT: Maybe we can . . . and . . . maybe we can't. I love to sing and dance. Can you sing, Rabbi? Can you dance?

ADAM: Can I sing? Can I dance? Watch this! (*Sings and dances.*)

SERPENT: Pretty good . . . But Rabbi, I love to smoke and drink and kick up my heels and shout, especially in synagogue.

ADAM: A wonderful fellow to wake up the congregation.

SERPENT: You don't know me yet. I love to gamble and steal and lie.

ADAM: Oh! There's a lot to learn about living.

SERPENT: That even you don't know, Rabbi.

ADAM: Is there more?

SERPENT: More? I'm just beginning.

ADAM: Go on. Go on.

SERPENT: I like to carry my passion to the limit.

ADAM: Good!

SERPENT: I like to blaspheme and slander my fellow man.

ADAM: Your way is very appealing. Let's go together.

SERPENT: But wait, Rabbi. You haven't heard me. I love to deny God's existence. And that's the road *I'm* taking to Jerusalem.

ADAM: Come, I think I can use you. I think you're just the man I've been looking for.

SERPENT: What! Chained for life to a virtuous man? I'll be damned! Nothing doing.

ADAM: Wait! I know your secret. Confess. Haven't you always had a secret longing for holiness?

SERPENT: How did you guess?

ADAM: You can't fool me. Evil is just *live* spelled backwards. You've got everything upside down.

SERPENT: At last. A man who understands me.

ADAM: Have some wine. We can go the way together. A part of my portion you shall have. When I eat, you shall eat. When I sleep, you shall sleep.

SERPENT: Things are getting better.

ADAM: When I pray, you shall pray with me.

SERPENT: Better and better.

ADAM: When I love, you shall love with me.

(*Enter Eve, who goes to another part of stage.*)

SERPENT: Hotter and hotter.

ADAM: For every rung I climb, you shall climb with me.

SERPENT: Agreed. (*They shake hands.*) Look in that rock.

ADAM: A book!

(*Enter Rebbe Gershon, in mime walk; goes to Eve.*)

SERPENT: The Book of Adam. Only seven men have ever read it. Abraham, Noah, David, Moses, Solomon, Elijah . . . you are the seventh man. This will teach you all you need to know on your journey.

ADAM: You'll never get away from me now. Come, follow after.

SERPENT: What's a poor devil to do?

ADAM: I'll introduce you to my wife.

SERPENT: I've met her already.

(*Adam and Serpent move away from Eve and Rebbe Gershon.*)

REBBE GERSHON: (*To Eve.*) The Divine Being is in exile and you have to pick a simpleton for a husband.

EVE: I must get ready for Shabbas.

REBBE GERSHON: Never has there been such a great crisis. Our people are fighting for their very lives and this man falls asleep in synagogue.

ADAM: (*To Serpent.*) I like you so much, I swear we'll never part.

SERPENT: Is that a promise?

REBBE GERSHON: Where is he now? Out in the fields, I suppose.

ADAM: By the living God, a promise.

REBBE GERSHON: You do all the work and he wanders to the mountain top.

EVE: That is as it should be.

REBBE GERSHON: His head is empty. He knows nothing.

SERPENT: Look in the Book. The first page. What do you see?

ADAM: A Great Man. His feet touch Earth; his head above Heaven.

REBBE GERSHON: Tell me something. He can't earn a living. A scholar he's not.

ADAM: His legs, the water and earth; his arms, the fire and air.

REBBE GERSHON: Tell me, what do you see in him? No, don't tell me. I give you a few dollars to buy this inn and make a living. You're my sister, after all.

ADAM: His genitals, all suns; his breast, the galaxies.

REBBE GERSHON: He has no head for business. You run things, but he can't even wait on the guests. He spills soup down their necks.

ADAM: His mouth, the sons and daughters of God.

REBBE GERSHON: He's a laughing-stock. A bumbling, crude, ignorant peasant. Well, I know. That is as it should be. Every day I teach him Torah. What's Torah?

EVE: I think it's the Ten Commandments.

REBBE GERSHON: You know, I've always wondered what the Torah was.

SERPENT: (*Calling to Rebbe Gershon.*) The Old Testament, the first five books of Moses.

REBBE GERSHON: (*Calling to Serpent.*) Oh, thanks. (*To Eve.*) Every day I teach him Torah, and every day he forgets. Not one word!

ADAM: His brain, all worlds.

REBBE GERSHON: He can't remember one word of Torah! Not a single word! My God!

EVE: To be sure, my husband is an ignorant man. But he does the right thing.

REBBE GERSHON: Listen, I'll tell you the truth. I'm ashamed of him. Think about divorcing him. I dreamed you would wed a great scholar, a light of Israel, who would bring honor to our name. Generations of scholarship in our family and we end up in disgrace.

ADAM: An entire universe.

REBBE GERSHON: The man is an offense against reason. Can there be a greater idiot in all of Poland?

SERPENT: That's you.

ADAM: Huh?

SERPENT: They're talking about you down there. Hurry, you're due in your next scene.

(*Adam goes to Eve and Rebbe Gershon.*)

EVE: My husband works hard.

REBBE GERSHON: What does he do? From morning to night he does nothing. And from night to morning he also does nothing.

ADAM: Shalom.[7]

REBBE GERSHON: Shalom.

EVE: Shalom.

REBBE GERSHON: Oh my God, Israel, you should watch where you're going.

ADAM: I'm so sorry, Rebbe Gershon.

REBBE GERSHON: Perhaps you're tired.

ADAM: Tired? Why should I be tired?

REBBE GERSHON: From all the work you do.

ADAM: Oh, it's nothing.

REBBE GERSHON: Yes, nothing. You learned Torah today, maybe?

ADAM: Maybe.

REBBE GERSHON: Maybe . . . and what have you got to give me?

ADAM: I . . . (*Spills wine on Rebbe Gershon.*)

REBBE GERSHON: Oy! This is what you have to give me!

ADAM: I'll fix it.

REBBE GERSHON: Don't fix it.

ADAM: I'm so sorry, Rebbe Gershon.

REBBE GERSHON: For what have you got to be sorry?

ADAM: I've ruined your suit.

REBBE GERSHON: It's only my suit. It's nothing. I can always get another.

ADAM: I'm glad you feel that way about it.

REBBE GERSHON: But my life, Israel, you're ruining my life! And that I can't get another.

ADAM: Oh.

REBBE GERSHON: Saddle my horses, Israel. I'm going.

ADAM: You're not staying for the afternoon meal?

REBBE GERSHON: No!

(*Exit Rebbe Gershon.*)

WITNESS: And so time went on. People came and went to the inn. They never knew; they never dreamed . . . by day he was a simpleton, by night a holy man, a hidden one, a Zaddik.[8] By day he saddled the horses, by night he studied the Book. By day he cleaned the barn, by night he studied the Book. By day he scrubbed the floors, by night he studied the Book. While others slept, he studied the Book.

ADAM: I've been chosen.

EVE: Chosen?

ADAM: I'm the one . . .

EVE: Yes . . . ?

ADAM: I have to go . . .

EVE: Go? Where?

ADAM: On the journey to Jerusalem.

EVE: I don't understand.

ADAM: It says, right here in the Book.

EVE: My God. It's wonderful.

ADAM: But why me?

SERPENT: The fool must go.

EVE: Why do you call him a fool? My husband's not a fool.

ADAM: It says right here in the Book: "The heavens said no. The mountains would not do it. Only man, foolish man, said 'yes.' He would carry the burden."

EVE: What does it mean?

ADAM: I must take all men with me on the journey.

EVE: To think that you've been chosen.

ADAM: I can't do it.

EVE: You must.

SERPENT: You both must. Look. Page three in the Book of Adam.

EVE: (*Reading.*) "Adam and Eve go on the journey together."

SERPENT: "With the Serpent."

EVE: Line?

SERPENT: Eve says: "I will go."

EVE: Yes, yes, I remember. Eve says . . . I say . . . I mean . . . I will go with my husband.

SERPENT: Right.

ADAM: I don't want to go.

EVE: You can't refuse. Can he?

SERPENT: Oh yes, he can refuse. It's in the script.

EVE: I won't let him.

SERPENT: That's in the script too. Good.

ADAM: I'm not a leader. I'm just an ordinary man. I'm dumb.

EVE: You are not.

ADAM: I don't know anything. Your brother is right. I . . . I . . . I can't remember the words.

SERPENT: Human learning is the whore of Babylon.

(*Enter Rebbe Gershon, who joins rabbis in background.*)

EVE: Listen to me. I believe in you.

ADAM: I don't know how to talk to men.

SERPENT: It's a magic book. It will put honey in your mouth. Read.

EVE: I love you, Israel. I have faith in you. It's your duty. I will always be at your side to help you.

ADAM: Jerusalem? I don't even know where it is, or how to get there.

SERPENT: Look under J.

EVE: J, J, J, "Jerusalem, a city in Palestine. Sometimes known as a place in the human heart."

ADAM: "Where all directions meet."

EVE: "And all hearts are One."

ADAM: I will go.

EVE: Yes my darling.

ADAM: Look, the Great Man I saw in the Book.

EVE: Where?

ADAM: Through the window!

EVE: Oh! Oh! (*Faints.*)

ADAM: Eve!

EVE: I'm all right. Is this happening?

SERPENT: Yes.

EVE: Is it real?

SERPENT: Yes.

EVE: But I really saw a gigantic man.

SERPENT: Naturally, you have to see him. He's in the play.
    (*Eve faints.*)

ADAM: Eve! Sharon!* Eve!

EVE: Is he gone?

ADAM: I think so. Yes.

EVE: The Titanic Man. What . . . who is he?

ADAM: He's . . .

SERPENT: You, Adam.

ADAM: Oh no he's not.

SERPENT: You don't believe me?

EVE: No!

SERPENT: Look for yourself. Here's the contract.

ADAM: What is this?

SERPENT: It's signed by God.

ADAM: What?!

SERPENT: You can read.

EVE: No! I don't want to.

ADAM: Why not?

EVE: I'm frightened.

ADAM: Don't be stubborn, Eve.

* Real name of actress to be used here.

SERPENT: You have to read it. Your next line in the play is . . .

EVE: Let me see.

SERPENT: That's right.

EVE: (*Reading.*) "The day had twelve hours."

ADAM: "In the first hour when God wished to create the world He began His creation with nothing other than man and He called him Adam."

EVE: "In the second he became a golem, an unformed mass."

ADAM: "In the third hour he stretched forth his limbs and they became a universe."

EVE: "In the fourth he stood on his feet."

ADAM: "In the fifth He cast a soul into him and he became a Titanic Man."

EVE: "In the sixth He showed him all the generations and their wise men in one moment of time."

ADAM: "In the seventh Eve was given him for a companion."

EVE: "In the eighth hour the two lay down in bed and made worlds."

ADAM: "In the ninth the prohibition was communicated to him."

SERPENT: "In the tenth he transgressed it."

EVE: "In the eleventh he was judged."

ADAM: "In the twelfth he was expelled and went out of Paradise."

EVE: And Adam does not remain one night in glory.

ADAM: But we are so tiny, and he is so great.

SERPENT: You will grow into him.

ADAM: How?

SERPENT: By taking the journey so you can reach your true size. That's what the play is about.

EVE: But the play doesn't make any sense. Our bodies can't get any bigger.

SERPENT: Look. Adam, Eve, you don't understand. The Grand Man is your spirit.

ADAM: Oh, he represents our spirit.

SERPENT: Yes.

EVE: He's a symbol.

SERPENT: Yes.

EVE: Oh. Well, why didn't you say so before?

ADAM: Well, when do we meet him again?

SERPENT: At the end of your journey.

EVE: In Jerusalem?

SERPENT: Yes.

EVE: Adam, I don't think we should go. Maybe it's better if we close the Book of Adam and never open it again. We're happy the way we are. It's too dangerous.

ADAM: No. It contains all the secrets of the universe. I must read on.

EVE: Yes, Adam.

SERPENT: He's hooked. (*To audience.*) They'll go on the journey.

WITNESS: Should I introduce him now as Israel ben Eliezer, the Baal Shem Tov?[9]

SERPENT: Yes, of course. How else will the audience know who he is? Now he's the Baal Shem Tov. He's accepted the journey.

WITNESS: Israel ben Eliezer . . . Men called him the Baal Shem Tov — the Master of the Good Name — the Master of the divine names of God.

SERPENT: I see a strange flame coming from the village.

RABBI CIARAMITOVSKY: It's mystical.

RABBI ZIEGLER: It's a mystical strange flame.

RABBI OZBORSKY: It's holy.

RABBI ROGGEVITCH: Maybe it's the Light of the Holy One.

REBBE GERSHON: We must go see it.

RABBI IMLAVITCH: We must investigate.

RABBI ZALZ: Where is it coming from?

SERPENT: Let's find out.

(*Rabbis approach in mime walk.*)

REBBE GERSHON: My brother-in-law's house, the village idiot!

RABBI HILSENSKY: Israel ben Eliezer.

(*Rabbis laugh.*)

RABBI ZIEGLER: Israel ben Eliezer, how can that be?

REBBE GERSHON: Is there a greater idiot in all of Poland?

RABBI HILSENSKY: The light of Israel, indeed!

SERPENT: How do you know that He would not manifest through a fool?

RABBI ZIEGLER: But Rabbi, the man is unlearned.

SERPENT: I know, Rabbi.

REBBE GERSHON: This is great foolishness.

SERPENT: Man's wisdom is foolishness in God's eyes.

REBBE GERSHON: Pffffffff.

RABBI ROGGEVITCH: Could it be, Rabbi?

RABBI OZBORSKY: It could be.

RABBI ZIEGLER: What is the harm in finding out?

REBBE GERSHON: What will you see, that he's the chosen one of God?

RABBI OZBORSKY: That is what we must find out, Rebbe Gershon.

REBBE GERSHON: You go if you want; you're wasting your time.
  (*Exit Eve.*)

RABBI ZIEGLER: That we will see.
  (*Rabbis enter house. Rebbe Gershon remains behind.*)

RABBI CIARAMITOVSKY: Look how he glows!

RABBI ZIEGLER: His eyes . . . !

RABBI OZBORSKY: They're on fire!

RABBI ROGGEVITCH: His whole body . . . !

RABBI HILSENSKY: A great light!

RABBI IMLAVITCH: So this is the flame we saw!
  (*Enter Eve with tray containing seventy shots of whiskey; places tray on table; exits.*)

RABBI OZBORSKY: Israel, we would have a word with you.

ADAM: A word is good. And with schnapps it's even better.

RABBI ZIEGLER: No. No. We must talk.

ADAM: The wine is good. Is it not written: "My word shall be like wine in thy mouth"? Have a drink.

RABBI ROGGEVITCH: That refers to holy matters, Israel.

ADAM: Isn't that what you came for?

RABBI ZALZ: This is an empty place. (*To Serpent.*) Who am I talking to when I say: "This is an empty place"?

SERPENT: There are only nine men.

RABBI ZALZ: So?

SERPENT: There has to be a minyan.

RABBI ZALZ: A what?

SERPENT: A minyan! Don't you understand? In the Hebrew religion, there have to be ten men for a prayer to reach Heaven.

RABBI ZALZ: All right, don't get sore. I was just asking. Why ten?

SERPENT: Look. (*Holds up his hands.*) What do you see?

RABBI ZALZ: Two hands.

SERPENT: No! Ten fingers.

RABBI ZALZ: Uh, huh . . .

SERPENT: And Ten Commandments. Ten is a key number in the Hebrew religion. There are ten Sephiroth.[10] There are ten . . . ah . . . oh, other things like that.

RABBI ZALZ: This is an empty place.

ADAM: It will be filled.

RABBI HILSENSKY: By whom?

ADAM: The tenth man.

RABBI IMLAVITCH: There is no one with us.

ADAM: Are you certain?

RABBI HILSENSKY: Yes.

ADAM: Perhaps someone will come.

RABBI IMLAVITCH: Who?

ADAM: Yes, who? (*Rebbe Gershon joins rabbis.*) Now we are complete.

RABBI IMLAVITCH: Israel, we came to find out if . . .

ADAM: How long will you carry your mother on your back, Rabbi Koch? She's been dead a long time. Bury her, and find her in your wife.

RABBI KOCH: Oh!

ADAM: Rabbi Ozborsky, look in your pocket. There's a message waiting for you.

RABBI OZBORSKY: (*Finds message.*) "The world was made for me." Wonderful!

ADAM: Look in the other pocket.

RABBI OZBORSKY: (*Finds another message.*) "I am nothing." Not so wonderful.

ADAM: Walk between. You know, Rabbi Ziegler, you mustn't be jealous of your wife because she loves the attention of other men.

RABBI ZIEGLER: Rabbi . . . Rabbi . . .

ADAM: Let her bring them to your home. Learn from her. She will teach you how to love men too. Once there was a man who despised himself because he was so small. "I am good for nothing," he said. "I am only a runt." Until one day he looked into his heart and saw it was as great as Heaven. And then what joy, eh, Rabbi Zalz?

RABBI ZALZ: Yes.

ADAM: Ah, Rebbe Gershon . . . Rebbe Gershon . . . What can I say to you? Incline to me. Once there was a drunkard. After the first drink (*All drink after each toast*) he started to relax. The second drink warmed him. The third loosened him up. With the fourth drink he began to forget his troubles and feel good. He couldn't stop now, and with the fifth drink he lost track of time. He didn't know where he was or who he was. And when he reached the sixth drink all he could say was . . . "Who?"

RABBIS: Who?

ADAM: Do you understand?

RABBI IMLAVITCH: He got intoxicated.

ADAM: Yes.

RABBI HILSENSKY: Bewildered.

ADAM: Yes.

RABBI OZBORSKY: And by the seventh drink (*All lift glasses*) he reached the end.

ADAM: Yes.

RABBI ZIEGLER: The Presence.

ADAM: Of Who!

RABBIS: Who! (*All drink.*)

ADAM: You understand?

RABBI OZBORSKY: What did he do then?

ADAM: He laughed; he cried; he shouted; he danced; he tore his hair out. People thought he was mad, but this was his service, you understand?

RABBI ZALZ: And then what happened?

SERPENT: Tell them.

REBBE GERSHON: People tried to reform him, naturally.

RABBI IMLAVITCH: Shh! He's telling the story. Go on.

ADAM: That's right, Rebbe Gershon.

REBBE GERSHON: What did I tell you? It turned out just like I said.

RABBI HILSENSKY: But it didn't work.

ADAM: No. He languished and fell into a melancholy, and from a melancholy into a deep sadness, and from a sadness into despair.

RABBI HILSENSKY: Life had lost its meaning . . .

RABBI IMLAVITCH: . . . its taste.

ADAM: "I am now like other people," he said, "but I am not happy."

RABBI ZALZ: No.

ADAM: He had lost his way. Until one day . . .

RABBI HILSENSKY: Yes?

ADAM: There was a wedding feast.

RABBIS: Uh, huh . . .

ADAM: And just to be sociable, he had a drink. (*Adam and rabbis drink.*)

RABBIS: Ahhhhh . . .

SERPENT: Costumes!

(*Enter Costumers; rabbis dress Adam in formal Hasidic regalia.*)

RABBI KOCH: And then a second!

RABBI HILSENSKY: And then a third!

RABBI OZBORSKY: From Paradise to Paradise.

RABBI IMLAVITCH: And by the time he had the fourth drink he began to forget his troubles and feel good.

RABBI ZALZ: He couldn't stop now and by the fifth drink he lost track of time.

RABBI OZBORSKY: From Paradise to Paradise.

RABBI KOCH: By the sixth glass he was in Heaven.

RABBI HILSENSKY: He lost track of himself.

RABBI ZALZ: He didn't know where he was.

RABBI IMLAVITCH: Or who he was.

RABBI CIARAMITOVSKY: And when he reached the seventh Heaven he was so dumbstruck, all he could say was, "Who?"

ALL RABBIS: Who! . . . Who! . . . Who! . . .

ADAM: He had found his way. Better drunk with God, than sober without Him. You understand, Rebbe Gershon?

REBBE GERSHON: I understand.

ADAM: Then dance! (*Rabbis dance.**) *And what you don't know, your feet will tell you. Dance! And let legs, arms, hands, speak for you. All flesh must dance for its Creator. Dance in joy to the Lord and His Shekinah. Dance to the joy of the King and the Queen. Dance and rejoice in joy at their meeting. Dance! Dance! Dance!* (*Enter crowd.*)

WITNESS: Out of the dark forests of Poland rode the Baal Shem Tov and his Hasidim,[11] relieving the poor, giving succor to the downtrodden, liberating the oppressed. In fervor they came: by horse, by cart, by carriage, by foot, pouring over every city and village, hamlet and byway of the land — 'til the holy sparks in men's hearts began to stir. In laughter they came: singing and dancing, telling stories and jokes. In the name of the Blessed One they came: raising men up to the Lord, 'til even in that dark time, that terrible time, the sparks ignited, caught fire, spread to every ghetto in middle Europe, 'til thousands and hundreds of thousands were on fire. The Baal Shem Tov and his Hasidim . . . how shall I describe them? They planted the Word of God in men's hearts. The Baal Shem Tov and his Hasidim . . . what shall I say? They taught the sparks to leap for God.

ADAM: I will bring Heaven down to Earth. I swear a vow, a holy vow, that I will not leave off 'til Heaven opens and Messiah comes.

RABBI HILSENSKY: What must we do?

ADAM: Sound the ram's horn with all thy might. (*Rabbi blows ram's horn.*) Messiah is coming. Blow with all thy strength, with all thy

*Music p. 255.

force. Call to him. Pray for him and he must come. (*To Serpent.*)
What comes next?

SERPENT: Jacob Frank.[12]

ADAM: Who is he?

SERPENT: The false messiah. He seduces the people, leads them astray
and breaks your heart. Places: Jacob Frank, false messiah.
(*Enter Jacob Frank, playing recorder.*)

RABBIS: Who is he?

RABBI KOCH: I don't know.

RABBI HILSENSKY: He says he's the Messiah.

RABBI ZIEGLER: I have never heard of him before.

REBBE GERSHON: Where does he come from?

RABBI ROGGEVITCH: You know more than I do.

ADAM: He's an impostor. He pretends to be the Messiah. He twists
our teaching. Stay away from him.

JACOB FRANK: It is true; I am an ignorant man.

RABBI ZALZ: Then why do they follow him?

JACOB FRANK: And it is because I am an ignorant man that I am
chosen; an Am Haaretz.[13]

(*Jacob Frank leads crowd around stage like Pied Piper.*)

RABBI CIARAMITOVSKY: The people are desperate.

RABBI ZIEGLER: They don't know what to do.

RABBI OZBORSKY: Times are so awful they'll follow anyone.

ADAM: You must go to the people. Warn them. There's not a moment
to lose.

JACOB FRANK: After all, are we not all one people? Are we not all part
of God? Is not His Presence everywhere?

ADAM: He will lead the people into bestiality.

JACOB FRANK: In all bestiality lurks not the Evil One, but the holy
sparks of God. Who shall release them?

RABBI CIARAMITOVSKY: We!

(*Rabbis, with exception of Rebbe Gershon, begin leaving the Baal
Shem Tov, one by one, to join the crowd.*)

RABBI ROGGEVITCH: The people have nothing.

RABBI HILSENSKY: We have promised them a Messiah.

REBBE GERSHON: What do you want to do?

ADAM: Protect the people!

JACOB FRANK: As children of one God, we have only to see that
everything is holy. By plunging into uncleanliness, and salvaging
the cleanliness within, you sanctify the holy name of God.

RABBI ZALZ: How can this man be an impostor? He speaks with the tongue of an angel.

ADAM: We must ransom the holy sparks from death and exile.

JACOB FRANK: By plunging into the filth and horror and sickness of life.

RABBI KOCH: He is the fulfillment of your teaching.

RABBI ZIEGLER: A walking Torah.

RABBI OZBORSKY: He is the Messiah.

ADAM: The perfect lie.

JACOB FRANK: And for this reason I have been chosen.

RABBI HILSENSKY: There is no longer any need to reach for Heaven, it is here before us.

JACOB FRANK: And for this reason have I come.

ADAM: No! Master of the Universe, how could you do this?

JACOB FRANK: To reveal that all is permitted.

RABBIS: At last, Heaven has opened. Hallelujah!!

ADAM: No! No! No!

JACOB FRANK: What need is there of Torah?

ADAM: Hell has opened.

JACOB FRANK: In God's name we shall break the law that separates and divides man from man. This is the message of your salvation.

ADAM: You are all asleep.

JACOB FRANK: And I am he who has been sent.

ADAM: You are not listening.

RABBI IMLAVITCH: But it is as if you are speaking.

ADAM: You can't see.

JACOB FRANK: I permit you everything.

ADAM: They're all asleep.

RABBI KOCH: Every word he speaks is yours.

JACOB FRANK: For you are All.

ADAM: I must warn them.

JACOB FRANK: And all that is, is yours.

ADAM: People! Listen to me.

JACOB FRANK: Be the gods you are.

ADAM: He is not the One.

JACOB FRANK: Dance and rejoice upon the land.

ADAM: You are being fooled! He is not from the Lord. He is from the other side. Don't listen!

RABBI HILSENSKY: Oh! My God! They are taking the Torah from the Holy Ark; they are carrying it off.

ADAM: Master of the Universe, give me strength!

(*Adam takes Torah from crowd; Jacob Frank wrests Torah from Adam's hands.*)

Master of the Universe, help me. Help me! Oh, my Lord God, what have You done?

JACOB FRANK: What need is there of Torah, when One is All and All is One?

(*Exit Jacob Frank, followed by rabbis and crowd; Rebbe Gershon remains.*)

ADAM: Have you no pity on Your creation? They must believe in You . . . they must. Be merciful; hear me . . . hear me. Have mercy, mercy!

WITNESS: The time was not yet. The Baal Shem Tov had failed. His generation was not accounted worthy. Messiah had not come.

(*Enter rabbis.*)

RABBI CIARAMITOVSKY: My God, what have we done?

RABBI ROGGEVITCH: We promised the people a Messiah and instead this man came.

RABBI OZBORSKY: How could we be so blind?

RABBI ZIEGLER: We've destroyed the Torah.

RABBI HILSENSKY: What fools we were!

RABBI IMLAVITCH: And we've left the Baal Shem Tov.

WITNESS: What made these rabbis come back and change their minds about the Baal Shem Tov? What happened?

SERPENT: Jacob Frank went off and burned the Torah. This they couldn't tolerate. They came back.

WITNESS: I see. ··

(*Enter Eve.*)

SERPENT: Eve, it's your line. Find out if he is alive or dead.

EVE: (*Calling.*) Israel.

REBBE GERSHON: Israel.

EVE: Israel!

SERPENT: "My soul."

EVE: My soul.

REBBE GERSHON: There he is!

EVE: Israel.

SERPENT: Jacob Frank, are you ready for the seduction?

(*Jacob Frank nods assent. Exit Serpent.*)

EVE: He's feverish.

ADAM: All for nothing. I have failed. Failed. Failed!

EVE: Shhhh.

ADAM: The great demon has shattered the world! Shattered . . . Too late . . . never . . . never . . . useless . . .

(*Adam collapses; rabbis carry him to bed.*)

EVE: My soul . . . my soul . . . my soul . . .

ADAM: It's all over! It's all over . . . my service was for nothing.

EVE: (*To rabbis.*) You've done this!

RABBI IMLAVITCH: No, he was our light, our life.

EVE: You betrayed him.

RABBI ROGGEVITCH: But we loved him.

EVE: You killed him.

RABBI ZIEGLER: But we didn't know.

RABBI KOCH: We studied with him.

RABBI HILSENSKY: We were fooled. We were fooled . . .

(*Exit rabbis.*)

REBBE GERSHON: The Angel of Death has cast his shadow.

EVE: He won't have him.

REBBE GERSHON: This has broken his heart.

EVE: He will grow a greater heart.

REBBE GERSHON: A man can bear only so much. Even he.

ADAM: Ohhhhhh . . .

REBBE GERSHON: He may not survive this.

EVE: He will survive. The world has need of him. He is the light of the world.

ADAM: Why? Why?

EVE: Hush my child. I will protect you, and heal you, and bring you back to life.

(*Enter Serpent, dressed as Death; watches from afar.*)

WITNESS: Thus began the Baal Shem Tov's long struggle with death. Feverish days and nights, with only his wife to nurse him. He was alone, while Death watched from a distance.

SERPENT: Enter Frank.

JACOB FRANK: (*Unseen, calling from offstage.*) Baal Shem Tov. Baal Shem Tov.

ADAM: Yes . . . ? Yes?

JACOB FRANK: Help me . . . help.

ADAM: I am coming. Who calls?

JACOB FRANK: It is I, Jacob Frank. I know you for a holy man.

ADAM: Go away!

JACOB FRANK: You will not leave a plea unanswered.

ADAM: Go away!

JACOB FRANK: Please . . . Baal Shem Tov!

ADAM: I cannot help you.

JACOB FRANK: I have lost my way. Let my soul come to you.

ADAM: No . . . no . . .

JACOB FRANK: If you will not pity me, pity the hundreds of thousands who have followed me into the world of confusion. You will not forsake them.

ADAM: No . . .

JACOB FRANK: They are bound to me.

ADAM: Bound to you . . .

(*Enter crowd of mourners. They stand at the Wailing Wall in the background.*)

JACOB FRANK: It is for their sake that I plead.

ADAM: For their sake . . . ?

JACOB FRANK: Lost and ruined souls wandering forever. You will snatch them from Sammael's hand, and restore Israel to the true path.

ADAM: I must restore Israel! But how . . . how?

JACOB FRANK: Let me come to you. We will do it together.

ADAM: I don't understand.

JACOB FRANK: You will work through me.

ADAM: Work through you?

JACOB FRANK: You will take my soul into your own. We will be as one.

ADAM: But I am not like you.

JACOB FRANK: Yes, yes, you are just like me. Don't you feel it?

ADAM: No.

JACOB FRANK: We are of one mind.

ADAM: No.

JACOB FRANK: No one could tell us apart.

ADAM: No.

JACOB FRANK: Think of what a great deed we shall do. We shall restore the Temple.

ADAM: But not in your name.

JACOB FRANK: No, of course not. In your name.

ADAM: My . . . name?

(*Jacob Frank's spirit enters Adam.*)

JACOB FRANK: There is no difference now. I am in your soul now . . . your very soul.

ADAM: Ohhhhhh!!

JACOB FRANK: Too late . . . I shall take you with me on the path of nothingness.

ADAM: Depart! Dybbuk![14] Depart!

JACOB FRANK: Too late! (*Laughs daemonically.*)

ADAM: In the name of the Almighty One, I command you to leave me. Eve! Eve!

EVE: I am here, Israel.

ADAM: Stay with me. Don't leave me.

EVE: I could never leave you.

ADAM: He is choking me. Here inside me.

EVE: Who?

ADAM: He is taking me with him.

EVE: Who?

ADAM: I am going under. My soul is dying. I am . . .

EVE: Israel! Israel!

ADAM: Oh!

EVE: Oh my God! What is it?

ADAM: Jacob Frank.

EVE: Cast him off!

ADAM: I can't . . . too weak.

EVE: I am with you, beloved. Use my strength. Cast him into Hell.

ADAM: One last effort. (*Struggling to rise from bed.*) In the name of my Beloved . . . I hurl you into the abyss! (*Collapses.*)

EVE: Pray! I must hurry.
(*Exit crowd of mourners.*)
(*Eve covers Adam; lights Sabbath candles. Serpent approaches.*)
Come in, Death.

SERPENT: You know me.

EVE: Yes.

SERPENT: I am not accustomed to being recognized.

EVE: You come swiftly.
(*Eleven gongs sound.*)

SERPENT: At the appointed time.

EVE: "The eleventh hour."

SERPENT: "The hour of Judgment." I have come for the soul of the Baal Shem Tov.

EVE: Yes, he is expecting you . . . (*Eve gasps.*) The Presence has entered.

SERPENT: Yes!

EVE: A good Sabbath to you, Death.

SERPENT: Good Sabbath.

EVE: You must be tired, Death, from going to and fro upon the Earth.

SERPENT: It is my service.

EVE: Still, you must be weary. Won't you . . . rest.

SERPENT: There's little time.

EVE: Just for a moment.

SERPENT: Only a moment then.

EVE: Have you had a pleasant day, Death?

SERPENT: Most pleasant.

EVE: You must be hungry.

SERPENT: I have dined already. I must be going.

EVE: So soon?

SERPENT: I have one final thing to do.

EVE: You have forgotten to celebrate the Creator of the universe. (*Pours wine.*)

SERPENT: I must hurry.

EVE: The Merciful One will be angry. It is the Sabbath meal.

SERPENT: Such distinctions do not apply to me.

EVE: A holy day. All the King's subjects must participate. (*Both drink.*)

SERPENT: I must go.

EVE: You must give me your blessing, Death.

SERPENT: Do not detain me.

EVE: You have entered my house on the Sabbath Day. You cannot leave without giving me your blessing.

SERPENT: You have it, only let me go.

EVE: One favor, then, Death.

SERPENT: Anything, but be quick.

EVE: Take me.

SERPENT: What?

EVE: Take me, Death.

SERPENT: It's not possible.

EVE: Ask.

SERPENT: It's not in my power.

EVE: Ask a greater Power.

SERPENT: It has never been done before.

EVE: Could you not love me, Death? Am I not fair?

SERPENT: Thou art fair.

EVE: Would you not love to take me in your embrace, and hold me in your arms forever?

SERPENT: Yes.

EVE: You can have me.

SERPENT: Heaven would not allow it.

EVE: Heaven has allowed stranger things. If your love were great enough, you would go before the Throne and ask.

SERPENT: Ask for thy soul?

EVE: Yes.

SERPENT: I would be ridiculed.

EVE: You cannot resist me, Death. Of all who come to you, only I come willingly. Only I yearn for your touch, your mouth upon my lips. You are my passion. Take me; I'm yours. Take me! Take me!

SERPENT: I am gone.

(*Exit Serpent.*)

EVE: (*Goes to Adam.*) I will be waiting for you, Israel. Oh . . . but if the answer is no? My husband must finish his work. We must flee Death. Israel, Israel! But if the answer is no . . . I must find another way. Oh, whatever ministering angels that be, minister now to me.

(*Enter two Angels, carrying Baal Shem Tov costume identical to Adam's. Enter Serpent; from afar shakes his head "no" to indicate that heaven has refused Eve's request.*)

EVE: I will say goodbye to my husband.

SERPENT: You have one minute.

EVE: (*As Angels dress her, unseen by Serpent, she begins to act for Serpent's benefit.*) Oh, my poor husband, my poor husband, how I shall miss you. I cannot live without you . . . What shall I do? Oh, what am I going to do? I can't live without you. Don't leave me. I'm frightened. Don't die. Please, you mustn't. (*Disguised as her husband she goes to Serpent.*) You know how women are. Can't control their tears. My soul is prepared . . . I'm ready.

WITNESS: The Baal Shem Tov and his wife, two halves of the same circle. Who can tell the difference? Not even Death could tell them apart. Hear the story of how Death was cheated.

(*Enter rabbis in background, carrying a bier.*)

ADAM: My soul is troubled. Eve! (*Rising from bed.*) Death, stop! I am the one you want.

SERPENT: Who are you?

ADAM: I am the Baal Shem Tov.

SERPENT: (*To Eve.*) Then you are . . .

ADAM: My wife.

SERPENT: I'm confused.

ADAM: Take me!

EVE: Goodbye, my love. Come for me.

(*Runs toward Serpent, who retreats; Adam follows.*)

ADAM/SERPENT: No!

EVE: (*Goes toward Serpent.*) I take you, Death!

(*Adam attempts to stop her.*)

SERPENT: (*Retreating.*) It's not possible.

EVE: We are contracted.

SERPENT: You cannot do this.

EVE: (*Embracing Serpent.*) It is finished.

(*Kisses Serpent, falls back onto bier.*)

SERPENT: It is not permitted.

ADAM: Eve! Eve!

EVE: Don't keep me waiting too long . . .

(*Eve dies; rabbis carry her on bier to bed; exit Serpent.*)

ADAM: Oh my Beloved, I thought I would be swept up to Heaven in a storm like Elijah.[15] But now I'm only half a body and I must live out the rest of my days on this poor Earth without you. Oh, when will Messiah come? When?! When?!

(*Blackout. Angels blow out candles. Exit all. During darkness, a double for Eve takes her place on bier and remains there motionless throughout play.*)

ACT II

SCENE 1: POLAND AND THE ROAD TO DAMASCUS

(*Adam, Witness, Rebbe Gershon, Rabbi Ziegler, Rabbi Roggevitch, and Rabbi Ozborsky discovered on stage.*)

ADAM: Why has He taken my beloved from me? I served Him faithfully, walked in His commandments, followed His laws. I asked for nothing . . .

WITNESS: Where do you go, Rabbi?

ADAM: . . . and now I, half a man . . .

WITNESS: Where do you wander?

ADAM: . . . must crawl between Heaven and Earth toward death. Am I a fool that worships that which despises me?

WITNESS: Why do you go, Rabbi?

ADAM: Shall I live every second, minute, hour . . .

WITNESS: Why do you wander?

ADAM: . . . in the light of that which is witness to my impotence?

WITNESS: Where, Rabbi?

ADAM: Oh, the Sun hath made me mad!

WITNESS: Where?

ADAM: Pluck it out. None shall see my shame.

WITNESS: Where do you go, Rabbi?

ADAM: I don't know.

(*Enter Serpent, dressed in Dervish costume.*)

SERPENT: Weren't you present in the first act?

ADAM: Yeah, I was here in the first act.

SERPENT: Well?

ADAM: I saw her die.

SERPENT: Of course. That's why you're going after her.

ADAM: But how can I find her if she's already dead?

SERPENT: Don't worry about it. Get into your costume and let's go. What are you wearing those rags for? Get into your costume now.

(*Enter Costumer, who places cloak on Adam, then exits.*)

ADAM: The rabbi costume?

SERPENT: What rabbi? You're a Moslem now.

ADAM: I'm a Moslem now?

(*Enter Hermit.*)

SERPENT: Well, of course. The play is not restricted to just Christians in New York, or Hebrews in Poland, or Moslems in Damascus, or Egyptians in Egypt. All right, Moslem Hermit: "There is no God . . ." say the line.

HERMIT: (*Chanting in Arabic, then English.*) La Ilaha Illallah Muhammad Rasoolullah. There is no God but Allah and Mohammed is His Prophet.

SERPENT: What are you rabbis doing here?

RABBI OZBORSKY: What do you mean, what are we doing here? This is our blocking.

SERPENT: No. The rabbis were in the last scene, in Poland. There are no rabbis here.

RABBI ZIEGLER: We thought he was still the Baal Shem Tov.

SERPENT: No. He's a Moslem. We're going into Moslem country now. Don't you understand?

RABBI ROGGEVITCH: Well, do you want us to get into Moslem costumes and come out praying to Allah?

SERPENT: Yes, of course.

RABBI ROGGEVITCH: Oh . . . O.K.

(*Exit rabbis except Rebbe Gershon.*)

SERPENT: Moslem Hermit . . . say your line.

HERMIT: (*Chanting.*) There is no God but Allah and Mohammed is His Prophet.

SERPENT: O.K., Witness . . . now you sing your song.

(*Exit Serpent.*)

WITNESS: (*Singing.*)* Living and dying I ply my trade . . .

ADAM: Salaam.

HERMIT: Salaam.

WITNESS: (*Singing.*) Dying and living, it's all the same . . .

REBBE GERSHON: Can't I say goodbye to him?

(*Enter Serpent.*)

SERPENT: Yes. Say goodbye.

(*Exit Serpent.*)

WITNESS: (*Singing.*) Shoes for the crippled . . .

REBBE GERSHON: O.K. Goodbye. Something for the journey.

(*Gives Adam a package.*)

* Music p. 255

ADAM: Thank you.

WITNESS: (*Singing.*) Shoes for the poor . . .

REBBE GERSHON: Goodbye.

ADAM: Goodbye.

WITNESS: (*Singing.*) Circling and circling throughout the world.

(*Exit Rebbe Gershon.*)

Of all the wonders I have seen, none more wonderful than this.

With a prayerbook and a shawl . . .

(*Enter Serpent.*)

SERPENT: No! Not a prayerbook and a shawl. He's not Hebrew. He's Moslem.

ADAM: What do they carry?

SERPENT: Just a stout walking stick and a big hat like a whirling Dervish.

(*Enter Costumer, who places Dervish hat on Adam; exits.*)

SERPENT: Witness, just give your last line.

WITNESS: At last he came to a hermit.

HERMIT: There is no God but Allah . . .

SERPENT: Wait a minute! Didn't you forget something?

ADAM: No, I've got everything.

SERPENT: No, you haven't.

ADAM: I've got my stout walking stick, my . . .

SERPENT: The Book . . .

ADAM: Oh . . . what about it?

SERPENT: You forgot to bury it.

ADAM: I did . . . ?

SERPENT: Yes. Bury it, bury it! Hurry! You've got to meet the Moslem Hermit now. It's the next event.

ADAM: Is that in the script?

SERPENT: It's all in the script.

ADAM: Where do I bury it?

SERPENT: The same place you found it.

ADAM: But I never found it . . . The Baal Shem Tov found it.

SERPENT: You were the Baal Shem Tov, don't you remember?

ADAM: Yes.

SERPENT: Yes. Only now you're a Moslem. So you have to leave the Book for whoever plays the Baal Shem Tov next.

ADAM: (*Replacing Book in rock.*) Who will that be?

(*Exit Serpent.*)

SERPENT: (*Shouting from offstage.*) Whoever selects himself.

ADAM: Is there going to be another performance?

SERPENT: The play's always being performed. You know that.

ADAM: Right.

HERMIT: There is no God but Allah and Mohammed is His Prophet.

ADAM: Salaam.

HERMIT: Salaam.

ADAM: Art thou alone?

HERMIT: Alone with the Alone. Poverty is my only glory.

ADAM: Canst thou direct me to the abode of Death?

HERMIT: Most men shun death, why do you seek it?

ADAM: Why do I seek Death now?

(*Enter Serpent.*)

SERPENT: Because you have to get your beloved from Death's arms, don't you?

ADAM: But you just told me . . .

SERPENT: You're mad with grief . . . you don't understand. You're going out of your mind. You can't live without her! You're going mad! Say your next line: "Oh, my beloved." You'll see what I mean. Follow the script.

(*Exit Serpent.*)

ADAM: (*To Hermit.*) Oh, my beloved.

(*Enter Serpent.*)

SERPENT: Not to him! He's not your beloved.

ADAM: Where is my beloved?

SERPENT: She's dead.

ADAM: For God's sake, how can I go on?

SERPENT: Exactly. You can't go on. You're yearning for Death. Life is no good without her. You know what it means to be in love, don't you?

ADAM: Yeah!

SERPENT: Look, just because you're a Moslem doesn't mean that you don't know what love is. Moslems fall in love too, you know. So play the scene.

ADAM: But I wasn't married to Eve.

SERPENT: Huh?

ADAM: He was . . . the Baal Shem Tov was.

SERPENT: No. Adam is always married to Eve. It's always Adam and Eve. Don't you understand? There's only one theme in this play — Adam, Eve and God.

WITNESS: And Witness!

SERPENT: And Witness. There are a thousand plots. This play could be plotted a million different ways. It's not the plot that matters . . . It's the theme that matters — Adam, Eve and God.

WITNESS: And Witness!

SERPENT: And Witness. And you can't live without Eve. Adam and Eve must be joined together inseparably forever. Right?

ADAM: Right.

SERPENT: Now, say your line, "We would be as the birds . . ."

ADAM: We would be as the birds in the air; the lilies in the field.

SERPENT: That's right, Adam and Eve.

ADAM: Oh, but to be caged in this dungeon of flesh and blood, condemned . . .

SERPENT: Do you know why you're condemned?

ADAM: Yeah, because I can't find my Eve.

SERPENT: Right.

ADAM: And I can't die, right?

SERPENT: Right. Now say the next line.

ADAM: Cursed be the day I was born . . .

(*Exit Hermit.*)

SERPENT: Right.

ADAM: Cursed the stars . . .

SERPENT: Put a lot into it. This is your tragic moment!

ADAM: I know. And doubly cursed the light of the Sun . . .

SERPENT: You're getting ready to slay God . . . that comes in the next scene. Go on.

ADAM: Out moon, Sun, lights. Now give me perpetual night.

SERPENT: What is thy wish?

ADAM: Out, out, blot out the Sun.

SERPENT: No! "To be with my beloved."

ADAM: To be with my beloved.

SERPENT: Right!

ADAM: Right.

SERPENT: Come with me.

ADAM: Where are we going?

SERPENT: To Hell.

ADAM: I don't want to go to Hell.

SERPENT: Of course you do.

ADAM: Why?

SERPENT: So you can seize your beloved.

ADAM: She's in Hell now?

SERPENT: She's in Death's arms. I've already told you that.

ADAM: And I've got to get her?

SERPENT: Of course. Besides, every hero has to be tested.

ADAM: Ah . . .

SERPENT: And how does a man have his mettle tested except by going through the trials . . .

ADAM/SERPENT: . . . and tribulations of Hell for his beloved.

SERPENT: It's beautiful!

ADAM: Right.

SERPENT: Right. Are you ready for the journey?

ADAM: I'm ready.

SERPENT: All right, let's go. Witness, tell the audience what it's about. Tell them where he's going.

WITNESS: Through the Valley of Despair, into the Pass of Defilement . . .

SERPENT: More mood, more atmosphere.

(*Enter men in a chain gang in loin cloths; Urael, Azarel,*[16] *who hang crucified upside down from crosses; Watchman.*)

WITNESS: To the place of excrement, deeper, deeper, into luciferic night. To the place of desolation, of utter abomination, the city of depravity, the city of the damned.

SERPENT: (*To Witness.*) All right, that's enough . . . Audience hears it. (*To Adam.*) Here's the gate. Knock. Knock.

ADAM: The mountains are trembling.

SERPENT: Of course. Witness!

WITNESS: Yea, though I walk through the valley of the shadow of death, I will fear no evil for Thou art with me.

SERPENT: Knock.

ADAM: The valley is on fire.

SERPENT: I know that.

WITNESS: He maketh me to lie down in green pastures. He leadeth me beside the still waters. He restoreth my soul.

ADAM: It is a fearful thing to go against the Lord.

SERPENT: Only he who does can stand beside Him.

(*Ten gongs sound.*)

ADAM: "The tenth hour."

SERPENT: "The hour of transgression."

ADAM: My soul is filled with dread.

SERPENT: Strike the gate.

ADAM: My hand will not obey.

SERPENT: Strike.

ADAM: I shall turn back.

SERPENT: You shall go on.

ADAM: No.

SERPENT: Yes.

(*Forces Adam to strike gate.*)

WATCHMAN: Who dares to strike at this dread hour of night?

ADAM: I do.

SERPENT: Right.

WATCHMAN: Who are you?

ADAM: I'm Adam.

WATCHMAN: What are you doing here?

ADAM: I don't know.

SERPENT: No! "I've come for my beloved," is your line.

ADAM: I've come for my beloved.

WATCHMAN: You've come to the right place.

ADAM: What place is this?

WATCHMAN: The city of the damned.

ADAM: Who is your king?

WATCHMAN: Phantasmagoria reigns here.

ADAM: I would see him.

WATCHMAN: Enter

(*Opens gate of Hell, exits.*)

SCENE 2: HELL

SERPENT: Put on this garment of slime and plunge into everlasting night. Come, give me thy left hand and fall to the bottom of the Earth.

ADAM: Oh God, when shall we arrive?

SERPENT: When we are at the place of nothingness, the eternal nightclub of Hell.

ADAM: What sight is this? Men chained to their shadows, pulled in tormented grief.

ADAM: Below, all is the reverse of above.

(*Exit Serpent.*)

(*Enter Satan, Moloch,*[17] */Belial,*[19] *Queen of Folly, King Onan*[18] *King Lucifuge*[20] *and Lilith.*[21] *Satan and Moloch share a single costume with a sword through their heads. King Onan/Belial masturbates under costume throughout scene. Lilith is a* *composite character, played by five actresses, one of whom is Eve. Music and drum rhythm throughout scene; Satan, Moloch, Queen of Folly and Lilith "speak-sing" unless otherwise indicated.)**

SATAN/MOLOCH: Welcome to Thaumiel.[22] We are the doubles of God. The two-headed Satan and Moloch. Rulers of the kingdom that takes darkness for light. Concentrate all thy force and spend it on delight. On the throne sits Folly, our most beloved queen. Incline toward her and satisfy thy every craving. Carouse and frolic 'til thy urge is spent. Then comes ease, satiety and sleep. What is thy wish?

ADAM: To be with my beloved.

QUEEN OF FOLLY: (*Spoken.*) No sooner said than done. Behold! The daughter of our union.

SATAN/MOLOCH: The jewel of our realm. Lilith!

QUEEN OF FOLLY: (*Spoken.*) Is she not beautiful?

ADAM: She shines in the darkness more brightly than the stars.

QUEEN OF FOLLY: (*Spoken.*) What will you pay?

ADAM: I'll serve you faithfully for a hundred years.

QUEEN OF FOLLY: Bzzz . . . A hundred years is barely time to go beyond her eyes. Observe her look of arrogance and pride. Only a hero could warm those eyes.

ADAM: Five hundred years.

LILITH: Tush . . . You underestimate the time it takes to be squeezed by these envious thighs.

ADAM: Eight hundred years of bondage then.

LILITH: Who would call it bondage to devour the flame of Lilith's lust?

ADAM: Nine hundred years.

QUEEN OF FOLLY: Bzzzz . . . Bzzzz . . . Why not say nine thousand? (*Enter Serpent.*)

SERPENT: Why aren't you getting more excited here? It's boring. Look, Adam, Lilith is everything you see on the streets today, every beautiful skirt that walks by. It's all carnality, pornography . . .

ADAM: But I'm a spiritual man. I'm not interested in Lilith.

SERPENT: Oh yes you are. Like all spiritual men, you suffer from a split between your body and your spirit. The idea is to become a

*Music p. 257

spirited man.

ADAM: What's the difference?

SERPENT: A spirited man's heart and sensuality are fused.

ADAM: Well, when do I become a spirited man?

SERPENT: Later on in your evolution. Take it from "Nine thousand years."

(*Exit Serpent.*)

QUEEN OF FOLLY: Why not say nine thousand?

LILITH: My gluttonous appetite seeks fulfillment. Sate my superhuman appetite 'til every tendril, fibre and particle of me burst and flood you in celestial juices.

LILITH/QUEEN OF FOLLY: One thousand years, no less. Well??

ADAM: Done.

SATAN/MOLOCH: She's yours; you're ours: our bondsman for a thousand years.

ADAM: But wait . . . Who are all these men trailing behind her?

SATAN/MOLOCH: Where? What men? I don't see any men.

ADAM: There! Hundreds and thousands in mournful columns.

SATAN/MOLOCH: An optical illusion. You're still too much in the light.

LILITH: Come little Adam, come my lord and master.

SATAN/MOLOCH: Drink this cup, and purge yourself of all illusion. Drink and be thou evermore a son of darkness.

LILITH: Drink!

QUEEN OF FOLLY: What sayest thou now?

ADAM: (*Singing.*) Thou art all beauty, within whose dazzling rays, the divine vision fadeth fast away. Farewell all joy, honor, bliss for one kiss from your lips.

SATAN/MOLOCH: Now is your union complete.

LILITH: What is thy name?

ADAM: A . . . d . . .

LILITH: Adam . . . (*Laughing.*)

ADAM: A . . . d . . . Ahhhhhhh!

LILITH: Poor little Adam. He's lost his tongue.

(*Laughter from Lilith, Satan/Moloch, Queen of Folly, King Lucifuge, King Onan/Belial.*)

SERPENT: That's enough!!

ONAN/BELIAL: (*Masturbating under costume.*) Hey, listen. Do I have to do this through the whole scene?

SERPENT: That's what we pay you for, Bob.* Let's cut this whole thing in half. You keep masturbating. You can't stop the goddamn thing . . . it's important.

ONAN/BELIAL: Got it.

SERPENT: O.K. Now it's clear. Don't you think it's clear to the audience that all of humanity down there is in service of Lilith, this gigantic, titanic female and that the energy of all the men is going into her?

URAEL: (*To Serpent.*) Hey, these explanations are terrific but we're hanging here upside down for a really long time.

SERPENT: Hey, listen. These guys are in pain. Let's hurry up. Now, let's have the angels speak before they pass out. O.K. . . . Cut to the angels.

AZAREL: Give us the cue line, "Crucified upside down."

WITNESS: Crucified upside down.

AZAREL: (*To Adam.*) Who art thou?

ADAM: A . . . aaa . . . d . . .

AZAREL: Who is man that thou shalt remember him?

ADAM: A . . . aaa . . . d . . .

AZAREL: A handful of dust, a groveling worm.

URAEL: (*To Azarel.*) Stay. Remember our curse.

AZAREL: How could I forget it?

URAEL: (*To Adam.*) Oh, thou seed of Adam, we are a portion of that heavenly host hurled from translunar light into this dark abyss because our rebellious tongue slandered thy name . . . Know thy name is Adam.

ADAM: Adam!

URAEL: And thy Creator's first fruits.

ADAM: Adam!

URAEL: Call on the Supreme One.

ADAM: Oh, Lord of Judgment!

URAEL: And in His name, pull forth the sword of self-satisfied reason from Satan's head, cut off the hand that conceals God's light. Then plunge it into the infernal abode of Lilith's night.

ADAM: You bitch. I'll kill you! (*Lunges sword into Lilith; all inhabitants of Hell collapse and die.*) Thou hast taught me well the hatred that can conquer Hell, or pull down Heaven from its

---

*Real name of actor playing Onan/Belial.

heights. Now will I rage, rage against the light.

WITNESS: (*Singing.*)*

Oh, my Lord
Be not wrathful with Thy servant, but
Hide Thy anger in Thy mercy and
Lead me forth.
Oh, my Lord and Master,
Show me Thy way.

ADAM: Thou art a deceiver . . . a lying, treacherous devil god who promises but does not fulfill. You have stolen my life. You gave me . . . Eve . . . Oh, my God, Eve . . . I have forgotten thee. Where am I? Am I in Hell? Eve! . . . Where have You hidden her? Answer me . . . lonely . . . so lonely . . .

WITNESS: (*Singing.*)**

Dying and living it's all the same.
Shoes for the crippled, shoes for the poor.
Shoes for those who have died in the war.
Shoes for the living but none for the dead.
Shoes for the man whose feet have bled.

ADAM: I shall summon all the hosts of Hell to burst this mundane shell, and batter down the gates of Heaven. There I shall force You to reveal where my love is. If Thou wilt not hear my prayer, let Lucifer[23] come. (*Raising sword to kill himself.*) Now to unlock Thy seal . . .

(*Enter Serpent, grabs sword from Adam.*)

SERPENT: He kills and He maketh to live. Wilt thou linger in Hell forever? Adam, thou must hurry, or suffer eternal damnation.

ADAM: Rather Hell with Eve, than Heaven without her. Did He who made us one, calculate the pain when He sundered us in twain? Can I forget how Eve lay slumbering in my breast 'til the Lord God, in jealousy of our bliss, opened my side and took her from me? From this day forth, I am the enemy of God. I break my covenant with Him. Lucifer, kneel, and by thy oath, promise thou shalt lead me through Heaven and Earth, paradise and Hell, 'til I be united with my love. Oh swear, or thou shalt break my heart. Why dost thou weep, Lucifer?[23] Canst thou know my pain?

SERPENT: Can I, who gazed upon the face of God . . .

*Music p. 270
**Music p. 271

ADAM: You mean you really gazed upon the face of God?

SERPENT: Yes, I'm the Serpent, aren't I?

ADAM: What's it like to look upon the face of God?

SERPENT: If you'll just continue on your journey, you'll find out for yourself.

ADAM: I will?

SERPENT: Yes. Can I who gazed upon the face of God, wrapped in the garment of His boundless light, not know the eternal ache within thy heart? He was my all; my life. Oh, it was bitter, bitter to be banished from His sight. Outcast in endless time, doomed to wander these infinite spheres — eternally alone. Oh Adam, what would I not give to be at one within His heart?

ADAM: I am sorry for thee, Lucifer.

SERPENT: And I for thee.

ADAM: Someone's crying. Eve . . . ?

SERPENT: Hush. It is the infernal abodes lamenting. They are calling home the dead.

ADAM: In all the worlds can there be such sadness? It is like a needle that penetrates my heart.

SERPENT: There is no greater terror than when the dead awaken and read the Book of Life.

(*Men in chain gang awaken.*)

Therein all their crimes are written. They are gathering for their journey. The caravan of truth approaches. We must hurry.

(*Nine gongs sound.*)

"It is the ninth hour."

ADAM: "The hour of prohibition." I am flesh and blood. I cannot steal into the caravan of the dead.

SERPENT: I know a magic spell that can unlock the gate of Hell.

(*Enter Dancing Serpent, hissing.*)

The great serpent coiled in the abysmal depths, that cast thee out, shall lead thee back to Paradise. Oh Adam, have no fear but follow after me and leap upon his back. Now be quick and leap! Hold fast to the serpent's back and we shall spiral up to Earth 'til we reach the ladder to the Sun.

(*All inhabitants of Hell spring to life. Exit chain gang.*)

LILITH: Adam! Adam!

SERPENT: Don't look back. If thou dost, thou shalt never return.

SATAN/MOLOCH: Spittle and dust, spittle and dust . . . man is but a brew of scum. Foul clay and bestial dust. Spittle and dust, spittle and dust.

SERPENT: Close up thy ears, or you shall be lost in the kingdom of lies forever.

QUEEN OF FOLLY: Thou wicked, evil, filthy thing, thou hast not kept thy bargain.

LILITH: I love thee, Adam.

QUEEN OF FOLLY: You promised to be my bondservant for a thousand years!

SATAN/MOLOCH: Spittle and dust, spittle and dust. Foul clay and bestial dust!

QUEEN OF FOLLY: A thousand years!

LILITH: Adam! Adam!

SERPENT: Look Adam, how the Sun bursts forth.

(*Exit all inhabitants of Hell, except for one member of Lilith who goes to background of Hell and remains motionless throughout play.*)

ADAM: How beautiful is the day.

(*Enter Eve and Death's Double, at a great distance, unseen by Adam. Eve wears a flowing Middle Eastern gown and her face is veiled.*)

What is that shadow moving across the sky?

SERPENT: The Lord of Death. His caravan and bride eclipse the Sun as they pass by.

ADAM: Every living thing is withered in their path, each goodly bud, each blade of grass.

SERPENT: All that lives must make obeisance to his might. See how millions follow in his path.

ADAM: Oh, the mournful voices of the dead.

SERPENT: Each is bound to the perpetual wheel of life 'til he pays for his every feeling, thought and deed.

ADAM: Where does he take them?

SERPENT: To Judgment — where all paths cross.

ADAM: I grow dizzy. There is a strange buzzing in my ears. Eve?

SERPENT: Death is singing. It is not meant for mortal ears.

ADAM: Eve? Death is coming closer. I cannot bear it.

SERPENT: You must. See him drive them on, seated there on his great white steed, his charger rearing in the air.

ADAM: Who is that lady by his side?

SERPENT: That is his bride.

ADAM: She is veiled. I cannot see her eyes. And yet, I feel . . . Eve?

SERPENT: She is beckoning.

ADAM: I feel . . . I know her.

SERPENT: Go to her.

ADAM: I cannot move.

SERPENT: She is beckoning to you. Go. Go!

WITNESS: From a great distance he looked. Long, long, he gazed.
   (*Adam and Eve call to each other from afar.*)

ADAM: You called.

EVE: Thou art alive, and yet dead.

ADAM: Art thou the bride of Death?

EVE: Yes.

ADAM: What is thy name?

EVE: Truth.

ADAM: I would see thee face to face.

EVE: No corrupted look can meet my gaze. What wilt thou pay?

ADAM: My life.

EVE: Come to my court tomorrow at high noon.

ADAM: What city? What city?

EVE: Damascus . . .

SERPENT: Let us go . . .
   (*Exit Adam, Witness; Death's Double gives robe of Death to Serpent, then exits.*)

SCENE 3: THIRTEENTH CENTURY DAMASCUS
DEATH'S HOUSE

EVE: I've died and lived a thousand times and always returned to your arms.

SERPENT: No mortal is worthy of your eternal beauty.

EVE: Shall no man ever take me from you, Death?

SERPENT: He who does must guess my secret.

EVE: Tell me thy secret.

SERPENT: You will betray me.

EVE: I am pledged to you.

SERPENT: A pledge can be broken.

EVE: Dost thou love me, Death?

SERPENT: This knowledge is not for your ears.

EVE: I am your bride.

SERPENT: Ask anything . . . golden cities in the Sun, the music of the spheres, but not this.

EVE: Do you fear the race of man?

SERPENT: No mortal can conquer Death. How many ages I've watched you lying in the arms of kings and emperors, of men in distant lands, and none could content thee.

EVE: Yes, Death.

SERPENT: How jealously I brooded over you and how I envied these wretched mortals their moment, until I held you in my arms once more. And yet always you return to life and betray me with the living . . . Why?

EVE: I cannot tell you, Death.

SERPENT: You seek a perfection that only I can give you. None can understand, none can love you as I do. Thou art my queen, my soul, my bride. Though all men vie for you, none can see you as you are. Why do you not forfeit your lives and stay with me?

EVE: Oh, but for the hope of something after death.

SERPENT: There is nothing after death.

(*Serpent claps. Enter two Servants.*)

I go a day's journey. Guard her well.

FIRST SERVANT: My Lord, there is a man outside the gate who seeks audience with thee.

SERPENT: He shall not enter. Have everything in readiness when I return.

(*Adam enters from afar, prostrate, struggling to rise.*)

Who is he that seeks me?

ADAM: A man, no less.

SERPENT: What is thy petition?

ADAM: Death.

SERPENT: Thy single life is of no account. Many wait for me.

(*Eight gongs sound; exit Serpent; enter Handmaidens.*)

EVE: "The eighth hour; the hour of Love." Bring the man within.

FIRST SERVANT: My lord and master bade me bring no man within the courtyard, on pain of his displeasure.

EVE: On pain of my displeasure, do as I command.

(*Servants drag Adam into courtyard.*)

(*Goes to him.*) Oh, my love! How long I have waited for thee!

ADAM: Eve! . . .

EVE: (*Whispering.*) Hush, we are in Death's dominion. Forgive me that I play with thee. (*To Handmaidens.*) I have heard an ancient story that our sages teach: When by Allah's hand Adam first was cleaved in half, he fell from Heaven like a thunderbolt upon these distant shores; he could neither eat nor drink nor move, so grievous was Love's fierce wound; and when he wakened from his swoon he would not take another, but compassed Heaven and Earth to find his Eve. Is it true?

ADAM: Thou knowest.

EVE: Why, I think there is no greater love in all of Islam. What thinkest thou? Hast thou heard of a greater love?

SECOND HANDMAIDEN: I have not heard of it, my lady.

EVE: Yet what of Eve? Was that lady faithful?

FIRST HANDMAIDEN: The Koran teaches she was faithless.

THIRD HANDMAIDEN: Scripture says she mated with the Serpent.

EVE: Had Allah made me Eve, scripture would have lied. I would have waited 'til the end of time. If I were Eve, I would stand before my Creator and cry, "Test me, prove me, I am faithful to my Adam."

ADAM: Oh God!

THIRD HANDMAIDEN: He faints.

EVE: Take him within.

FIRST SERVANT: As thou commands.

(*Servants carry Adam into inner chamber and place him on couch.*)

EVE: Gently.

(*Exit Servants.*)

SECOND HANDMAIDEN: My lady, shall I call a physician?

EVE: I shall be all the medicine that he needs.

ADAM: I thirst.

EVE: Bring him drink.

FIRST HANDMAIDEN: Yes, my lady.

ADAM: Is this the cup of love?

EVE: Drink deep.

ADAM: Eve . . .

EVE: Hush . . . this will slake your thirst.

ADAM: Oh God. The great Hand that pours the pitcher fills the cup. He who drinks can never drink enough.

EVE: You must rest.

(*Exit Handmaidens.*)

ADAM: Strange . . . the music . . . the music they are playing.

EVE: The story of the maiden.

ADAM: It moves me so. Why? It pierces my heart as if it would break.

EVE: It is her song of love.

Listen! Oh listen to my tale.
In the Holy Land, in the heavenly city,
In the city of Jerusalem,
In my Father's house, there lived a maiden.
A great king came; he was my betrothed.
His hands enthroned me
In the temple of Love.
His eyes dressed me in Splendor.
I drank the wine of Love from his mouth.
Face to face he whispered unutterable words,
Secret words for my ear only.
Death came, with a cruel army.
He tore me from my Beloved's arms.
He stripped me of my garment of glory.
I cried to Heaven to see my shame . . .
But Heaven did not hear me.
I begged Earth to hide me.
But Earth did not heed me.
I was alone.
I called out his name.
I asked the stars where I could find him.
Stars did not know.
I asked the Ocean.
Ocean did not know.
Death took me
To his windowless house,
The House of Forgetfulness.
But I remembered my Love,
His touch.
I left Death's house to search for him.
I covered my nakedness in strange garments
And wandered many lands.
I lived many lives. I died many deaths.
Cruel men dressed me in rags,
I wept as they defiled me.
Their scorn broke my heart.
I became tarnished.
I lost my splendor.
You who have heard my story,
Have pity. Tell me where my Beloved is.

Tell him I wait for him
To restore me to my Father's house,
So I can once more lay in his arms.

ADAM: Oh, to be thy king.

EVE: And, oh, to be thy kingdom.

ADAM: We would traverse all the worlds; space and time would be our dominion.

EVE: But, a king must have a crown, lest Death take his kingdom from him.

ADAM: Show me the way, love, and with wings of love, I'll reach it.

EVE: It hangs high up on the immortal Tree of Life. Not even Death can seize it.

ADAM: And the means?

EVE: Thou must mount the steed of Death and ride into the highest Heaven. But how shalt thou outwit him?

ADAM: Since Love's my God, I shall call on Him and He shall find a way. But first I would see thy face.

EVE: My face shall burn. Love is a holy fire.

ADAM: It shall be my Paradise.

EVE: Paradise is not enough. Oh Adam, could we but cling in holy remembrance past all forgetting. But Death will come and take me from thee. Go to the six directions of the world and he is there to the outmost boundary.

ADAM: When I am far removed from thee I die, but when I cling to thee I live in death.

EVE: Wouldst thou die for me?

ADAM: Aye. Unveil. Thy face shall be the moon and stars. (*Eve unveils.*) Oh my love, thou art blind.

EVE: From gazing into eternity.

ADAM: Thou dost not know me.

EVE: Yes, Adam. I know thee from the Beginning.

ADAM: But thou canst not see me.

EVE: (*Touching his face.*) These ten vessels shall trace the lineaments of thy face. Thy cheek, brow, mouth shall be my sacraments.

ADAM: Then come, anoint my lips, for thy mouth shall be the prayer that wakens my sleeping will. (*They kiss.*) From thy head a thousand worlds hang flaming on each hair. Thy cheeks are sapphires that light the sky, thy lips the entrance to Paradise, thy neck the milky white dew of Heaven. Oh, let me nestle there.

EVE: Oh, Adam!

ADAM: How can I enumerate the Book of Love?

EVE: Turn the page and read. I would hear more of thy doctrine, love.

(Enter First Handmaiden.)

FIRST HANDMAIDEN: He comes! Death comes, my lady!!

(Exit First Handmaiden; enter Serpent.)

SERPENT: Aiiiiiiiiii . . . *(Eve faints on couch.)* I am the master of this house. What mortal dares to be within these halls, sup at my table, drink my cup? Who living would lay his head upon my couch?! Who would steal my bride?!

ADAM: Thou art the thief, Death. She is mine.

(Adam, unable to rouse Eve, goes to meet Serpent.)

SERPENT: What art thou that I should heed thee? A moment and thou art dead.

ADAM: That moment fills immensity. It is written in the Book of Life: the woman is mine.

SERPENT: I shall catch thee both in my net.

ADAM: We shall fly from thee.

SERPENT: There is no flight. I am the Lord of Death. No mortal can stand before me.

ADAM: Hath not the Living One said, "Thou shalt bend thy knee to man"? I shall yoke thee and put thee to service.

SERPENT: Who dares to question me?

ADAM: I will know thy mystery.

SERPENT: In the day thou knowest thou wilt surely die.

ADAM: Then I die.

SERPENT: Art thou certain? Wilt thou give up life?

ADAM: I will have the woman.

SERPENT: Thou knowest we both shall have her.

ADAM: Never!

SERPENT: Thou hast betrothed her to me.

ADAM: Liar!

SERPENT: Hast thou forgotten? What is mine is thine, you said.

(Adam runs from Serpent to Eve.)

ADAM: What is this thou sayest?

(Adam rouses Eve, both try to flee Serpent who blocks their way and begins to stalk them.)

SERPENT: "We will go the way together," remember? "A part of my portion you shall have," remember? "When I eat, you shall eat," remember? "When I sleep, you shall sleep," remember? "When I pray, you shall pray with me," remember? "When I love, you shall love with me," remember? "For every rung I climb, you shall climb with me," remember?

ADAM/EVE: AHHHHHHHHHHHHHH!!! Sammael!!!

(*Blackout; exit all; enter Adam's and Eve's doubles in Damascus during blackout, who remain in Damascus motionless throughout play.*)

SCENE 4: JERICHO

(*James, Nathan, Adam, Eve, and Witness discovered on stage; Adam and Eve lie prostrate on the ground; Eve wears white cloak.*)

WITNESS: If thou hast followed thus far in our tale, hear how Death put the first man in his spell. Hear how Adam and his Eve fell into a swoon and plunged into the dreaded body of Leviathan,[24] the great whale that encircles all the world. Watch through our eyes as they cut their way and swim, exhausted, to the shores of the Dead Sea.

NATHAN: Hail to thee, daughter of God.

EVE: What land is this, and who art thou?

JAMES: This is the Promised Land and we are friends, disciples of the Fisher King.

EVE: The hills of Judea. My heart leaps at sight of thee. How beautiful thou art. I will hug thee as I run out to meet thee. How the sunlight kisses thy peaks, and the fleecy clouds nuzzle 'gainst thy earth. Oh Adam, we are at journey's end. They have fished us from the sea; they have saved us.

NATHAN: The Lord hath done it.

JAMES: He hath used our hands.

EVE: (*Tries to awaken Adam only to discover . . .*) He's dead!! Oh no, my lord is dead!! The Evil One hath done this; he hath severed us . . . How quiet all is here. It is as if the breath of God had stopped. Oh Adam, we would have lived forever in this holy land bathed in sweet peace. I would have filled thy mouth with kisses, and clung about thy neck and we would have studied all the ways of love. But thou art dead, and I of women most forlorn.

(*Eve breaks down weeping. Enter Serpent in loincloth.*)

SERPENT: Go on.

EVE: I can't go on. He's dead.

SERPENT: So?

EVE: Don't you understand, he's dead.

SERPENT: He's supposed to be dead.

EVE: He can't be!

SERPENT: He has to be! It's in the script.

EVE: My life is over.

SERPENT: No, it's not. You've got to get to Jerusalem.

EVE: It's my fault. I killed him!

SERPENT: No, no, that's not your line!

EVE: He died trying to save me. Every time we meet, we lose each other! Why? Why?!

SERPENT: No, your line is . . .

EVE: If I hadn't called you to Death's house in Damascus, you'd be alive now. Of, if only we were back in Damascus, I'd do it all differently.

SERPENT: Forget Damascus. You've got to get to Jerusalem!

EVE: I don't care about Jerusalem. I don't care about anything now.

SERPENT: But you must go on! Your line is, "I must get to Jerus . . ."

EVE: I can't go on without him!

SERPENT: What are you talking about?

EVE: You promised me we'd go to Jerusalem together.

SERPENT: Yes, I . . .

EVE: Back in Poland, you swore to it.

SERPENT: I . . .

EVE: You've cheated me of my love!

SERPENT: The play must go on!

EVE: Why must it go on? Don't you understand I'm suffering? Can't you see what love is? No! You don't care about anything but your play.

SERPENT: Look, honey, I know you're upset. But I promise you . . .

EVE: Don't promise me anything. You'll only break your word.

SERPENT: I promise you there'll be someone along soon to help you.

EVE: (*Wailing.*) AaaaEeeeIiiiOoooUuuu.

(*Enter Serpent's Double from afar wearing loincloth and white hooded cloak, calling, "Why dost thou mourn, sister?"*)

SERPENT: You see? Here he is now.

(*Serpent slips into the white hooded cloak as his double exits.*)

EVE: My lord is dead and there is no man to restore him to me.

SERPENT: (*From afar.*) He but sleepeth. Thou shalt see him at thy side.

EVE: Who art thou? I know thee, yet I know thee not. I have seen thine eye and face before, but where or when I cannot say. I remember and I remember not. But why callest me sister, my Lord?

SERPENT: Were thou not imprisoned in matter thou wouldst know.

EVE: I am clay and water.

SERPENT: Is thy Creator so poor that He made thee only of this?

EVE: I know not, my Lord.

SERPENT: Thou art fallen and thy soul wanders, else thou wouldst remember when thou abode with me in the supernal light.

EVE: When did I abide with thee, Lord?

SERPENT: When thou clung to the paps of our heavenly mother and ate of her light and drank of her milk.

EVE: Thy word piercest my heart. But . . . oh, I cannot live without my Adam. My soul cries out for him.

SERPENT: Thou shalt give birth to him. He who was thy husband shall be thy son. Thy heart shall be the entrance to his life.

EVE: Where is the way to this?

SERPENT: Through the gate of Life.

EVE: How is the way to this?

SERPENT: Beyond space. Beyond time.

EVE: What is the way to this?

SERPENT: He who is beyond existence shall tell thee.

EVE: Who is He that thou lovest so?

SERPENT: (*Trembling.*) I am called to the Kingdom of Light. I must journey to Jerusalem that scripture be fulfilled.

EVE: I will walk by thy side.

SERPENT: Thou canst not go my way now.

EVE: When?

SERPENT: When eternity is rent by time and bleedest upon the cross of matter.

EVE: Yet will I follow from a distance.

SCENE 5: JERUSALEM

(*Enter Crowd.*)

WITNESS: Oh Father of boundless light, who sendest Thy Son perpetually into eternal night, suffer Thy mystery to be born, be crucified, and rise in me, for if it take place not within my soul, what profits it to me?

SERPENT: Thou hast heard that I suffered and yet though I suffered, I suffered not. That my flesh was torn, yet it was not. That I was crucified, yet was I not. That I was hung upon the tree and slain, yet dying, I lived. For while Jesus wept, the Christ I am rejoiced. From the All I came, to the All I shall return.

WITNESS: Who hath heard a greater mystery? That Love eternally walks the road to Calvary alone, a plank upon His back, in perfect obedience to the ineffable commandment from above.

EVE: Oh, that the stars would reverse their course!

JAMES: Suffer this to be, else the Teacher of Righteousness hath done his work in vain.

EVE: Will no man help Him? Then must I.

NATHAN: Pray.

WITNESS: All men stood lining the Via Dolorosa,[25] each called to play his part—disciples, pharisees, high priests, revolving in the timeless mystery, and watched the Just Man made perfect, lift humanity through the fourteen stations of the cross. At the first station the Kingdom of Gluttony trembled. At the second, Anger bowed its head. At the third station Greed bent its knee. At the fourth, He faltered, 'til Simon held Him up and Sloth lay prostrate at His feet. At the fifth station the Kingdom of Vanity fled. At the sixth, Lust fell down and worshipped. At the seventh station of the cross, Pride witnessed the masterpiece of creation and abased itself in the dust.

Thus the seven deadly sins, the seven kingdoms of the world, the seven lords of contention were turned, healed, converted. And from their ranks stepped forth seven princes who, following His wake, vied to be His footstool as He mounted to the cross. As He marched the last seven stations of the cross, the planetary lords cried to the Holy One and wept for the body they had made in torment and tears of sweat. The precious vessel soon to break. At last it was done. Upon the cross Eternal Beauty bled.

(*Everyone, including all of Adam's and Eve's doubles, who had remained motionless throughout play, begin to tremble.*)

EVE: Oh, my Lord, my Lord.

ADAM: (*Rising.*) Eve . . . !

EVE: Adam . . . thou livest!

ADAM: What hath happened?

EVE: Oh, Adam . . . He died that ye might live.

(*Seven gongs sound.*)

EVE: "The seventh hour."

ADAM: "The hour when Eve was given to Adam as his companion."
(*Blackout.*)

SCENE 6: EGYPT

(*Lights up on: Ayi,*[26] *Tyi,*[27] *Nurse, Harmhab,*[28] *Priests, Moses, Crowd, Standard-bearer and Witness all frozen as Hieroglyphs; Eve dressed in ancient Egyptian costume; Adam wearing a Pharaoh's hat and jeweled neckband.*)

ADAM: I cannot preach love and go to war.

AYI: Wilt thou lose Egypt?

ADAM: If I must. But I cannot lose the Lord.

AYI: Shall an empire be lost for love?

ADAM: Yes.

EVE: We must part then. Is that what my Lord hath said? Oh royal
Mother, am I never to hold him in my arms again? Oh tell him he
does not mean it. Oh please, someone speak for me. Ayi, I know
my Lord does not mean what he is saying. It is all a dream. Thou
wilt tell me so . . . Ayi . . . Ayi . . . Ayiiiii! Thou wilt not leave
me.

ADAM: Oh, Nefretete.[29]

EVE: Do not weep, my heart. Do not weep, my love.

ADAM: My heart.

EVE: I have waited so long for thee. So many lifetimes, and now thou
art taken from me. Ohhh . . .

ADAM: No . . . I cannot let thee go.

(*Eve breaks down crying. Serpent runs in dressed as Hermes
Trismegistus,*[30] *carrying staff of Caduceus.*[31])

SERPENT: Eve! Eve! Stop the action . . . Hold the show!

EVE: Ohhhhh . . . I can't bear it. I can't stand it. I won't allow it. It's
too much!

SERPENT: Eve, it's only a play. Don't you understand?

EVE: Why do we always have to lose each other? What do we keep
doing wrong?

SERPENT: Eve, control yourself!

EVE: I can't control myself. (*Passionately kisses Adam.*) I really like
this guy. I don't see why we have to keep splitting up. This evening
is driving me crazy.

SERPENT: Just say your lines.

EVE: Shhh . . . I will live a queen, alone,

Within these marbled halls.

I shall . . .

(*Witness attempts to put a costume on Adam.*)

ADAM: What the hell are you doing!?

WITNESS: I'm putting on the thighs and belly of a woman.

ADAM: What do I want with the thighs and belly of a woman?

SERPENT: It's in the script.

ADAM: I don't understand what that has to do with Ikhnaton.[32]

SERPENT: It has everything to do with Ikhnaton. He's the Pharaoh of Egypt.

ADAM: I don't see what being Pharaoh has to do with having the thighs and belly of a woman. You're not going to make a fruitcake out of me. I'm not going on with this play.

EVE: Neither am I. I will not be separated from him again. Why can't we just end this play beautifully?

SERPENT: You don't understand.

ADAM: I'm a man!

SERPENT: Yes, of course you are. And also a woman.

ADAM: No, I'm not. Ask Eve.

(*Eve smiles coyly.*)

SERPENT: How can I explain this? Everybody has a masculine and feminine side. At this point in your development, Adam, when you play the role of Ikhnaton, both sides of your nature are united to show thy body is a sacred Hieroglyph, the signature of the Lord, wherein is written that thou art His elect. And it shall be a divine omen for the people. And it shall be for them a sign that He hath given thee a portion of soft woman's nature to stem the cruel fury of the world and gentle all the land. In other words, you're a normal man.

EVE: Honey, I don't mind if you have the thighs and belly of a woman. It's O.K.

ADAM: You mean you'll still love me if I look like that?

EVE: Yes.

SERPENT: All right. Let's go on.

(*Serpent starts to exit.*)

EVE: I will live a queen, alone,

Within these marbled halls.

I shall . . . Wait a minute! (*Serpent stumbles.*)

You still haven't answered my question, why we have to be separated.

SERPENT: (*Trying to recover.*) Don't you remember at the end of the last scene. (*Tripping over staff.*) Christ! . . . when you were reborn, both of you?

ADAM/EVE: Yes.

SERPENT: All right. Now, in this next hour of your life, what do you think you've been trying to do, you two?

(*Adam and Eve look bewildered.*)

Tell them Witness.

WITNESS: Picture if you can, these two high priests of love — the first man and woman of the land — traveling on their barge of splendor up and down the river of life, the holy Nile. Clasped in one another's arms, they taught by every act and gesture, the holy ritual of love.

SERPENT: In other words, you try to create a kingdom of love right here on Earth. Ikhnaton and Nefretete are the first people in the world who ever tried to do it. You even try to do it before Moses. And then what happens?

EVE: Everybody becomes jealous of us?

SERPENT: Of course. Ayi . . .

AYI: The priests daily incite the people against thee. Great Queen, thy and thy lord's bond of love is too strong. They want it broken before the people's eyes.

SERPENT: Of course. Mother . . .

TYI: The devils! The devils!

SERPENT: Harmhab . . .

HARMHAB: How long can an empire be ruled from under the skirts of women?

SERPENT: Priests . . . (*Priests speak.*) People on the bank . . . (*Crowd speaks.*) Egyptians . . .

(*Everyone speaks at once causing uproar; Serpent restores order.*)

In other words, things haven't changed that much on Earth in the last few thousand years. All right, now will you please say your next line?

ADAM: What is my next line?

(*Serpent at his wits' end, exits laughing hysterically.*)

EVE: Shhh . . . I will live a queen, alone,

Within these marbled halls.

I shall not cry out nor mourn the time,

For in memory's enchanted hall

I will see thee everywhere

In the faces of our little ones,
In every arbor, grove and park.
I shall mingle in thy presence.
I shall grow old, but
Our love shall not stale.
It shall be forever young, for
It shall be the keys that house
The inner chamber of my heart.
And from its fabled treasure
I will relive our life forever.
I shall not be sad, for
I have known the beauty of the world
Thy face, thy walk, thy heart.
I will recount the glories of our time and
I will wait until
Thou shall return to me.
I will wait until
Thou come.

ADAM: Oh my love, there is no place on Earth for us.

EVE: Beyond Earth there is a place where we two shall meet as One.

ADAM: In God's arms.

EVE: Farewell my love.

ADAM: Farewell my life.

(*Exit all except Adam, Witness, Moses, Standard-bearer.*)

WITNESS: A solitary figure crosses the desert, his shadow cast by the setting sun. Twilight. He who was once great Pharaoh, now outcast, alone.

ADAM: I will go to
The Valley of the Kings
Where my fathers lie.
I will enter the tomb
And find my eternal home.
And pray God give me rest.
Great Sphinx,
There is but a little light
Before my life is done.
I perish, but you go on.
Thou art silent. But I remember
In the morning of my life
How many times hath God

Risen on us both.
I, naked in thy presence,
Seeking to gain thy wisdom,
Thrilled by thy mystic song,
The sublime secret that dwelled
Within my heart . . .
Then I was thy beloved.
You sang to me of greatness . . .
Oh, if I could once more
Hear thy immortal song
Or borrow thy wings
And fly to lands undreamed;
All would be well.
(*Moses approaches Adam in mime walk.*)
Moses! Thou must be gone. I have failed. Thou must go on. Take
thy people and journey to Jerusalem.

MOSES: Great Pharaoh, I will stay by thy side.

ADAM: The greatness of Egypt is fled. Thou must take her wisdom
into the desert with thee.

MOSES: Where shall I hide me?

ADAM: The Lord will guide thee.

MOSES: Shall I not see thy face again?

ADAM: We go our separate ways. When this generation is past, thou
shalt return and forge of the Hebrew slaves a new nation. Thou
shalt break the power of Egypt. Thy deed shall resound
throughout the ages. In that I shall be with thee.

MOSES: Will they receive the God of Truth?

ADAM: Only he who knows he is enslaved, outcast and despised can
receive the God of Freedom. Only he has need of it.

MOSES: Thou art my teacher, I have studied at thy feet.

ADAM: Thou shalt succeed where I have failed. The soul of man must
not perish from the Earth.

MOSES: What of thee?

ADAM: God is with me. Dost thou understand?

MOSES: I hear and I obey . . . I hear and I obey . . . I hear and I obey.
(*Moses, in mime walk, disappears across the sands of Egypt.*)

ADAM: How can I tell Moses to journey to Jerusalem when I'm going
there?
(*Enter Serpent.*)

SERPENT: So you can meet him there.

ADAM: I meet Moses again in Jerusalem?

SERPENT: Yes.

ADAM: But we're going in opposite directions.

SERPENT: Right.

ADAM: He's going into the future and I'm going into the past; how can we meet?

SERPENT: Because it's in the script.

ADAM: But that's impossible!

SERPENT: How do you know that?

ADAM: Because I know! How is it possible for us to meet if he's going one way and I'm going another way?

SERPENT: The journey doesn't take place in time, but eternity — and in eternity time is a circle.

ADAM: That means the play eternally recurs . . .

SERPENT: Of course.

ADAM: And I'm doomed to repeat every word and gesture forever and ever.

SERPENT: Just as the author wrote it. Everything is predetermined.

ADAM: But that's unbearable. I want my choice.

SERPENT: Then you must spiral out of the circle.

ADAM: What spiral? Where?

SERPENT: There has to be a spiral. Otherwise you wouldn't have any freedom.

ADAM: But then I'd be contradicting the author. You just told me everything is predetermined.

SERPENT: Not if you decide to change the script.

ADAM: But I can't change the script.

SERPENT: Yes you can.

ADAM: But that's not in the script.

SERPENT: Yes it is. It's all in the script. The author wrote it that way. You create the play.

ADAM: Do you mean every time the play is performed, it's a different play?

SERPENT: It has to be; otherwise it wouldn't contain all possibilities.

ADAM: All possibilities? Well, when does that happen?

SERPENT: When do you want it to happen?

ADAM: Now.

SERPENT: Why didn't you say so before? Then that's the next scene.
   (*Enter Nefretete's Double who remains motionless in Egypt throughout rest of play.*)

ADAM: Great Hermes, dost thou mock me? All is lost.

SERPENT: Oh, son of man, dost thou forget so soon? Why dost thou condemn thyself to this single life? Body is but the tomb of soul.

ADAM: Egypt . . .

SERPENT: Egypt and this little round of time is but a dream. Now Adam, stand upon thy feet and follow me. Wilt thou wander in darkness forever?

ADAM: Who shall teach me Wisdom, Lord?

SERPENT: Thou shalt learn it from . . . (*Opening his hand.*)

ADAM: A worm?

SERPENT: Look once more.

ADAM: A chrysalis.

SERPENT: And now . . . ?

ADAM: A butterfly!

SERPENT: See how all creation testifies against thee? This is the excellence of God — that He made all things that thou might see Him all in all.

ADAM: Oh, my Lord!

SERPENT: Canst thou not follow the least in God's creation? Gather up thy life and hold it in thy grasp. See that thou art all thy life. Gaze upon thy future, present, past.

ADAM: The Sphinx, the Sphinx is singing in my ears! Great riddler, I remember thy secret!

SERPENT: Put on thy wings. Follow that which was once a worm through the gateway of the stars, and thou shalt gain eternal life.

ADAM: I am a man, my Lord.

SERPENT: Thou enters a man. Thou shalt leave a god.

VOICES OF THE PYRAMID: Know all . . . dare all . . . be all . . . do all . . .

ADAM: The Pyramid is alive.

SERPENT: It is the tomb of God. Hear His soul whispering within thee.

VOICES OF THE PYRAMID: Leave thy body and follow me.

ADAM: The song of immortality.

SERPENT: Dost thou hear?

VOICES OF THE PYRAMID: Conceive nothing impossible to thee. Know all sciences, all arts, the nature and way of every creature. Be fire and water, the dry and the moist, know thyself to be in every place . . . in Earth, in sea, in Heaven, in the unbegotten, in the womb, in the young, in the old, in the dead. Grasp all things at once . . . all times, places, deeds and qualities.

ADAM: God's melody has ravished me. His many voices have loosed me from myself. He hath split and broke me into a thousand pieces. I am all in one.

SERPENT: Wilt thou be purified?

ADAM: Yes, yes!

SERPENT: Go Adam, ever deeper, 'til thou reach the inmost room.

ADAM: I know not where I am, my Lord.

SERPENT: Thou art in the Hidden of the Hidden, the King's chamber. Here thy heart shall be weighed.

VOICES OF THE PYRAMID: Who art thou?

ADAM: I know not.

VOICES OF THE PYRAMID: What art thou?

ADAM: I know not.

VOICES OF THE PYRAMID: Where goest thou?

ADAM: I know not.

SERPENT: Now thou shalt become what thou were before thou wast born.

VOICES OF THE PYRAMID: SILENCE!!

(*Six gongs sound.*)

ADAM: "The sixth hour."

SERPENT: The hour of Wisdom.

ADAM: "And He showed them all their generations and their wise men in one moment of time."

SERPENT: Up, up through the Pyramid's top, 'til thou stand upon the infinite point where all directions meet.

ADAM: A great bull, a great lion, a great eagle, a great man clamber up the Pyramid's sides. Lit from within . . . Oh God, am I mad!? Each beast has for arteries and veins, billions of tiny men and women, numerous as the sands.

SERPENT: All humanity.

ADAM: Where do they go?

SERPENT: To the heavenly city.

ADAM: The beasts. The beasts! They shall devour me!

SERPENT: Hold fast.

ADAM: I am being crushed! The four are blending into one. Hermes, save me!

SERPENT: I am ever with thee.

ADAM: Aiiii!! They have transformed into the Sphinx. He is singing. My mind, oh, my mind is breaking on the rack of his song.

SERPENT: He is singing to the Madonna of the Stars.[33]

ADAM: Black Goddess of the great night.

SERPENT: She is his Beloved, contracted by the Lord above, before time had begun its course. See the twelve virgins of the light as they make their circuit round her in the sky! Oh, heavenly Pyramid, whose point doth touch our own, and whose life doth nourish us below!

ADAM: The riddler flaps his wings.

SERPENT: He woos her in the darkness of the night.

ADAM: Why, oh why?

SERPENT: From her mankind springs, and to her man must eternally return. While all men sleep, he brings them to her heavenly arms. There all humanity is nourished at her breast. Revitalized, refreshed, he hies them back to Earth before the break of dawn. Watch him take wing on his holy pilgrimage of love.

ADAM: He flies.

SERPENT: Straight to her heart. Now, Adam, take wing.

ADAM: I shall fall!

SERPENT: Be the equal of God!

ADAM: Oh, Lord, I shall die!

SERPENT: Dost thou love me, Adam?

ADAM: Aye!

SERPENT: Then soar!

ADAM: Into eternal life or death, I know not . . . As long as thou art at my side.

(*Blackout. Five gongs sound. Exit Adam, Serpent and Standard-bearer.*)

SERPENT: (*From offstage, during blackout.*) "The fifth hour."

ADAM: (*From offstage.*) "He cast a soul into him and he became a Titanic Man."

SCENE 7: PARADISE

(*Lights up. Enter ten actors and actresses who form human Tree of Life.[34] Enter Serpent, dressed in a golden costume with cape. Enter Eve, wearing long flowing dress. Adam discovered lying on ground, asleep, costumed in same suit he has worn throughout play, a garland of flowers upon his head.*)*

*Music p. 275

SERPENT: Adam . . . Adam . . . Adam! Adam who art David, King of Israel, Messiah . . . Awaken!

EVE: He sleeps, my Lord.

SERPENT: Wilt thou sleep through all eternity? Call him to thy side. I shall show thee a tree of immortality, a kingdom that fadeth not from view!

EVE: Adam . . . Adam . . . the tree, the tree in the midst of the garden is singing. Hear its celestial song? I hear God singing.

ADAM: Can it be the Lord?

(*Four gongs sound.*)

EVE: "The fourth hour."

ADAM: "The hour when he stood on his feet."

EVE: The tree is calling to us.

ADAM: No, do not go.

EVE: I must.

ADAM: Eve . . . !

(*Tree of Life sings throughout.*)

TREE OF LIFE: I am Victory.

I am Splendor.

I am Justice.

I am Mercy.

Come, enjoy the fruit of God.

Pluck me and be King of Heaven.

Eat and be Queen of Love.

Taste me and know all Beauty.

Gain my secret and know thyself.

Reach and thou shalt have Wisdom.

Reach and ye shall win a crown.

EVE: What does it all mean, Adam?

SERPENT: Thou shalt know all. Ye shall be as gods.

TREE OF LIFE: Gain my secret and know thyself.

Reach and thou shalt have Wisdom.

Reach and ye shall win a crown.

EVE: Oh Adam, shall we be as wise as God?

SERPENT: Come, I will pluck for thee.

ADAM: Shall I steal God's Wisdom?

SERPENT: Stolen fruit tastes best.

(*Enter animals who wander throughout Garden of Eden.*)

ADAM: (*Holding apple.*) Remember!

SERPENT: Now, thou alone shall be God!

ADAM: No! I have done this thing before.

EVE: Adam, shall we not eat of the forbidden fruit?

ADAM: Nay, for in the day we do, we are dust.

TREE OF LIFE: Come, enjoy the fruit of God!

EVE: But it is so pleasing to the touch. See how it glitters in the light.

ADAM: Illusion! That shall make us wander forever lost in time.

TREE OF LIFE: Eat and be immortal.
Taste and be all wise!

ADAM: We shall lose Paradise! Eve, dost thou not remember how the Lord God drove us from the Garden?

EVE: Remember . . .

TREE OF LIFE: Eat and be immortal.
Taste and be all wise . . .

ADAM: We have done all this before! Stood before the Serpent, ate the sacred fruit and fell.

EVE: Did we fall, Adam?

ADAM: Into time's dream.

EVE: Time's veil is rent. The centuries reel by. Now I see clearly. If we eat the forbidden fruit we must be servant to the Serpent until the end of time.

ADAM: I shall once more be Ikhnaton, great king, driven into exile.

EVE: And I, Nefretete, who waits for him forever.

ADAM: I shall be the Baal Shem Tov, Master of the Good Name. And I shall be the man who curses God and is slain by Death.

EVE: Oh, and I shall be the woman who hated thee, and thou me.

ADAM: I am all men who have ever gone on the journey.

EVE: And I am all women who have ever gone on the journey.

ADAM: Now will I break with thee, for I am God's man forever.

SERPENT: Oh Adam, behold the nature of thy adversary.

(Serpent transforms into an angel with gold wings.)

ADAM: Lucifer!

EVE: The Christ!

SERPENT: I am both. Thou fell with Lucifer; ye shall rise with Christ.

ADAM: But thou art . . .

SERPENT: Yes . . . Death, and Hermes Trismegistus, Sammael, and all the other names men have called me; always changing yet always One, until I awakened in thee the immortality of which I myself partake. It was for this thou journeyed from trial to trial; that ye might learn the knowledge of thy Self. Now Adam and thy Eve, rise up and follow me. I am the Way, the Truth and the Life!

ADAM: Where do we journey?

SERPENT: To Jerusalem, the heavenly city, we three in One.

ADAM: How shall we go?

EVE: We are made of dirt.

SERPENT: He who planned thee hath made provision for thy journey. He hath taken dirt from all seven worlds to make thee. The highest is divine, of One substance with thy Creator; the lower dirt thou shalt leave behind.

EVE: Glory!

ADAM: In the name of the Lord!

SERPENT: Up the Tree of Life!

TREE OF LIFE: Ten sapphires sparkling bright.
Ten sapphires in the Tree of Light.
If thou wouldst gain the meaning,
Seek to know all.
Strive to be all.
Dare to be the friend of God.

ADAM/TREE OF LIFE: I am Victory.

EVE/TREE OF LIFE: I am Splendor.

ADAM/TREE OF LIFE: I am Mercy.

EVE/TREE OF LIFE: I am Justice.

SERPENT: (Singing.) I am the Beauty that accomplishes all.

TREE OF LIFE: Pluck me and be King of Heaven.
Eat and be Queen of Love.
Taste me and know all Beauty.
(Three gongs sound.)

ADAM: "The third hour is striking."

EVE: "The hour when he stretched forth his limbs and they became a universe."

ADAM: Eve! Look! The Grand Man I saw in my youth.

EVE: The Titanic Man!

SERPENT: Thou art that. In His image are ye made. Now Adam, enter into thy full height and depth; thy length and breadth. Be what thou art, and Eve and thee shall be healed.

ADAM: Ahhhhh!!! I am being stretched to the boundaries of the world.

SERPENT: To infinity!

ADAM: The universe is entering me. I am inside the Grand Man. Oh God, I am He. Eve!

EVE: At One with thee at last.

SERPENT: Thy rib is healed.

ADAM: And thou?

SERPENT: I am thee.

TREE OF LIFE: Gain my secret and know thyself.
Strive and thou shalt have Wisdom.
Reach and thou shalt be as . . .

ALL: (*Singing.*) God . . . God . . . God . . .
(*Two gongs sound. With the exception of Adam and Eve, everyone, including the doubles of Adam and Eve, begin slowly rotating in place. Serpent stands motionless in background.*)

ADAM: "The second hour. The hour when he became a golem, an unformed mass." Thou hast accompanied me on my journey. Now I will accompany Thee.
(*One gong sounds.*)
"Twelve o'clock." We are at the beginning.

EVE: And the ending. "The first hour."

ADAM: "When God wished to create the world, He began His creation with nothing other than Man . . ."

EVE: "And He called him ADAM."

ADAM: We've always been on the journey.
(*Witness gives shoes to Adam. He puts them on.*)

EVE: Yes, that's what it means. Every One is on the journey.
(Blackout.)

SCENE 8: NEW YORK

(*Lights up on Adam and Eve in their original positions and costumes at end of first New York scene. Bodies slumped on couch, heads thrown back, apparently unconscious. Garden of Eden ensemble continues to circle throughout scene.*)

EVE: (*Awakening.*) Oh God, what's happening to me?

ADAM: I . . . I . . . I . . . never felt this way before.

EVE: Neither have I.

ADAM: Toward anyone?

EVE: No one.

ADAM: Oh my God . . . Eve . . . I love you.

EVE: Oh Adam . . . Adam . . . We've found each other. Is it true?

ADAM: Yes . . . yes.

EVE: Where is he?
(*Adam rises, looks for Serpent, pauses, and discovers . . .*)

ADAM: (*Touching his heart.*) He's here.

EVE: We're not dreaming . . . ?

ADAM: No. Don't you understand? It's real! *Real!* I love you!

EVE: Dear heart . . . kiss me, kiss me.

ADAM: Yes!

(*They kiss.*)

EVE: Ohhhh! I love you . . . What comes next?

ADAM: Jerusalem.

EVE: Where all directions meet.

ADAM: And all hearts are One.

SERPENT: Who will play Adam next?

(*Entire ensemble continues to circle slowly in place. Adam and Eve watch from couch; Serpent motionless in background. Follow-spot recalls to memory each scene of the play in sequence by focusing briefly upon: doubles of Adam and Eve; Witness; Tree of Life; Serpent; finally returning to Adam and Eve on couch as the play ends.*)

MUSIC

BY MACK SCHLEFER

LYRICS BY A. F. HORN

NIGUN

WITNESS SONG

MUSIC FOR ACT III SCENE 2, HELL

On the throne sits Fol - ly, our

most be - lov - ed queen. In - cline and sat-is-fy thy ev - ry

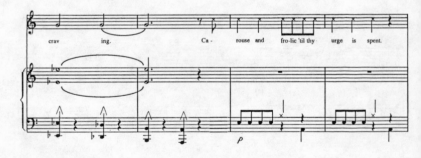

crav ing. Ca - rouse and fro-lic 'til thy urge is spent.

Then comes ease,   sa - tie- ty and   sleep.

TRPT.

ff
A tempo

VOICE

What is thy   wish?

"To be with my beloved."   *"No sooner said than done. Behold, the daughter of our union."*

Electric Piano

The

(Dialogue continues)

(shouted)

jew-el of our   realm.   Liljth!

Repeat 4 times

Adam   S+M

Done! She's yours;   You're ours: our bonds-man

for a thous-and years.

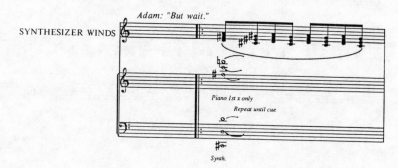

Adam: "But wait."

SYNTHESIZER WINDS

Piano 1st x only

Repeat until cue

Synth.

Adam: "...trailing behind her?" ♩ = 288   S+M

Where? what men? I don't see an-y

sfp pui mosso

Adam: "There..."   S+M

men. An op - ti - cal il -

Lilith

lu - sion. You're still too much in the light. Come lit - tle Ad - am,

S+M

Come my lord and mas - ter. Drink this cup and purge your-self of

all il - - lu - - - sion. Drink and be thou ev - er -

Queen/Lilith

more a son of dark - - ness. Drink! What sayest thou now? Thou art all

beau - - - ty with - in whose dazz - ling rays. the di - vine vis - ion

fad - eth fast a - way.   Fare - well

all   joy,   hon - or,   bliss

for   one   kiss   from your

lips.   Now is your un - ion com -

S+M

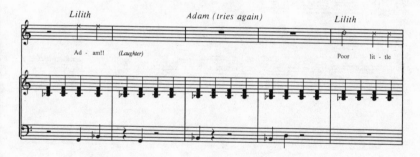

(Dialogue continues)

Cut on cue: Serpent: "That's enough."

Cue: Witness: "Crucified upside down."

Andante

Dialogue continues

Alto recorder

Azarel: "A handful of dust..."

Urael: "O thou seed of Adam..."

accel.

ad lib.

f

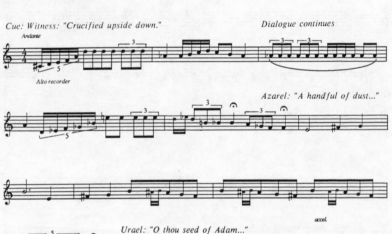

♩ = 132   Cue: Adam: "...lonely...so lonely..."

Dy - ing and liv - ing it's all the same.

Shoes for the crip - pled,

shoes for the poor. Shoes for those who have died in the war.

Shoes for the liv - ing but none for the dead. Shoes for the man whose

Dialogue continues

Clarinet

feet   have   bled.

Solo piano

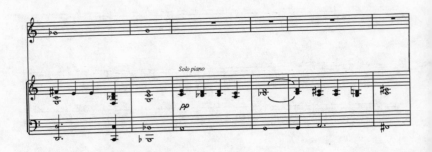

pp

Cue: Adam: "Let Lucifer come."

Fade
Cut on cue

Lilith

thing, thou hast not kept thy bar - gan. I love thee,

Queen

Ad - am. You pro-mised to be my bond - ser-vant for a thous - and years!

Satan/Moloch

Spit-tle and dust, spit-tle and dust. Foul clay and

Queen   *Lilith*

best - ial dust! A thou-sand years! Ad - am! Ad - am!

Flute

Hi-hat

Piano

Repeat and fade till next scene

MUSIC FOR ACT III SCENE 7, PARADISE

Eve: "He sleeps my Lord..."

no Ped.

Serpent: "Call him to thy side."

"...Tree of immortality."

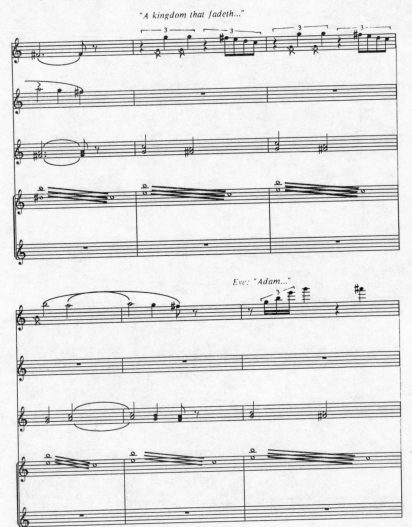

know   thy - self. ____   ____   Reach ____

____ and thou   shalt have   wis - dom. ____

Continue on cue: "Nay, for in the day we do..."

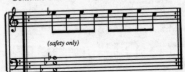

(safety only)

Eve: "But it is so pleasing to the touch..."

Come, en- joy the fruit of God!

Cue: Adam: "...wander forever lost in time."

Eat and be im - mor- tal.   Taste and be all

Cue: Eve: "... remember..."

wise!

Eat and be im - mor- tal.

Serpent: "It was for this thou journeyed."

Adam: "Where do we journey?"

poco a poco cresc.

Eve: "Glory." Adam: "In the name of the Lord."

Tree of Light

Ten   sap - phires   spark - ling

Tree of Light

Taste me and know all Beau - ty

Eat and be Queen of Lo - - - - - - - ve.

Serpent: "Be what thou..."

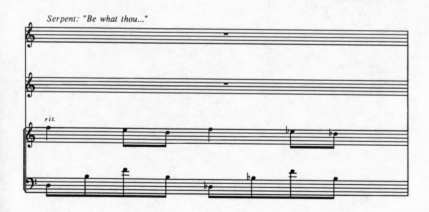

Adam: "The universe is entering me..."

Cue to continue: "And thou? I am thee."

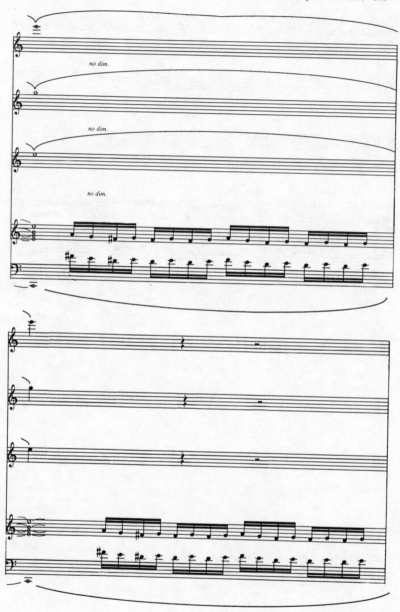

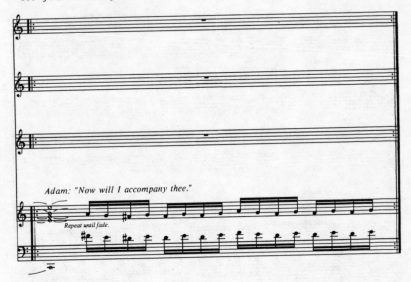

THE ARGUMENT

A Play in One Act

1972

CHARACTERS

First Man   Second Man

THE ARGUMENT

FIRST MAN

We've taken the garment of the earth and made it useful, taken minerals from the ground. Our metallurgy's transformed the world. Copper, nickel, lead — the raw material of our ambition has been transformed into gleaming brass, resolute steel, mighty iron — the framework of our nation, the guts of the world. Our factories singing in the night, our dynamos humming, our alchemy, more fabled than any Arabian adventure, have revealed the mysteries of the sea, turned forests into paper, the desert into glass. We've lowered man toward the flaming center of the earth and the bottom of the ocean. We've changed salt sea marshes into resorts of pleasure. We've planted our derricks into soft yielding dirt, drilled through resistant bone rock and tapped the most precious blood of earth — oil, that makes the world go round. We've mined the veins and arteries of the planet to bedeck and dress the world; gold and silver, platinum and diamonds have we found; treasure beyond compare, no pirate on the high seas could have dared. And all this secret knowledge we've lifted from the obscurity to the earth to the light of reason. These dark precious jewels we've used to beautify women and give pride to men. Our winged jets have unified the nations, broken through sound to make Peking and New York twin brothers. Our copper cables transposed into the nervous system of the earth carry brain waves within seconds. We've knitted the fellowship of sound into one great masterpiece of mass communication. We've conquered gravity, the earth, and made that madcap fellow, the moon, our dominion. Our cyclotrons have broken the power of the sun; the atom's won. The electron and all that's in it is ours. We'll melt the polar caps, throw domes of radiant energies across our cities, and span continents in glass, impervious to nature's wishes. We'll turn day into night, night into day. We've conquered air and sea and land and fire, and made them servants of our desire. Now light will soon be ours to command. The elusive speed of light we'll capture, and then the world is ours! Our rocket ships will circle Mars and Venus, and this decade will see the solar system within our grasp. Our laboratories have penetrated the gene, the chromosome, the sperm, the secret of the enzyme, the catalyst of life. We know the secrets of aging and of youth, the processes of quickening and slowing down. We've transplanted hearts and spermatic lives and every organ of the body. We can turn a man into a monkey and monkeys into men. We've replaced the human mind. It's now outmoded. The cornerstone of the new age is the computer, which we've created from scraps of metal and glass and wired all together. Since nature always was a sorry worker and life emerged by accident, there is no design or moral purpose. We've improved on nature beyond all conception. You must admit we're clever. We are the conquerors of time and space, the creators of life, the conquerors of the solar system, the masters of the universe. There are no other gods but us, no other intelligence greater than our own. What have you to say to that? What have you to match it?

SECOND MAN

One Socrates is greater than all that. One flower in all its raiment. One child's laughter. The smile of an old woman as she comes to rest. What are your factories, your buildings, your laboratories to that? What are your corporations, your industries, your boards to the transcendental glory that creates worlds? One redwood towering to heaven in true worship can teach man more about his source — where he comes from and what he must do — than all your products and all your theories. A blue jay on the wing is a lesson in grace no picture can equal. The elk is a treatise in pride defying all description. The bird of paradise whispers celestial secrets in my ear. The mockingbird mocks not me, but all your vain ambitions. Great nature standing stalwart throughout the ages cannot be trespassed, encompassed or betrayed. Your factories whistling in the night, the humming dynamo, the winged jet — what are they to the Song of God — the screeching of the bat, the billowing whale, the majesty of mountains, the cycling seasons. Sing you a tale for a day? I will sing you a tale for all days and all seasons. Ninety billion years of your time, a wink from the galaxies; three hundred million quadrillion years, a mere breath — the birth, growth, death of a universe: one breathing in and out of that First Principle. Your atomic bombs — the buzzing of a fly. Your science — the rustling of a mouse. Understand the blinking of an eye and you'd impale ten thousand atheists upon a nail. The power of a billion solar systems, locked up in the secret of a thumb. The Mind of man, faster than the speed of light. Send the fastest rocket across the bloodstream of light, Mind will be there first. Aeons hence, traverse the galaxies, Mind will be awaiting you and come out to greet you. Let your ultimate daring, billions of years hence, be to traverse a universe, Mind has traversed all universes, backward and forward turning. Do you say man is little, brother, to be bent and turned and twisted on your lathe? I say he is immense. I, a man, a citizen of the cosmos Earth, declare man's tyranny shall end; for until that ends, nation shall rise against nation, and the Earth shall know travail. I, just one of billions, one drop of the ocean, eternal by that reason; a citizen of the solar system, a citizen of the Milky Way and of the universe beyond, a citizen of all creation — by virtue of Mind. Through Mind I squeeze into the smallest, expand into the largest, contract into the infinite, expand into the limitless. From infinite to infinite is my domain — worlds without ending. Do you say man is little? I say he is immense, the wonder of creation — the reconciler of heaven and earth. In me lies all creation, all of heaven and hell. Of every soul and state of man, of all the stuff of worlds, of all that's man and bird and twisted form am I. Within me the rose, and the muck from which the rose has climbed — the lily and the slime. I am the murderer and the victim; in me the hero, the clown, the doubledealer, the coward's fear. Of every station, state, degree am I, the spanner of continents; black, red, yellow, white, brown man, all within. Every varied hue and shade am I; no color more distant than another. Within me, God and the devil do contend. Is the Sun far? In me, the message of the ages. I declare I am made of sunlight. Each electron of light locked within a molecule of air. Each molecule imprisoned in a cell. Change the scale, each cell a solar system. Each electron does dutifully revolve around its proton, as do Mars, Jupiter, Saturn, Earth around the Sun — each one bound in its accustomed place. In me the refuge of billions of lives, each cell container of quadrillions more, who are born, mate, live and die, as do I, their galaxy. And I, to a Greater, but a petty lump of flesh and blood, their god, to whom they lay all their oblations. In fifteen seconds of my life, four centuries of theirs do pass. God must be justified upon this Earth, brother. Out of this dark agony of night, out of your black satanic mills, man will awaken and sing the beauty of the Earth from pole to pole. The Earth will awaken and sing the glory of creation; each molecule, cell, electron, leaping, swirling, twisting, turning in its accustomed place. The dance of all creation: each cell to every cell does sing; each particle of light with every other rejoices in common harmony. And I, a simple, ordinary man, the heir to all creation. For me the orbs did all arise, form, coalesce and condense. For me the winged bird did fly, so that I, with watchful eye could catch the meaning and seeing, say, oh, yes! and return the knowledge to its source, its great Creator, the Master of the workshop, waiting to see if I, His puppet, would guess the meaning. The wind, the water, the earth, the fire and I. In me, the purpose of all creation, I, transformer of continents, peoples, worlds, I, make to rise and fall. The voice of God, my own. Every particle — flesh, blood, hair, eyes — God's. He enters to possess and ravish me. He becomes I, and I, He . . . for there is only One.

Appendix

THE FANTASTIC ARISING
OF PADRAIC CLANCY MULDOON

1 *The gods*, refers to the ancient idea that people are influenced and controlled by higher forces of which they are not aware. The Greeks placed these forces at the level between the sun and the earth, personifying the planets as gods, beings with intelligence and purpose.

2 *Dover Beach*, by Matthew Arnold, British poet (1822-1888).

3 *Lazarus* of Bethany, brother of Mary and Martha in the Gospels. Moved to compassion by the death of his friend Lazarus, Jesus traveled to his grave and restored life to him after four days of death. The raising of Lazarus from the grave symbolizes the death and rebirth which all the great religions teach. (St. John, Chapter 11.)

4 *Lysistrata*, Greek for "demobilize the troops," a comedy by Aristophanes, first performed in 411 B.C., the twentieth year of the Peloponnesian War between Athens and Sparta which was destroying classical Greek civilization. In the play, Lysistrata, an Athenian woman, rallies the women of Greece to withhold their love until the war is ended. Although they agree reluctantly and participate less than wholeheartedly, her plan works. The men are taught by women that Love is the greatest warrior and the gentlest of friends.

5 *Parnell*, Charles Stewart (1846-1891). One of Ireland's great leaders in her century-long struggle for independence from England.

6 *Beelzebub*, in the New Testament is portrayed as the prince of devils. In *Paradise Lost* Milton places the fallen angel second only to Satan in power. In Hebrew Beelzebub means "Lord of the Flies," a denigration of the name Baal-zebul which means "Lord of the High House." The high houses or high places were altars of the Baal or gods. So the root meaning of Beelzebub is "leader of idolatry," the enemy of the call, "Hear O Israel, the Lord our God, the Lord is One."

7 *Hans Christian Andersen*, Danish (1805-1875), Author of *Andersen's Fairy Tales*. Great Grandfather's story is the first in *The Snow Queen*, "A Tale in Seven Stories."

8 *Christ is risen from the dead . . . ,* from the Russian Orthodox Easter Matins. "For since by man came death, by man came also the resurrection of the dead." (I Corinthians, Chapter 15, verse 21.)

9 *The Hapsburgs*, of the Austro-Hungarian Empire were the ruling family of central Europe from the Renaissance to World War I. Through astute politics and intermarriage their influence became so powerful that the Hapsburg bloodline found its way into many of the ruling houses of Europe. Like the Medicis, who created the Renaissance, they were able to sustain and dominate the culture of Europe for hundreds of years.

10 *The poets of Provence*, the "poets of love" in southern France from the tenth to the thirteenth centuries. Dante, Petrarch, de Ventadour, de

Born, Daniel, de Borniel, Rudel and the other troubadors were combining elements of the Sufi, Arabic, and classical Latin traditions with the Christianity of the Cathars (pure ones) of Albi, a sect which was continuing the ancient tradition of esoteric Christianity stemming from the Gnostics. Their aim was to meet with influences coming from northern Europe where Christianity was leaving the Ark of the monasteries, as Noah had when the flood receded, to recultivate the earth with the Gothic Cathedrals. This union of the masculine and feminine poles of the religion of Love would have created the greatest civilization Europe had ever known were it not for the Albigensian Crusade (1208-1230) of Pope Innocent III and the fires of the Spanish Inquisition which reduced medieval Christianity to ashes.

11 *St. Lama*, founder and originator; from him followed an unbroken line of lamas – from the Tibetan word "blama" which means chief or high priest. Lamaism is noted in the *Tibetan Book of the Dead* as a form of Tantric Buddhism which began there in the eighth century A.D. The first community of lamas was established in 749 A.D. by Padma Sambhava (in Tibetan, Pedma Jungne which means "the Lotus-Born"). He was known as Guru Rin-po-ch'e, the "Precious Guru."

THE LEGEND OF SHARON SHASHANOVAH

1 *Michael Chekhov*, nephew to Anton Chekhov; one of the most brilliant students of Stanislavsky; an actor of genius who headed the Second Studio of the Moscow Art Theatre and made further contributions to the art of acting as a spiritual discipline. See his book, *To the Actor*.

2 *Eugene Vakhtangov*, trained by Stanislavsky, he was the most inspired director to come out of the studio tradition. He worked closely with Michael Chekhov on contributions to the art of the theatre and directed some of the most beautiful productions of the twentieth century.

3 *Moscow Art Theatre*, founded in 1898 by Konstantin Stanislavsky and Vladimir Nemirovich-Danchenko. Based on the inner truth and feelings of the actor and an organic method of recreating man and his spirit on stage. The playwright Anton Chekhov worked in association with the theatre.

4 *Theseus and Ariadne*, a Greek legend. Every year, Athens sent seven youths and seven maidens as tribute to Minos, king of Crete. They were killed by the Minotaur, a bull with the head of a man, that lived in a maze called the Labrynth. Theseus went to Crete in disguise to kill the Minotaur. Ariadne, daughter of Minos, fell in love with Theseus and decided to help him. She gave him a sword to conquer the Minotaur and a thread. She held one end of the thread so Theseus could find his way back from the maze. Ariadne left her father's house and journeyed with Theseus. Theseus later deserted her on the island of Naxos, where the god Dionysius came and possessed her.

JOURNEY TO JERUSALEM

1 *Calico Pie*, from *Book of Nonsense* by Edward Lear, British humorist (1812-1888).

2 *Rebbe Gershon*, Israel ben Eliezer's brother-in-law, and at first his

detractor, he later became one of the most devout of the Hasidim. Rebbe Gershon was a scholarly man who was respected by the community. With the Baal Shem Tov's help he developed great heart and exemplified the Law *(Torah)* in his life.

3   *Shekinah*, in Hebrew "to dwell," meaning a revelation of the Holy in the midst of the profane. The Shekinah is the "Presence" or bride of God, His feminine aspect, by which a place, an object, an individual or a whole people is sanctified. She is the immanence of God in the world. See the appendix note for *Ten Sephiroth*.

4   *Carpathian Mountains*, the eastern wing of the great central range of Europe. The Carpathians extend from Poland to Romania.

5   *Sammael,* the Evil One, destroyer of Jews. On the Tree of Life Sammael represents the Sephira *Geburah* (Severity), fear of judgement, and is the antagonist of the Archangel Michael, who represents the Sephira *Chesed*, grace or mercy. In the guise of a serpent he tempted Eve in the Garden of Eden. He is sometimes called the tester, the bringer of death, which has earned him the name "venom of God." He is powerless only on Yom Kippur, the Day of Atonement. Sammael corresponds to Satan in the Christian tradition. "Satan" is Hebrew for adversary.

6   *Davening*, a way of prayer. During the act of fervent and intense praying the body shakes and trembles so that mind, heart and body are united by the Presence of God.

7   *Shalom,* Hebrew for "peace" and commonly used as a greeting.

8   *Zaddik*, Hebrew for "righteous," a man who devoted his life to the service of God and man, guiding his work with study of the *Zohar* and the *Kabbalah*, as well as *Talmud* and *Torah*. On the hearth of the Law burned a passionate love of the beauty of the universe, which the Zaddik kept hidden until he was strong enough to reveal it through his own life.

9   *Baal Shem Tov*, Hebrew for "master of the good name" (1700-1760). This most recent Jewish prophet taught that man's first duty is to seek God in everything, to serve Him through simple prayer, emotional fervor and joyful living — even though, at that very time, his people were being persecuted and killed in the Pogroms. His teachings brought warmth and joy; he warned against sadness and mortification which stultify the heart. Born Israel ben Eliezer, he was a simple man who spent long hours in solitude and meditation in the woods and fields. After he married he discovered for himself the central pillar of all great teachings: love for God, His Law *(Torah)*, the community of Israel and all creation.

10   *Ten Sephiroth*, Hebrew for "numerations." The Kabbalistic idea of ten Sephiroth on the Tree of Life forms the very basis of thought which surfaced during the flowering of Jewish mysticism in the Middle Ages. They are the principal keys by which the secret doctrine of the *Torah* can be unlocked, which Moses understood in writing the first five books of the Old Testament. They had been passed on to him from Abraham through an unbroken oral teaching in which it is said that the lightning flash of the creative impulse of God, the unmanifest, unknowable *Ain Soph*, passes through *Kether* (Crown), *Chokmah* (Wisdom), *Binah* (Understanding), *Chesed* (Mercy), *Geburah* (Severity), *Tiphereth* (the King of Beauty), *Netzach* (Victory), *Yesod* (Foundation) and *Hod* (Glory) and creates the manifest world, *Malkuth* (the Kingdom, the Shekinah).

11   *Hasidim*, Hebrew for "the devout." The coming of the Baal Shem Tov and his followers (the Hasidic movement) rekindled a spark in the Jewish people that within three generations reconnected them through

the line of their fathers from David to Moses to Jacob to Isaac to Abraham to Adam, giving them new faith and purpose in their religion — a rebirth. The essential duty of these men was to attain "devekut," or cleaving to God, in every action of their lives: in eating, walking, talking, praying, loving and the study of *Torah*, the inner act was to bind the soul to God.

12 *Jacob Frank*, (1726-1791), the last of the false Messiahs stemming from the messianic movement begun in 1665 and which eventually enveloped Turkey, Poland and Galicia. His demonic influence was so powerful that it led to the only burning of the *Torah* in all of Poland's recorded history. Jacob Frank's method was to play on the sincere wish of the people to find salvation through a Messiah. By almost imperceptible distortions of the truth he led his followers, by a process of logic based on false premises, to an orgiastic lust for self-destruction, disillusionment with the ideal of family and chaotic disruption of tradition.

13 *Am Haaretz*, Hebrew for "man of the earth," in Jewish tradition a common man, a man who works hard, values nature and neighbor, and instinctively understands the place of God in the universe.

14 *Dybbuk*, Hebrew for "attachment," the disembodied spirit of a dead person which, finding no rest from sins during its life, seeks a living person to inhabit, acting as an evil influence. Possession by a dybbuk is often taken as a sign of a person's hidden sins.

15 *Elijah*, a prophet of the Old Testament who dared chastise a king for looking to Beelzebub instead of God. God sent a chariot and horses of fire and lifted him up to heaven in a whirlwind. In Hasidic legend he is said to have foretold the coming of the Baal Shem Tov. He appeared with Moses during the transfiguration of Christ. (II Kings, Chapters 1 and 2; St. Mark, Chapter 9, verses 1 to 13.)

16 *Azarel and Urael*, refers to the two angels "Aza-el" and "Uzza" who set out to prove man's wickedness before God. When they came to earth they sinned with mortal women and were exiled by Him; but they are still alive and are responsible for some of the evils of this world — the teaching of sorcery and showing women how to allure and seduce men through the illusion of false beauty and glamour. (Genesis, Chapter 6, verse 4.)

17 *Moloch*, Hebrew for "king," the Canaanitish god of fire to whom children were sacrificed.

18 *Onan*, the grandson of Jacob, son of Judah. He was told by his father to fulfil the wife of his dead brother, Er, by planting his own seed in her. Choosing to spill it on the ground instead, Onan displeased God and was put to death. (Genesis, Chapter 38, verses 1 to 10.)

19 *Belial*, Hebrew for "worthlessness," whether material or spiritual: also demon of lies and bearer of guilt.

20 *Lucifuge*, a combination of two Latin words, "lux," or light and "fugere," or to flee. He is the demon who perpetuates the darkness of hell by preventing even a ray of light from entering it.

21 *Lilith*, Hebrew for "night monster," a female demon who was the mistress of Sammael. She disguises herself as a voluptuous harlot to seduce and destroy unsuspecting men by feeding on their blood. The union of Lilith and Sammael forms the Great Beast. She was the mother of Adam's demonic offspring before his union with Eve, and threatens evil to all children.

22 *Thaumiel*, "thauma" is Greek for miracle, "miel" is French for honey:

the land of illusion whose king is Phantasmagoria.

23 *Lucifer*, was cast down from heaven "For thou hast said in thine heart, I will ascend into heaven, I will exalt my throne above the stars of God." (Isaiah, Chapter 14, verses 12 to 20.) In *Paradise Lost* John Milton says:
"Fallen Cherub, to be weak is miserable,
Doing or suffering; but of this be sure—
To do aught good never will be our task,
But ever to do ill our sole delight,
As being the contrary to his high will
Whom we resist."
There is an ancient legend that an emerald fell from Lucifer's forehead as he plunged from heaven to earth. The search for this jewel is said to be the Quest for the Holy Grail; or in another tradition: the Emerald Tablets of Hermes which will give birth to divine knowledge in any man who can find it.

24 *Leviathan*, in Jewish mythology, the female monster of the sea, whose male counterpart is Behemoth, monster of the land. One day the two will fight a mighty battle for control of the Earth. In the story of Jonah, Leviathan is the whale that swallows and keeps him captive in its belly for three days. She is so powerful that God warns Job, "Lay thine hand upon him, remember the battle, do no more." (Job, Chapter 41, verses 1 to 11.)

25 *Via Dolorosa*, Latin for "sorrowful way," the way of crucifixion, the "Fourteen Stations of the Cross" on the way to Calvary.
The First Station of the Cross "And they stripped him, and put on him a scarlet robe. And when they had platted a crown of thorns, they put it upon his head." Humility.
The Second Station of the Cross That the prophecies might be fulfilled and mankind redeemed from the sins of Adam, he receives the Cross.
The Third Station of the Cross Jesus falls. Sustained by matter.
The Fourth Station of the Cross He meets his mother and overcomes all earthly temptation.
The Fifth Station of the Cross Simon bears his Cross. "Blessed art thou, Simon . . . and I say also unto thee, That thou art Peter, and upon this rock I shall build my Church."
The Sixth Station of the Cross The woman, Veronica, wipes his face with her veil. Divinity's countenance imprinted on matter, eternity's trace in time.
The Seventh Station of the Cross He falls a second time. Sustained by soul.
The Eighth Station of the Cross The Earth weeps. "Weep not for me," he says to the women of Jerusalem, "but weep for yourselves and your children."
The Ninth Station of the Cross He falls for the third time. Sustained by spirit.
The Tenth Station of the Cross They cast lots for his garment. Oh God, Oh God, I am nothing.
The Eleventh Station of the Cross Christ nailed to the Cross. The still quiet center of the World sustaining all.
The Twelfth Station of the Cross Death. "Father, why hast thou forsaken me?" "I thirst." The sop of vinegar. "It is finished."
The Thirteenth Station of the Cross Taken down from the Cross, laid in the arms of his mother. Rest in the womb of God.
The Fourteenth Station of the Cross Christ laid in the sepulchre . . .

Divinity entombed in matter, only to be reborn again. The Resurrection.

26 *Ayi*. Ikhnaton's most trusted priest and advisor. He eventually succeeded to the throne several years after Ikhnaton's death.

27 *Queen Mother Tyi*, wife of Amenhotep III and mother of Ikhnaton, who took a prominent role in government during her son's reign.

28 *Harmhab*, an army general during Ikhnaton's rule, and his deputy in several lands. He conspired with rebellious priests and other forces seeking to overthrow Ikhnaton. Increasing his power during the eight years following Ikhnaton's death, he ascended to the throne in 1350 B.C.

29 *Nefretete*, Egyptian for "the beautiful one is come," she was the mother of seven daughters and Queen of Egypt. She was known as the most beautiful woman in all of Egypt.

30 *Hermes Trismegistus*, (literally Hermes thrice great), the name given by the Greeks to the Egyptian god, Thoth, believed to be the origin of all wisdom of the universe and the soul of man, and the inventor of all arts and sciences. A second Thoth is said to have lived around the time of Moses who restored the teachings of Hermes by translating and explaining the emerald tablets he had carved, stone tablets said to contain all the secrets of the universe.

31 *Caduceus*, the staff of the messenger of the gods, usually made of olive wood crowned by two intertwined serpents. Hermes found the two serpents fighting and mediated between them with his staff. It became a symbol of reconciliation which, in his hands, led the souls of the dead to the world below and the souls of the living back to their source. The intertwined serpents joined by the staff symbolize the evolutionary and involutionary movements of the universe, the spiral of eternity and regeneration. The symbol of the staff itself appears throughout history in the possession of men like Moses, who told Aaron, "Take thy rod, and cast it before Pharaoh, and it shall become a serpent." When Pharaoh's magicians did the same, "Aaron's rod swallowed up their rods." (Exodus, Chapter 7, verses 10 to 12.) The difference between the two staffs is the source of their power, the level to which they were receptive – the magicians' to the lower level, Aaron's up through Moses to God.

32 *Ikhnaton*, taught the idea of monotheism before Moses transmitted it to the Hebrew people (Aton, the One Supreme God of Truth). Ikhnaton means "spirit of Aton" (the spiritual power which blazes forth from within the sun). He and his wife, Nefretete, were more devoted to the growth of this religion than to the expanding of the empire. Consequently they met with fierce opposition from the priests of the former gods and from the military. Despite this opposition they began to change the entire direction of Egyptian civilization until these forces combined to overthrow them. He was finally driven into exile. He was originally called Amenhotep IV and was the last ruler of the Eighteenth Dynasty (1375-1358 B.C.)

33 *The Madonna of the Stars* represents the Milky Way. She bears the Christ of the Sun in her arms. From him spring and to him eternally return the circle of physical life, weighed down by the moon, and the circle of invisible life ascending to the stars.

34 *The Tree of Life* and the Tree of Knowledge of Good and Evil exist in the Garden of Eden simultaneously and are one. The two Trees represent the two souls of man, the higher and the lower. The lower soul has as its host the corporeal body and is directed toward carnal gratification.

Thus Adam the man, and Eve the spirit of the living, are tempted by the Serpent, that is, desire and lust, and fall from the Tree of Life to the Tree of the Knowledge of Good and Evil or the dualistic world of materiality. The higher intellectual soul has its place in the world of the Divine at the Throne of Glory (Shekinah) where it delights in the glorious and tremendous Name of God and is known as the Tree of Life consisting of pure light. It is only with the knowledge and understanding of the Center Pillar of the Tree (Crown, Beauty, Foundation and Kingdom) that a man escapes from dualism and realizes that the good (the Right Pillar), the evil (the Left Pillar) and that which reconciles them (the Center Pillar) are one in the Tree of Life.

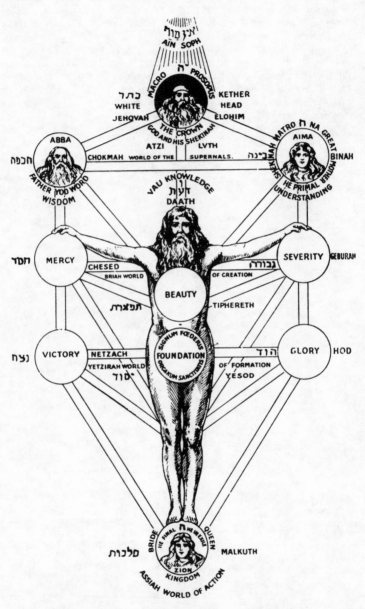

THE SACRED TREE OF THE SEPHIROTH

The Fantastic Arising of Padraic Clancy Muldoon
was first performed in 1973, and *Journey to
Jerusalem* in 1976 under the direction of Sharon Gans.
The Legend of Sharon Shashanovah
was first performed in 1979 under the direction
of A. F. Horn.

The author wishes to thank Michael Hilsenrad, Andrew Robinson, Andrew Cort, Paul Levine, Terrence Christgau, Matthew Fitzgerald, Ed Cohen, John Mahnke, Erik Sherman, Jonathan Weinert, Cathy Buckley, Michael Peipman, and Brad Smith, for help in the preparation of this manuscript. And my friend, Robert Klein, who has been of great help to me.